Women Pilots of Alaska

D1452258

Women Pilots of Alaska

37 Interviews and Profiles

SANDI SUMNER

McFarland & Company, Inc., Publishers
Jefferson, North Carolina, and London

Library of Congress Cataloguing-in-Publication Data

Sumner, Sandi, 1942–
Women pilots of Alaska : 37 interviews
and profiles / Sandi Sumner.
p.   cm.
Includes index.

ISBN 0-7864-1937-7 (softcover : 50# alkaline paper)

1. Women air pilots—Alaska—Interviews.
2. Air pilots—Alaska—Interviews.
3. Aeronautics—Alaska—Anecdotes.
I. Title.
TL539.S826   2005   629.13'092'2798—dc22   2004028957

British Library cataloguing data are available

On the cover: *top:* Keli Mahoney flying a Cessna 185
in the McKinley range, Alaska; *bottom:* Caren della Cioppa in
fur parka, standing beside a Cessna 140, Palmer, Alaska.

Manufactured in the United States of America

*McFarland & Company, Inc., Publishers
Box 611, Jefferson, North Carolina 28640
www.mcfarlandpub.com*

To my grandmother, Lillian Little,
who continues to inspire me;
to Keli Mahoney, Mike Jacober, and Dottie Magoffin,
who lived her dreams;
and to my father, Ross Edward "Ted" Jones,
who always told me, "You can do anything!"

Acknowledgments

This book came to fruition because the Alaska Ninety-Nines, women pilots, embraced the project, provided names (not limited to their members), and assisted with editing and technical advice. Every pilot whose story appears between these pages is acknowledged for trusting me to tell her amazing story.

Thanks are also extended to the Alaska Aviation Heritage Museum, the Smithsonian Air & Space Museum, the WASP Archives, the National Aviation Hall of Fame, the National Park Service, the Alaska Airmen's Association, Women in Aviation International and librarians and archivists throughout Alaska.

Every organization and every individual responded to my requests without hesitation. To my new friends I made during this project and to my lifelong friends, particularly other writers, I wish to express my heartfelt appreciation for your enthusiasm and help. And in my case, it was the man standing behind the woman — my husband, Jim Sumner — who deserves kudos for his patience and support.

Table of Contents

Table of Contents

Preface

In 1997, while serving on the board of the Alaska Transportation Museum in Wasilla, Alaska, I learned that Alaska's women pilots had never been recognized. Their amazing stories had yet to be collected. Fellow board member Ruth Martin Jefford's story appears in one or two books about bush pilots, along with Mary Barrow Worthylake's story, but this was the extent of women's aviation history in Alaska as far as the public knew.

By the spring of 2002, the seeds had germinated and I set out to meet and interview Alaska's aviatrixes. The Alaska chapters of the International Organization of Ninety-Nines—women pilots—provided a list of 60 women to interview. In some cases, personal interviews were impossible, as in the case of Marvel Crosson, the first known women pilot in the Last Frontier. Marvel died while participating in the 1929 Powder Puff Derby. My research took me to newspaper accounts, museum archives, and relatives, acquaintances, and peers of the pilots I would never get to meet. In rare cases, their stories were recorded in a book that was another resource I employed as a research tool.

I set out to learn why each woman desired to fly, where she learned, when she soloed, and what it meant to her to become a pilot. Most of all, I wanted to know why they chose the skies of Alaska rather than the plains of Nebraska or Kansas, where you could land in a wheat field instead of the gravel runways, glaciers, and sandbars more the norm in Alaska.

My research also took me to the air, where I sat in the cockpit, observed the abilities of these women, and enjoyed the same feelings they expressed of "freedom, peace, and being with God."

I learned about the challenges many of the women faced in order to succeed in a nontraditional role. I learned that becoming a pilot affected each one's entire life; the pilots in turn affected me. I learned that when these women decided to become pilots, the question was not so much "Why?" The question was: *Why not?*

Introduction

"Even if you're on the right track, you'll get run over if you just sit there."
— Will Rogers

When most women were getting married, having children, and fanning the home fires, a few nonconformists were taking to the air. In 1911, only eight years after the first powered flight by Wilbur and Orville Wright at Kitty Hawk, North Carolina, Harriet Quimby became the first American woman to receive a pilot's license. In 1921, Bessie Coleman broke the color barrier and became the first African American female pilot, obtaining her license in France. And in 1914, when Marvel Crosson was 14, she saw her first airplane, proclaimed that it was the only thing in the world she wanted and said she would be "an aviator" too. Marvel would later become the first female pilot in Alaska.

That same year, Jeanette Rankin from Montana was elected to the United States House of Representatives, even though women could not vote in elections. Women began to campaign for the right to vote in 1910 but the 19th amendment to the U.S. Constitution was not signed until June 4, 1919. In the meantime, 11,000 women enlisted in the Navy during World War I, serving as clerks and stenographers.

From 1910 to 1920, women bobbed their hair, discarded corsets and petticoats, drove cars, smoked cigarettes and declared their independence. In a letter to a friend, famed aviatrix Amelia Earhart wrote, "I cannot claim to be a feminist but do rather enjoy seeing women tackling all kinds of new problems—new for them, that is."

"In the meantime, in between time, ain't we got fun?"—these were the words to a popular dance tune of the 1920s, reflecting the carefree, live-life-to-the-fullest attitude of young people across the country. H. L. Mencken described the attitude of Puritans during this era as "the haunting fear that someone, somewhere, may be happy."

In 1927, the first "talkie" movie—*The Jazz Singer*, with Al Jolson—appeared on the silver screen. Baseball great Babe Ruth hit a record 60 home runs. And in May of 1927, Charles A. Lindbergh successfully flew a small plane across the Atlantic ocean in 33.5 hours, landing in Paris and making aviation history. With Lindbergh's single event, the world suddenly became smaller. The possibilities were endless for dreamers and entrepreneurs, and some of them headed north for the "last frontier": Alaska.

In 1927, Marvel Crosson packed her bags and followed her brother Joe Crosson to Fairbanks, Alaska. Marvel had already accrued 200 hours in the air before leaving San Diego, California, where the brother-sister flying team first dreamed of criss-crossing Alaska with U.S. airmail contracts. The press nicknamed the daring young woman "Pollyanna of the North."

In spite of bears, mountains, glaciers, downdrafts, updrafts, wind shear and completely unpredictable weather, aviators like Marvel and her brother Joe sought adventure and the opportunity to carve their future in the untamed wilds of Alaska. Once the mail routes were established, flying took the place of dog sleds or horse teams pulling wagons. Trappers and miners were happy to get their pelts and gold to market in Seattle in a few days, not months. Before airplanes, they had to depend on oceangoing vessels, the only connection to the Lower Forty-Eight. Airplanes provided Alaskans with food and supplies and much needed medical care in a more timely manner. This is still true today. Most of Alaska's 365,039.104 acres of land and 6,640 miles of coastline (33,904 miles of shoreline that includes islands) are still remote and unreachable without an airplane.

Alaska is the last frontier in America, comprised of 100,000 glaciers, 3,000 rivers and over three million lakes, plus 17 of the highest peaks in the United States, including 20,320' Mount McKinley. The vast state is also home to bears, caribou, moose wolves, whales, and walrus. Pilots in Alaska are often faced with negotiating landings with a bear, a moose, or a few caribou in their intended path — on an unmanned, unpaved runway in a remote area, often a sandbar.

To enjoy the wilderness and make a living in Bush Alaska, pilots depend on float planes to land on lakes and rivers where there is no other place to put a plane down. Most pilots in the Last Frontier fly their planes year-round by changing from floats to wheel skis in the winter months. Large spongy tires known as "*tundra tires*" make off-airport landings feasible and safer. Many runways are not maintained. There is no snow removal in the winter months, and frost heaves cause paved runways to spall and crack. Broken glass, rocks and debris are common, and fuel is often nonexistent — yet nothing, absolutely nothing keeps Alaska's pilots grounded.

"Alaska's a jumping-off place — the melting pot of the world. It's not even a state! You're gonna freeze," pilot Ruby Bennett's mother told her when the adventurous, high-spirited young woman agreed to leave Nebraska and travel to Anchorage, Alaska, in 1957 to marry George Pappas.

When Alaska became a state in 1959, one in 17 people owned an airplane. According to the Federal Aviation Administration (FAA) in 2004, one in 45 people in Alaska has a pilot's license — six times the national average. And of the 10,000 pilots in Alaska today, 6 percent are women. During the interviews for this book, it became clear these women are not recreational pilots taking a short hop on Sunday afternoons. They are flight instructors, commercial pilots, medevac, tour operators, airline, helicopter and ultralight pilots, and air traffic controllers. These women land on glaciers and mountain knobs, and some even prefer to jump out of perfectly good airplanes! Some seek the adrenaline rush of performing aerobatic stunts. When they're not flying, they are mothers, wives, and business owners.

Marvel Crosson, Ruby Bennett Pappas, and the other women whose stories appear between these pages became pilots for various reasons. But for all of them, when they soloed their self-confidence soared. As Ginny Jacober of Anchorage, Alaska, described it, it was like "a spiritual elevator" in the skies above earth.

Irene Ryan traveled from Texas to Anchorage in 1931, she explained, "There was no work at home. I took my savings in search of adventure." Her meager savings were $25 in severance pay when she left Texas. Irene soloed on June 23, 1932, at Merrill Field in Anchorage, Alaska, then went to New Mexico to get her degree in geology. She returned to Alaska and carved a place in the history books. Irene was recognized as Alaskan of the Year in 1986.

The second woman to solo in Alaska was Mary Barrow Worthylake, who said, "I had always wanted equal rights with my brothers—it hadn't seemed fair that boys got to do all the exciting things. I just wanted to prove that I could learn what Amelia Earhart once called a 'woman's reason.'" Mary soloed on July 27, 1932, at Merrill Field in Anchorage at Star Airways.

Many of the women interviewed were inspired by Amelia Earhart, like aerial photographer Amy Lou Barney from Juneau. Amy Lou flew "by the seat of the pants," hanging out an open door of the cockpit to take pictures of glaciers, mountains, lakes and rivers. Family physician Dr. Nancy Sydnam of Anchorage said there were no heroes for women until Earhart entered the picture, making her record-setting flight across the Atlantic ocean in 1932. In 1935, when Amelia Earhart flew from Hawaii to California, President Roosevelt wisely said, "Aviation is a science which cannot be limited to men only."

Bush pilot Ruth Martin Jefford arrived in Anchorage in 1941, already an experienced pilot. "In the Lower Forty-Eight you can drive to the next town, but not here. You have to fly," Ruth said. "That's one thing I liked."

Schoolteacher Pearl Laska Chamberlain arrived in Fairbanks in 1944, after ferrying airplanes for the military during World War II. Pearl expected to be hired on immediately, but she had to travel to Nome, Alaska, where she took a job at the North Pole Bakery, finally getting hired when one of Frank Whaley's regular pilots showed up drunk.

During the 1929 Powder Puff Derby, one male critic said, "Women pilots are too emotional, vain, and frivolous to fly, and are hazards to themselves and others." Patty Wagstaff learned to fly in Alaska and is a three-time United States National Aerobatic Champion. Patty is living proof of the fallacy of one man's judgment of women pilots.

Roberta "Berta" Degenhardt, now a pilot with FedEx based in Anchorage, received her aviation degree at prestigious Embry-Riddle Aeronautics University (ERAU) in Florida. Her last semester of college, Berta applied to be a Navy pilot. She was turned down because she wasn't male, but her career still soared. Berta is dual-rated in fixed-wing aircraft and helicopters, one of approximately 530 women with this designation in the entire United States.

Ellen Paneok, an Inupiaq pilot from Kotzebue, Alaska, admits she might have gone astray if she hadn't decided to start taking flying lessons when she turned 16. Ellen obtained her private pilot's license at the age of 20 at Merrill Field in Anchorage before she learned to drive a car. Ellen went on to become one of the best-known women in aviation ever born in the Arctic Circle.

The stories between these pages begin in 1927 and reach to the present day. The stories are unique, amazing, funny, and sometimes tragic, but they provide insight into why these pilots chose nontraditional roles and what it meant to each of them. These personal vignettes are intended to give Alaska's women pilots their rightful place in history and allow them to be an inspiration to all.

1

Stand Up, Stand Out:
MARGO COOK

"If the WACS and WAVES are winning the war, what the hell are we fighting for?" This was the cry from men during World War II when women were recruited to ferry planes and relieve male pilots for combat missions overseas.

Margaret Anne Cook, known to her friends in Alaska as "Margo," was teaching school in Downey, California, in 1941 when she read about female flying ace Jackie Cochran. "I wanted to do something different," Margo said. "I liked to be the first to try new things, so I quit my teaching job and signed up for the Civilian Pilot Training [CPT] program." This was the first step towards becoming a Womens Air Service Pilot, or WASP.

At the time the government offered this free program, only one in ten trainees could be a woman. Margo acquired her private pilot's license in June of 1941, but without the minimum of 100 hours in the air, she couldn't follow in Jackie Cochran's steps and become a WASP. She went to the desert in Blythe, California, where every waking minute she was flying to accumulate the required hours.

Margo—or "Cookie," as her classmates nicknamed her—became a WASP in 1943 based in Houston, Texas, where the women had to be housed off base in motels and eat at local cafes and soda fountains. Margo recalled their clothes. "We called them zootsuits. They came in three sizes: large, larger and extra large. They were basically jumpsuits. They also gave us heavier fleece-lined pants and jackets to wear because we flew open-cockpit BT-17s and when the wind blew—which it always did around Houston—it was very cold. The wind sock always stood out straight."

Margo completed her primary training, followed by basic training in a Vultee Vibrator, a popular nickname for a plane "that shook a lot." A few days before Margo's class was to be transferred to Sweetwater, Texas, where they would be housed at a military base, Margo and her classmates engaged in a softball game. The ball came flying across the field. Margo and a friend both chased it, ready to catch it in their mitts. Instead of catching the ball, the women collided, head to head. Unfortunately, this ended Margo's career in the WASP. Her left ear had to be re-attached and she

Margo Cook on a BT-17, or Basic Trainer, when she was a WASP in Houston, Texas, in 1943.

lost her hearing in that ear. Although disappointed, with no severance, or disability pay, or benefits, Margo considered this event a turning point for the good.

A friend who owned a Taylorcraft that she called *Private Willis* asked her to fly with her to Harrisburg, Pennsylvania. "Every time we touched down, the men would yell that WACS and WAVES were winning the war…. They resented women pilots."

"We flew on to Wayne, Michigan, and my friend asked me to look after a Stinson, which I gladly did," Margo said. "The people at Stinson were impressed with my knowledge and gave me a job as a compass compensator. One day when I was sitting in the cockpit, making the compass adjustments, a young man named Boots came to help me. Before long, they advanced me to a better position—A & E mechanic—and that was fine. Eventually, I became the assistant crew chief."

Margo laughed as she recalled an incident while she was working at Stinson. "I am deathly afraid of bees. I had climbed into the plane and closed the windows, unaware there was a bee inside. As soon as he made his presence known, I shut the engine off and jumped out!"

Margo didn't dwell on her fear of bees, explaining that she obtained her commercial license in *Private Willis* and continued to fly to Detroit City Airport where Stinson Aircraft asked her to become a test pilot in their L-5. Her technical experience at Stinson was the ticket to becoming one of the first-known female test pilots in the United States. "As at test pilot I did what's called 'squawking'—putting the aircraft through various maneuvers to be sure it was air worthy and didn't have any problems with the wings or the mags, and would fly straight and level." A civilian, she not only flew test runs right off the factory line for the military, she also gave demonstrations and taught herself to do aerobatics. "I loved to fly upside down," Margo said. "The belly of the plane would be streaked with oil and the crew was not happy about cleaning up the mess. They threatened to make me clean it, and met me with solvent and rags one time when I landed, but I refused."

Margo was employed and considered herself lucky in December of 1944 when the WASP program ended and her classmates couldn't find a job flying. Her fiancé was killed in World War II and Margo didn't pursue marriage again.

Margo talked of stunt flying for a Hop Harrigan movie in the Stinson airplane filmed at Thunderbird Field in Phoenix, Arizona. "I had to fly around wearing Hop's huge hat and when I landed, I'd fall on the floor of the plane and he'd put on the hat and take credit for my efforts. I really thought I was the hero, not him. There were two other pilots, men, and when I found out they were being paid more, I placed a phone call in the middle of the night and demanded equal pay. And I got it," Margo said, matter-of factly. "I also acted as technical advisor on the movie because I had more knowledge than the other pilots."

Margo could have continued to do movie stunts, but she noticed a lot of pilots had ulcers and weren't having much fun flying for other people. She opted for one movie and quit.

"Following the movie work, I was asked to take a Stinson back to Dreyfus, New York, for interior design changes," Margo said. "I'll never forget it. The workers couldn't believe I was flying the bigwigs around—the administrators. When we'd take off, they'd stand on the ground, their fists raised in the air to protest."

Stinson merged with another

Margo Cook with a Stinson L-5 (a 1945 Stinson aircraft) in Wayne, Michigan (adjacent to Willow Run Air Force Base).

9

company in 1946 and Margo returned to teaching until a former roommate suggested that she should come and teach in the Last Frontier. Margo did some flying at local flight services after she arrived in Alaska, and taught high school and became a counselor. In 1954 when the Alaska Ninety-Nines were created, Margo became a charter member. She is still an active member today.

Ralph Campbell first met Margo Cook when he and his wife lived in an apartment building in Anchorage where Margo was during the disastrous earthquake of 1964. He was a pilot and often took Margo flying in his Tri-Pacer with a 160-horsepower engine (originally 150 horsepower). "She wrung that plane out!" Campbell said. He explained that meant Margo put the plane through stalls and flew inverted just like she did as a test pilot for Stinson Aircraft. "She made me sit up and take notice! Margo's one hell of a pilot and I'm not exaggerating. Don't get me wrong; she's not a daredevil, she just knows what she's doing."

Flying is what made Margo the happiest. "I liked to do dangerous stuff like fly just above the trees and buzz farmhouses before I moved to Alaska," she said. "The farmers would get mad, but it never stopped me. It was fun."

On one flight, Margo was determined to find a small field where she could land the Stinson L-5, but it seemed to be unrecognizable. She landed at an unknown field and since she was in a military plane without proper identification, she had to wait to be cleared for take off. Stinson received a call and confirmed that yes, Margo "Cookie" Cook was the pilot authorized to fly the L-5. "When I returned to base, the crew came running outside and hung a big sign around my neck that read 'Property of Stinson Aircraft. If found please return to Wayne, Michigan.'"

Margo said, "I've been very independent all my life. I had two Master's degrees—one in Science, the other in Guidance Counseling—and my commercial flight instructor's license." She retired from Anchorage School District in 1982.

Pat Haller, a member of the Alaska chapter of Ninety-Nines, recalled when she took classes from Margo in high school. "She was tough, but she was very good." Asked if she remembered Margo touting her background as a civilian test pilot or World War II WASP, Haller didn't recall any time when it came up until they reconnected as members of the Ninety-Nines. This was no surprise because Margo doesn't brag, but she will talk about flying if approached, and her eyes light up when she shares her story.

Margo continued to fly just for fun at Spernak Airways at Merrill Field in Anchorage, and also helped to schedule the airplanes at Wilbur's Flight Service, also based at Merrill Field, but her paid flying career ended when she came north in 1953. "My friends in the WASP program continued to pursue flying in the Lower Forty-Eight with the hope of getting to fly into space, but it didn't materialize," Margo said. When asked what her goal would be if she were a young woman taking flying lessons today, Margo replied, "I'd want to be an astronaut."

I wonder if NASA would let Margo do aerobatics with the space shuttle. It's a sure bet she'd want to put the shuttle through its paces!

2

A Natural Gift:
Marvel Crosson

The press nicknamed Marvel Crosson "Bird Girl" and "Pollyanna of the North" because she was the first female pilot in the Alaska Territory when she arrived in 1927. Marvel followed her brother, Joe Crosson, to Fairbanks, Alaska, after she saved up enough money working in a camera shop in San Diego, California. Marvel was admired for her "pluck and resourcefulness," news reporters wrote in the 1920s.

Marvel and her brother grew up on a Kansas farm. She was 14 and Joe was almost 11 when they saw their first airplane, barnstorming across the wheat fields. In a September 1929 article in *The Country Gentlemen*, Marvel recalled their first reactions: "Joe grabbed my shoulder and began to dance up and down. 'I'm going to be an aviator. I'm going to be an aviator!' he shouted. And I agreed with him that it was the only thing in the world and said I was going to be an aviator too. This did not seem to be strange to Joe because we had always been partners and I could do anything he could."

It was no surprise, when the family moved to San Diego, California, that the sister and brother team saved up $125 and bought a wrecked Curtiss N-9 seaplane. Marvel and Joe scrounged for parts in junkyards and bought an old OX-5 engine from a boat dealer. In her account of the 1929 Powder Puff Derby, Gene Nora Jessen wrote, "When they tested the engine in the backyard, they simultaneously tested their mother's love and patience by plastering her chickens up against the fence."

Lillian Crosson, Joe's widow, confirmed the story for me when we talked on the phone. She and Marvel became close friends while Lillian was in college at the university in Fairbanks, before she met and married Joe Crosson. Lillian said, "Yes, they built an airplane in their backyard, and they flew it!"

Again combining their hard-earned cash, they decided that Joe would take flying lessons first; then he would teach Marvel. He did. The first time Joe turned the controls over to Marvel at about 1,000 feet, she said her heart was in her throat. The skeptics on the ground didn't want to believe a girl could fly an airplane, so when Marvel made a pass by the airport, Joe climbed out on the wing to prove that he wasn't piloting the aircraft.

"When we got in, the gang would not believe that I was piloting the plane!" Marvel wrote. "They would not believe that Joe was willing to risk his neck to a girl. Joe got peeved and we trundled the ship back to the line and took off again. This time I flew her much lower and we shot over the hangars with Joe on the wing waving like all possessed. This time they believed that I was piloting and there was a very different tone to their good fellowship from then on. They knew how Joe felt about it — he would never get out on the wing with any other pilot but me, and they knew it."

In 1926 Joe set out for even greater challenges in the Alaska Territory. "Joe received a long telegram from a man in Alaska asking him to come there and fly passengers and mail. What was more exciting, the man was willing to pay Joe $350 a month. Joe would have to be his own mechanic and take care of his planes, but even at that it seemed almost too good to be true. As Joe said, 'Just think, Marvel, he wants to pay me to fly!'"

Lacking enough money for the sister and brother team to both head north, Marvel stayed in California and logged in a couple hundred hours in the skies above San Diego. But when she had saved enough money, she joined Joe in Fairbanks. Lillian Crosson said Marvel once told her, "I want to race just like the men." Lillian recalls that Marvel obtained her commercial license in a check ride with Ben Eielson, the

Marvel Crosson, 1927. Kay Kennedy Collection, Alaska and Polar Region Archives, Rasmussen Library, University of Alaska Fairbanks.

father of aviation in Alaska. The year was 1927, but the precise date is unavailable. The previous year, the Air Commerce Act made it necessary for pilots to be licensed and the aircraft had to be certified air worthy.

In a news article in the *Ketchikan Chronicle* dated December 23, 1928, they picked up an interview Marvel gave in San Diego. "Aviation is here to stay," Marvel said. "People don't know what to use it for. Up north — beyond the railroad — it's transportation. It's there to stay." Of course, Marvel was speaking of Fairbanks. She was asked what would happen in case of a forced landing. "We doctor the motor and stretch the glides. Two hours out by airplane might mean a month of walking to get back."

Marvel and Joe had visions of crisscrossing Alaska with U.S. mail contracts, which was not well received by locals as a popular concept, especially dog mushers. Airplanes brought competition. Signs were blatantly posted at roadhouses that offered food and lodging to dog mushers: "NO DOGS NOR PILOTS ALLOWED."

In 1928 Joe traveled to New York to raise money for the airmail company he and Ben Eielsen planned to start in Alaska. Marvel would be one of the pilots. While in the Lower Forty-Eight, Joe was wooed by Sir Hubert Wilkins to be part of an expedition over the Antarctic, along with Ben Eielsen. Joe went to California to pick up a new Lockheed Vega and wired Marvel in Fairbanks to meet him in San Diego to help him ferry Wilkins' new monoplane to New York. They took turns sleeping and piloting as they flew across-country to deliver the airplane.

Marvel returned to San Diego following the cross-country trip with her brother. On May 28, 1929, she topped Louise Thaden's previous altitude record of 20,270 feet. The new record Marvel attained was 23,996 feet in a Travelair J-5. Two weeks later, she planned to compete in the first Transcontinental Air Derby, which was set to start in Santa Monica, California. It was an event that would take eight days to complete, ending in Cleveland, Ohio. Marvel planned on marrying aviator Emery Bronty when she reached Cleveland. Next on Marvel's agenda, after the air race, she planned to capture a new endurance mark.

The Powder Puff Derby, so named by Will Rogers, would have been but one in many more feathers in Marvel's aviatrix cap. She was the first to take off from Santa Monica when the race began, arriving at their first stopover safe and sound. Marvel was expected to win the race, but on the second day of the event, August 19, 1929, she crashed in Arizona. Crosson's crumpled body was found outside the airplane, her parachute unopened. There were rumors of acid that damaged wires in the engine, possibly a case of sabotage. As recent as 2002, a firsthand account from a young man who was at the crash scene tells a very different tale. Marvel probably suffered from carbon monoxide poisoning. Louise Thaden, the winner of the race, had a clear case of carbon monoxide poisoning in a plane she flew prior to the race. An air tube fed into the cockpit kept her from suffering the same fate as Marvel during the air race.

Male critics of women taking to the air in the 1920s were quick to blame the beautiful aviatrix' death on the inability of women to handle an airplane. Typical comments went like this: "Women pilots are too emotional, vain, and frivolous to fly, and are hazards to themselves and others." As for Marvel Crosson, nothing could have been further from the truth.

Lillian Crosson said, "Marvel was like a big sister to me. I looked up to her. She was eight years my senior, but we became close even before I met Joe. Marvel had personality. She was a wonderful person who loved people and flying. When Marvel was in Fairbanks she flew with Noel Wien and Ben Eielson, and of course, Joe," Lillian said. "Joe was in Cleveland, Ohio, waiting for Marvel to arrive when the air race ended. He was devastated to hear she crashed, of course. They were very close. I was on a train from Fairbanks and when it pulled into the station in Anchorage, Ben Eielson met us and told us about Marvel's death. I was shocked and saddened."

Eielson, Wien and Joe Crosson left permanent marks on Bush flying history in Alaska, and no doubt Marvel would have too if she had returned unscathed from the Lower Forty-Eight.

An excerpt from a letter Marvel wrote to her mother preceding the air race was very revealing: "Don't worry, every flyer would rather go out with her plane instead of a more lingering way. Just think of the thrill of making immediate contact with the spiritual while doing the thing one loves to do."

To have known Marvel personally would have meant being in the company of an ever-smiling, high-spirited woman on a mission to show the world that women were very capable pilots. She had a natural gift. In a news article a year after Marvel learned to fly, she said it best: "There is nothing in the world to rest your body after a long, tiresome day at work like a flight in an airplane up above the clouds. A half hour's sail onto the great blue expanse of the heavens, playing hide and seek with the clouds, inspires and rests you, and you return to earth invigorated and rejuvenated."

3

First to Solo:
IRENE IRVINE RYAN

Irene Irvine Ryan first had the thrill of being airborne in Border, Texas, in the late 1920s when she worked for a construction company as a bookkeeper after finishing high school. Her employer had the contract to build houses for the crews on the gas pipeline, and Irene flew with her boss to the sites to do the payroll and keep track of construction costs.

"That's when Mom fell in love with flying," Marcella Ryan Sharrock said. "When her Uncle Matt Neiminen came to visit from Alaska, he told stories of bush flying and Mom was hooked."

Irene arrived in 1931 and quickly landed a job as a waitress at the Anchorage Grill, followed by a job as a bank teller at National Bank of Alaska. Irene once told a reporter, "There was no work at home. I took my savings in search of adventure." Her boss at the construction company had given Irene $25 in severance pay.

Adventure turned into history-making firsts for the petite, 105-pound, brown-eyed brunette. At age 22, Irene became the first woman to solo in the Territory of Alaska on June 23, 1932, at Merrill Field in Anchorage. This feat is attested to in a letter signed by C. H. Ruttan, manager, and Jack Waterworth, instructor, for Star Air Service. Her instructor urged her to solo because Mary Barrow was also taking lessons. Barrows soloed July 27 of the same year, and received her license in September.

When Irene soloed, it was a clear and sunny day according to the United States Weather Service, with a high of 61 degrees and a low of 42 with zero precipitation. It is unknown how many hours of instruction Irene had in the T. P. Swallow open-cockpit airplane before her solo flight. Her fear and apprehension, or sheer excitement and elation, were never documented in articles written during her lifetime, and no diary has surfaced that might provide insight. But for most pilots — not only women — the single most confidence-building event of their life is when they solo in an airplane.

Learning to fly was only the first in a long string of significant challenges Irene

Ryan would take. Soon after this feat, Irene left Alaska and enrolled in the New Mexico School of Mines. She was the first woman geologist to graduate at NMSM. She married her classmate John Edward "Pat" Ryan and in the winter of 1941, with newborn Marcella Ryan in her arms, Irene and her husband settled into a 10' × 10' tarpaper shack he built at Merrill Field in Anchorage, Alaska. That first home was close to the power plant where Pat Ryan worked, but before long they moved into an unfinished cabin across town, "in the country" in an area known as Spenard, her daughter, Marcella, recalled. When they lived at Merrill Field, Marcella remembered her parents saying they had no running water and went into town to the Finn baths once a week. "Mom washed my diapers in a bucket and hung them on my stroller to dry in minus-30 degrees while she took me to the babysitter's house."

In an interview with the *Anchorage Daily News* in 1997, Irene described Anchorage in 1941: "So great was the crush of people arriving during that spring and summer of 1941 that many had to sleep in the lobbies of the hotels, in the restaurants and even in the jail."

In December 1941, when Pearl Harbor was attacked, Irene was working for the Civil Aeronautics Authority (CAA), designing and constructing airfields in the Territory, so her job was considered essential during wartime: "I did not have to join the exodus of wives and families from Anchorage and Alaska during 1942."

Following the war, Ryan helped design Anchorage International Airport and numerous other airports in Alaska. She was a consulting civil, mining, geological and petroleum engineer, employed during her long career by the CAA, Birch-Johnson-Lytle Construction Co., Thomas B. Bourne Associates, Fluor Corp. Ltd., Shell Oil Co., and Lyon & Associates. She also had her own consulting firm.

Ryan is best known for serving in the Alaska Territorial House of Representatives in 1955 and 1957, which met for 60 days every two

Irene Irvine Ryan, Star Airways, 1932, Merrill Field, Alaska. Kay Kennedy Collection, Alaska and Polar Region Archives, Rasmussen Library, University of Alaska Fairbanks.

Left to right: Nell Scott, pilot Harry Blunt, Irene Irvine Ryan. Kay Kennedy Collection, Alaska and Polar Region Archives, Rasmussen Library, University of Alaska Fairbanks.

years. In 1959 Ryan served in the state senate after Alaska became the 49th state. She not only filled these offices, she championed the development of resources such as oil. Her stepfather was a tool dresser and the family followed him through the oil fields of Oklahoma and Texas. In high school Ryan worked after class plotting graphs from drillers' logs and screening well cuttings for fossils. In Alaska, during his term in 1977, Governor Egan appointed Ryan to a cabinet post as Commissioner of the Department of Economic Development. It was Irene Ryan the legislators looked to for expertise in oil and mining, which was not typical in a male-dominated legislature.

Former Attorney General John Havelock, who worked alongside Ryan, said, "It was really extraordinary that woman could make her way in a man's world, in a man's topic."

In 1959 Irene put it in her own words. "I have found that the best way to be accepted on equal ground is just to go ahead and quietly do the job at hand."

Her daughter Marcella described her mother as "a woman who had inner strength of conviction. She didn't speak often, but when she did, people listened." Marcella also suggested that if her mother had not been an engineer she would have been a philosopher.

"I miss the old days," Marcella said as we looked at a showcase of family photos in the hallway of her home. In her office, filled with family history and mementos, Marcella proudly pointed to political posters when Kennedy and Johnson were running for president and vice president, inset photos of her mother and other Alaska Democratic candidates pictured with the national candidates. "Politics were the main topic at dinner when Mom and Dad were alive … forever. We always had people sitting around the table who cared about the future of Alaska and its people."

I was puzzled why Irene Ryan and not her husband, Pat, pursued an unlikely career in Alaskan politics. Marcella said it was because her father was employed in a federal civil service job at Fort Richardson and could not speak out. "They would attend meetings and my father would elbow my mother to speak up. That's how she got thrust into the political arena."

Irene Ryan was awarded an honorary Doctor of Science degree from Alaska Pacific University in 1985 and was named Alaskan of the Year in 1986. When she passed away at age 88 in 1997, the Alaska Legislature honored her with a proclamation and Governor Knowles ordered flags across the state flown at half mast. Listed among her achievements were the design of the military pipeline from Skagway through Canada to Fairbanks and geologic maps and surveys developed for Anchorage Gas & Oil Development, Inc.

Daughter Marcella said her mother was happiest in a pair of jeans and wool shirt, working in the outdoors at a mine site or oil drill site, "sitting on the well" taking core samples.

In one interview before her death, Irene Ryan said, "When we see something that we feel needs to be done, we can't sit still and let Henry do it."

Irene Ryan first came north for the adventure, but she stayed in Alaska and became a shaker and a maker, a doer. But first she was a pilot.

4

Why Not?
MARY BARROW WORTHYLAKE

"Would you like to take an airplane ride someday?" Joe Barrow asked the pretty young schoolteacher from Grants Pass, Oregon, in the spring of 1924.

Mary Barrow Worthylake, in her book *Up in the Air*, wrote, "Until that moment I had never desired to leave the ground, but suddenly flying was the one thing I had always wanted to do."

Two days later, Mary went for her first flight in a JN4D, or "Jenny," a World War I airplane. She wore goggles, a leather helmet over her long hair, and a long, tight skirt that made it awkward to climb into the cockpit. Mary said, "I had wanted to bob my hair but my Oregon school superintendent said he wouldn't have a bobbed-haired teacher in his county. A teacher couldn't possibly maintain either dignity or discipline with short hair!" (This was also the era when women did not wear slacks or trousers.)

Within a month, Joe Barrow proposed and made plans to return from California to marry his bride. When the chairman of Mary's school board heard about her wedding plans he said, "Better get him to take out lots of insurance. An aviator's wife is sure to be a young widow."

Mary's friends expressed their concern too. "Of course you'll get him to change his occupation. Surely you don't want a husband who *flies*!"

Mary and Joe married in September of 1924 and off they flew on their honeymoon in a Hisso-Jenny that Mary remembers "was mortgaged from the propellor to the rudder."

When they were planning to marry the couple talked about coming to Alaska, but six years passed before Joe and his business partner decided that Pacific International Airways (PIA) should expand into Alaska from British Columbia. They planned to bid on mail contracts that had been served by men with dog sleds.

Mary's elation and plans for a romantic trip north in 1930 soon vanished. Two planes were waiting at the airport. Joe would fly the trim-bodied Fleetster he had brought out from the East. His partner, Harry Blunt, would fly a Fairchild. When

19

all the gear and luggage was loaded the planes couldn't lift off. Everything was repacked and some things were discarded. Mary, along with Harry Blunt's wife, was left on the runway "amidst a pile of gear," she wrote. "They told us to meet them at Whitehorse when they departed." The two women traveled by steamship through the inside passage on board the *Princess Norah*. Mary's exquisite descriptions of her first trip north are worthy of sharing here:

"The trip up the Inside Passage is delightful, between wooded islands and steeply rising mountains where waterfalls tumble over crags and snow caps the peaks. At Alert Bay we saw our first totem poles in front of weathered cabins where Indian families lived. It was snowing in Ketchikan so we didn't do much sightseeing. Again at Juneau we tramped on snowy streets, the soft crunch of snow delightful to Californians.

"On a windy, blustery morning we steamed up Lynn Canal and docked at Skagway. The rocky cliffs above the pier were covered with paintings, insignia of boats and a huge painted skull of Soapy Smith — the bandit who had terrorized Skagway in the early days of the gold rush. The captain hurried the unloading so that he could be out of the canal in daylight as there were icebergs floating in the water."

Mary waited in Skagway for word from her husband but learned that Harry Blunt had crashed at Telegraph Creek and both his legs were smashed when the motor folded back on him. Joe Barrow tried to taxi across the ice to rescue his friend but his Fleetster aircraft dropped through a weak spot in the ice. Joe escaped the icy water through a trap door in the top of the cockpit. Both men were cared for at a small infirmary at Telegraph Creek by a veterinarian.

"There was nothing I could do but wait," Mary explained.

Mary Barrow Worthylake, 1932, Merrill Field, Anchorage, Alaska. Kay Kennedy Collection, Alaska and Polar Region Archives, Rasmussen Library, University of Alaska Fairbanks.

The Fleetster was recovered from the icy waters and Joe flew it back, but soon afterwards he decided that Mary should return to

Victoria while he went on to Fairbanks. Six months later, in June, Joe sent a telegram from Anchorage that read: "Catch the next boat north." Within 24 hours, Mary and their two children were on board the *SS Aleutian* as it steamed out of Puget Sound.

Mary discovered Anchorage to be "moderately new and up to date, comparable to a progressive small town in Montana." However, her first living quarters in Alaska proved to be quite a contrast from her seven-room home with all the city amenities in Victoria, British Columbia. Mary described their apartment in Anchorage:

"The living room contained a pull-down bed, the kitchen had a three-burner kerosene stove and a dry-goods box nailed outside the window for a cooler. Beyond was a room with twin beds for the children. The rent was $62.50, which seemed exorbitant, but would be far less than staying in a hotel and eating in restaurants. I unpacked our clothes and started housekeeping, discovering in dismay that the prices of food were double what they were 'Outside.' Everything had to be shipped by steamer, and then brought to Anchorage over the railroad from Seward."

Two weeks later Mary flew with Joe along the proposed mail routes. By November, Joe planned to begin mail service along the Yukon and Kuskokwim rivers so they stopped at the villages on the route to meet the people, to appoint agents, interview postmasters, select places for gasoline storage and winter supplies before the rivers froze over. Returning to Anchorage, Mary wrote, "Anchorage looked like a metropolis after the little native villages and trading posts where we had stopped."

Mary didn't have a chance to find a house for her family in the "metropolis" before Joe whisked them off to Fairbanks to another bare-bones apartment. Even though it seems hard to imagine being uprooted every few months, living out of a suitcase, Mary dutifully followed her husband's lead. In Fairbanks, Mary says she felt even more at home in Alaska.

"There was an atmosphere about this friendly town which I liked. Anchorage might be a town in Montana or Idaho, but Fairbanks could be nowhere but in the interior of Alaska. The Northern Commercial Company store displayed skis and dog harness and mukluks and dehydrated potatoes in the windows. Jewelry stores featured nugget jewelry. The telephone central office asked for the name of the person you were calling instead of a number, and often told you where you might find the person."

Mary wrote of the thermometer remaining at minus-32 degrees for six weeks, and she recalled one of PIA's planes taking off at Birches, on the Yukon River, when it was a mere 72 degrees below zero. Most Alaskan pilots today are reluctant to fly when the temperature is minus-40 degrees.

In her book, Mary recalled, "Frozen noses, frozen knees, frozen toes were commonplace."

The pioneer aviators in Alaska were often faced with unpredictable weather conditions. Mary compiled a list from the pilots' log books of January 16, 1932. All around the interior, from Fairbanks to McGrath, Ruby, Kaltag, Nulato, Unalakleet, Flat, Takotna and Tanana, temperatures ranged from minus-51 to a high of minus-40 degrees. A few days later, in the same villages, visibility was listed as "nil" or "snowing," but the pilots were still airborne as soon as conditions allowed.

Even though Mary's husband had a contract to deliver the mail, he and the other pilots accommodated the trappers who wanted to get their furs to market in Seattle. Orders for eggs, fresh meat and perishables were delivered along with mail.

Mary and her children were uprooted once again when Joe convinced her to return to Washington and wait for his instructions. She protested leaving her new-found friends, in spite of miserable winters and inadequate housing. But Mary and the children rode the train to Seward and the steamship to Washington, again. In the summer of 1932, they returned to Anchorage. Joe was on the East Coast arranging for financing for PIA. To keep busy and to prove something to herself, Mary decided to take flying lessons.

"For eight years I had wanted to fly, since I took my first ride in the cow pasture in San Jacinto [California]. I had never been physically active, had not cared for athletics. But I had always wanted equal rights with my brothers— it hadn't seemed fair that boys got to do all the exciting things."

When Mary asked her husband if she could have the money for lessons, he said, "You can't learn to fly. You get airsick too easily, but I'll let you hold the stick sometimes when we are in the air."

Mary didn't explain where the money finally came from for lessons, but she wrote of feeling like she was floating on air after the required physical exam. "I had closed my eyes and stood on one leg to see if my sense of balance was all right. I sat at one end of a room and pulled little strings to align bolts in a box seemingly a quarter of a mile away. This was a depth perception test."

Her doctor said, "Well, you passed for a private license. Your eyes aren't good enough so that you could ever get a transport license unless they should improve. Now go on and learn to fly — but be careful."

Mary didn't plan to be a commercial pilot or fly the mail or pilot a transport plane. "I just wanted to prove that I could learn, what Amelia Earhart once called a 'woman's reason.' Pilots stood around the field when a woman took off as if they considered every flight a potential crack-up."

In her book, Mary described the airport in Anchorage where she was first airborne: "Merrill Field, named for an early-day pilot, Russell Merrill, was about a mile from town, along a lovely country road, bordered in June with delicate pink wild roses and masses of flaming purple fireweed." In July of 1932, the airport had been relocated from a grass strip downtown. The community had purchased the land and developed a gravel runway a mile east of town. Only a handful of wooden hangars and shacks lined the north side of the airfield in 1932 when Mary learned to fly. In later years, Merrill Field became a hub of aviation activity, including air taxi operations, airline services, and flight schools. Today, four-lane streets border the north and south side of the original runway, and the University of Alaska's School of Aviation is located near the east end of the runway. A hospital, fire station and shopping center are within walking distance of the airfield.

Mary took lessons from Steve Mills, one of three owners of Star Air Service, the first flight school that opened at Merrill Field. She climbed into the open cockpit of Mills' Fleet biplane wearing jodhpur breeches, a blazer jacket made from a Hudson's Bay blanket, goggles and a borrowed leather helmet.

"Some days I felt that I was learning rapidly," Mary wrote. "I was master of the plane and it obeyed my commands. Other days were a constant battle with controls and perverse winds and air pockets. Then the plane took the bit in its teeth, so to speak, and no matter how tightly I clung to the stick, I had a feeling that its racing horsepower was mocking me — that I would never be able to subdue it."

Mary ground looped the biplane on one attempt at landing and a fellow student was quick to criticize. "Too bad, but women aren't supposed to fly anyway. A woman's place is in the home."

Mary reflected: "Perhaps I was too ambitious, attempting something for which the Lord hadn't intended me — or He would have given me wings. Here I was, a mother of two small children, risking my neck in so foolhardy a fashion. Had I any right to take such chances?"

Known for being even tempered, very focused, and self-disciplined, Mary continued taking lessons. She piled up seven hours of instruction time, 20 minutes a day, and felt a little ashamed because her brother Frank had soloed in just over four hours. She mentioned Jinks Ames, a mechanic who worked for PIA, had soloed after one hour and 20 minutes of dual instruction.

Finally, instructor Steve Mills cut Mary loose to solo, tying his white handkerchief to a wing strut to let everyone know a novice "was trying the air on wobbly wings."

In an open-cockpit airplane, without the benefit of large spongy tundra tires used today, no doubt Mary's takeoff on the gravel runway was bumpy at best. She had no radio or instruments to guide her flight, only an airspeed indicator. The biplane rolled down the gravel airstrip at Merrill Field, past the wooden hangars and shacks. Through her writing, we're able to relive the experience in Mary's own words:

"I didn't hesitate, but opened the throttle and went down the field. The tail came up. I was in the air. It had been a good takeoff. And not until that minute did the realization come to me that I was up — up in the air all alone. The front cockpit loomed big and empty without Steve's familiar head and shoulders up there. The engine throbbed with power as I banked and made a climbing turn."

Steve and his partners Jack Waterworth and Charley Ruttan watched as their lone plane flew overhead. If Mary crash-landed, their flying school would be out of business.

"I dreaded to start down; I was safe as long as I stayed in the air. I remembered a student who stayed up, flying round and round, afraid to come down, until he ran out of gas. I prayed, 'The Lord will preserve me from evil.'

"Down, down toward the field. I was a little high after all as I came over the edge of the brush to the runway. I touched the ground. The plane bounced. For a fleeting second I panicked. Was it a high bounce? Should I give the motor the gun and go on up again? No, the plane settled down onto the runway. I held the stick back firmly against my stomach and clamped on left rudder to counteract a ground loop. Then gently I applied both brakes. The Fleet slowed to a stop. I kicked it around, opened the throttle slightly and taxied up in front of the hangar. With one motion I cut the gas and the switch and then sank back, breathing a great sigh of relief. It was over. I was safely down.

"I took off my helmet and found that my forehead was wet with perspiration. I unfastened my safety belt with suddenly clammy fingers and, as I climbed out of the cockpit, I realized that my heart was pounding and my knees were rubbery. Reaction had set in and I was more nervous than I had been in the actual flight."

Mary's young children raced across the field to congratulate their mother. A telegram to her husband in New York, announcing her accomplishment, went unacknowledged, but Mary continued to fly, practicing figure eights and spirals and spot landings in anticipation of the semi-annual arrival of the inspector from the Department of Commerce: "My log book recorded just twelve hours of solo time when the Inspector arrived."

When it was her turn, Mary climbed into the plane and listened to the inspector's instructions. He told her to make figure-eight turns and to make a spiral from 2,000 feet to a spot landing in front of McGee's hangar.

"Those figure eights almost got me — vertical banks without gaining or losing altitude were no cinch for a student with twelve hours of solo! Then I climbed up to two thousand feet, shut off the motor, made three 360-degree turns, and at last brought the wheels down to the airport for a spot landing."

Mary, the only woman among 12 students, didn't expect to pass her exam.

"How incredulous I felt when the Inspector got out a pencil, rested his pad on his knee, and wrote me out a Letter of Authority. I had passed! I was a licensed pilot!"

Ironically, the young German pilot who criticized Mary when she ground-looped during training did not pass his exam. Only four of the 12 students passed that day, and Mary was the only woman.

Joe and Mary Barrow parted company for the last time in 1938 and Mary returned to teach school in Washington, later remarrying. Her son, Frank, learned to fly, as did his two daughters and son.

Dr. Maria Barrow, wife of Mary's son, Frank, fondly remembered her blue-gray-eyed mother-in-law: "I envied her ability to read without distraction. She was very active all her life in clubs and church. Mom enjoyed life and people. No matter how many times she moved, even after she remarried, she took it in stride. She loved to travel to numerous places around the world, often returning to Alaska."

Mary Barrow soloed on July 27, 1932, at Merrill Field in Anchorage, Alaska, and went on to become licensed in September of the same year.

5

One Woman's Journey:
MARY JOYCE

Mary Joyce is best remembered for mushing a team of dogs from Taku Lodge, forty miles upriver from Juneau, all the way to Fairbanks, Alaska, in 1936 — a 1000-mile trip. When she first talked about the trip she planned to make to Fairbanks, people in Juneau scoffed. Mary said, "The people in Juneau said it would take me two years to drive to Fairbanks and that I would be pulling the dogs in. They also said that I would eat the dogs or the dogs would eat me." Mary left on December 22, 1935, and with the help of Alaska Natives to guide her, arrived in Fairbanks on March 26, 1936.

Mary Joyce is also remembered as the first woman radio telephone operator in the Territory. With better than average hand-eye coordination, she was also known for her ability to drive a boat and shoot a gun as well as any man, maybe better, it's been said.

In some accounts, Mary is remembered for first piloting a plane in 1943, but Bud Bodding, when he spoke with me by telephone, remembered taking flying lessons with Mary and said she soloed in Juneau in 1937 after five hours of training. "About the same time I soloed," he said from his home on Douglas Island near Juneau. "Jimmy Rinehart was Mary's instructor. The C-3 Aeronca was on floats when both of us soloed."

There's more. Mary, who was also a nurse, was employed the by L. C. Smith family of Smith-Corona typewriter fame to care for their alcoholic son, Hack Smith. It is well publicized that Mrs. Smith bought the Twin Glacier Camp to house her errant son, Hack, and keep him out of the public eye. Mary inherited the camp when Hack died of a heart attack and she renamed it Taku Lodge. Mary turned it into a popular tourist stop on the Taku River.

In Juneau in the 1930s, gold mining was king. The Alaska-Juneau Mine employed almost 1,000 people. The men worked seven days a week in wet, cold underground tunnels with no safety devices and no first-aid kits. They had two days a year off— Christmas and the Fourth of July. Although air travel was becoming more common, marine transport brought goods and people to Juneau. When maritime strikes kept the ships from operating, old-timers said it was hard to get groceries.

When Pearl Harbor was attacked by the Japanese in December 1941, one Juneau man took his rifle to the Douglas Bridge and shot out the navigation lights in Gastineau Channel. Juneau never was attacked, but 150,000 soldiers and sailors passed through town. Fights broke out from Percy's Cafe on Front Street to the end of South Franklin.

"South Franklin was lined with bars with names like Bloody Bucket and Blackey's Bar. Near present-day Marin View Apartments was the red-light district. The houses had red lights and the women showed themselves in pictures windows," said John Dapcevich, who was a customer at Percy's Cafe when he was a teen.

Government replaced mining in Juneau, and after the Territory of Alaska became a state in 1959, it remained as the State Capitol.

Mary Joyce was in Juneau when mining was the main breadwinner; she was there when World War II broke out; and she probably raised her glass to celebrate

Mary Joyce holding onto the dog sled while competing in Fairbanks in the Miss Alaska Pageant of 1936 after mushing her dog team from Juneau, Alaska. Alaska Aviation Heritage Museum, Anchorage, Alaska.

statehood in 1959. Unlike her friend Bud Bodding, who became a Navy pilot and later flew for Alaska Airlines, Mary had a minor collision with a boat in Gastineau Channel in an Aeronca C-3 and hung up her wings. Fellow pilot Bodding said, "Mary only flew to and from Taku Lodge and Juneau because it's how you get around in Alaska."

It's no wonder that Mary became disenchanted or fearful of flying. Bodding said, "There are lots of steep mountains and it's hard to get in and out of Juneau. The winds from the Taku River into Juneau hit you in front one minute and in the next they smack you from behind. It's very unpredictable. That's why the legislature gathers in Anchorage or Fairbanks when they're weathered out of Juneau, or that's their excuse," he added with a wry chuckle. "With modern technology flying in and out of Juneau is a lot easier."

As for Mary Joyce, Bodding said, "She was an attractive woman with black hair when I met her in the 1930s. She liked to hang around men and airplanes and mush dogs across the glaciers. She was quite a character."

Mary went from pilot to stewardess for Pan-Am and Northwest Air, but that's not all. In the 1940s, Mary hauled radio equipment with her team of dogs for the U.S. Navy. When she sold the Taku Lodge she worked as a nurse at St. Ann's Hospital in Juneau. Apparently, Mary was also quite an entrepreneur. She bought the Top Hat Bar and the Lucky Lady Saloon, and for several decades Mary greeted her friends and customers from behind the bar.

Jim Ruotsala, author of the book *Alaskan Wings*, remembers talking with Mary at the Top Hat Bar. "She told me she had a picture of herself, and she'd sell it to me for $50.00. For that price she'd autograph it too!"

In a newspaper article about Mary after her death in 1976 from a heart ailment, a friend said, "Mary Joyce was one hell of a woman and lived a life that any man could envy."

Mary was a pilot, a nurse, and a barrista in later years. She mushed dogs a thousand miles across Alaska from Juneau to Fairbanks. She was a radio telephone operator who could handle a boat, fly a plane and shoot a gun. Mary Joyce was a Renaissance woman and Alaskan pioneer.

6

Alaska's Favorite:
RUTH MARTIN JEFFORD

With the determination of a grizzly bear, nothing seems to hold her back. Ruth Martin Jefford was the first woman pilot licensed to instruct students at Merrill Field in Anchorage. She was also the first female commercial air taxi operator in the entire state of Alaska. This pint-sized woman arrived here in 1941, stayed and gained the respect of all of Alaska's pilots.

Over the years, Ruth has received numerous awards, including recognition by the Alaska Airmen's Association for "excellent contributions made to general aviation." She is a member of the prestigious OX5 Hall of Fame, having soloed in an aircraft powered by the OX5 engine prior to 1941. Ruth is a lifetime member of the Ninety-Nines, and she has been recognized by the Smithsonian Air and Space Museum as a "frontier aviatrix." On the occasion of her birthday in July of 2002, Ruth was recognized by Alaska state senator Lyda Green for significant contributions she has made as "an Alaskan aviation pioneer, as a great mentor and ambassador for the 49th state."

The earliest memory Ruth has of airplanes was of a large plane landing on floats while she was on vacation with her parents in Lake George, New York. "I had never been off the ground," Ruth said when we met at her home in Wasilla, Alaska, "but that night, I dreamed I flew that big plane over the Adirondack mountains!"

Years later, when Ruth was 16, her family lived in Fremont, Nebraska. "I ran outside to watch a barnstormer flying overhead," she said. "He landed on the west side of town, and I raced across the fields on my bicycle to have a closer look. He asked me if I wanted to go for a ride. I didn't hesitate. Away we went, staying airborne so long that he ran out of gas and couldn't taxi when we finally landed."

Ruth was determined to learn to fly, so not long after, her mother drove her to Lincoln, Nebraska, every day for a month, where Jim Hurst, the barnstormer, gave Ruth lessons before he started work at eight in the morning.

Nestled into the cushions of her living room couch, no longer able to fly because

Ruth Martin Jefford, when she soloed at Lincoln, Nebraska, in an Arrow Sport with a Ford V-8 engine.

of failing eyesight, Ruth remembered that day when she soloed, as if it was yesterday.

"The plane was an Arrow Sport, with a big Ford V-8 engine manufactured by Henry Ford. The problem was that it landed so darn fast that no one else wanted to try to fly it. All the operators came out to watch me solo. When I landed, the other pilots were amazed so I guess you could say that was my *chalk mark*. In other words, I flew and landed that airplane!"

Ruth later married Jim Hurst, her flight instructor, in New York City. "We moved to Washington, D.C., but he never liked city life," she said. "I remember going to tea at the White House and meeting Eleanor Roosevelt before my husband accepted a job with the Civil Aeronautics Authority [CAA] in Anchorage, Alaska. The CAA was the predecessor to the Federal Aviation Administration [FAA]." Ruth smiled. "Jack Jefford, a barnstormer Jim knew in Nebraska, recruited my husband for the job with the CAA."

Ruth and Jim Hurst returned to Nebraska in 1941 to say good-bye to Jim's family. Before they boarded the boat in Seattle to head for his new job in Alaska, Pearl Harbor was bombed.

They arrived in Anchorage when it was a small town with about 3,500 residents. Fourth Avenue was the main street for commercial activity. Fort Richardson Army Base and Elmendorf Air Force Base were being constructed on the outskirts of Anchorage. The city would go through a boom, then decline again when the war ended in 1945. As late as 1950 there were only two paved streets with one stoplight on Fourth Avenue.

Within the first month, Ruth met Lorene Harrison, choir director at the Presbyterian church. Never one to sit idle, Ruth told her she could play the violin. "I never had a free moment again," Ruth said with a laugh. Lorene Harrison was also in charge of the USO and recruited Ruth to help make the soldiers feel welcome in Anchorage. Ruth also participated in the Red Cross Motor Corp, rising at all times during the night to go to headquarters because of blackout orders.

"It was pretty scary, driving in total darkness, especially in the winter," Ruth remembered. "We'd have to drive to headquarters when there was the possibility of an air attack ... when an unidentified aircraft was overhead. Then we'd deliver medical supplies to the various nursing stations. When the alarm was over, we'd go collect all the supplies and return them to headquarters. When I'd return home, Jim would say, 'Hi, honey, how's the war going?'"

Ruth and her husband started International Air Taxi Service at Merrill Field in Anchorage. "We were fortunate to have one of the few year-round mail contracts," Ruth said. "I flew to Skwentna, Alaska, on a weekly basis for more than 20 years, delivering mail and supplies." She is the only female pilot from that era who flew year-round in the Last Frontier. Others flew during the summer months only. Ruth also gave flying lessons, took people sight-seeing, booked charters and ferried planes from manufacturers on the East Coast to Alaska.

"I like Alaska because there are few roads, and were even fewer when I arrived in the 1940s," Ruth said. "In the Lower Forty-Eight you can drive to the next town, but not here. You have to fly. That's one thing I liked."

Even though Ruth taught people how to take to the air in her 1941 Taylorcraft, on wheels, skis or floats, she says she didn't particularly enjoy instructing.

"I had one student that I didn't dare let solo even after 30 hours. A woman, who after 20 or 30 attempts to land, I thought she should give it up. Her every attempt to land was crash and bang. This was my airplane she was crashing and banging every time she tried to land. I thought about how to tell her I wouldn't let her solo and decided to say, 'You probably have the wrong instructor.' I heard later that she soloed in a float plane, landed on water and took off from a sand bar."

I asked Ruth if she ever wore a parachute. "I don't think it's necessary. They're heavy and bulky and useless if you have a catastrophic failure and you're not wearing it at the time. Overloaded planes, bad weather, or turbulence cause crashes. If I was doing aerobatics I'd probably wear one, but when my first husband, Jim, tried to teach me, I was all over the damn sky! Aerobatics are fun and a good way to make money as a performer when you get tired of the old straight and level."

Postmaster Joe Delia with Ruth Jefford delivering the U.S. mail in Skwentna, Alaska.

Without pausing for a breath, Ruth added, "I prefer straight and level!"

Even now, in her late 90s, with macular degeneration taking its toll, Ruth walks a quarter mile up a steep grade every day to get her mail. "I fell once this winter," she said, "so now I take along two ski poles. I need to stay active. Walking is good for me." Her airplane is parked at water's edge outside her living room window. There's also a power boat. And somewhere at her house a motorcycle is tucked away — all there to remind Ruth of the good times, the adventure, and the sheer fun she's always had.

"I went to Pennsylvania once to pick up a plane and ferry it back and that's when I learned the hard way that it's a good idea to fly a new plane once before you make a long trip. My sister agreed to come along because she'd never been to Alaska. We landed in Cleveland, but not without ground looping that airplane. It must have looked funny if you saw us out there — the plane spinning around one way, then I'd get control of it and it would spin around the other way. When we came to a full stop I told them the parking brake on the right hand side seemed to be the problem. It was. There was a manufacturing defect in the Piper Cub.

"The one accident I had wasn't my fault. The mechanic doing maintenance moved the plane by the lockable tail where he loosened the brakes too much. I flew to Skwentna where there were very high crosswinds and I needed workable brakes.

In a heavy crosswind the plane tends to go into the wind and since the brakes were loosened, I ground looped left with the wingtip and left stabilizer. The FAA inspector checked out my plane because it was a commercial flight. When he was done, he handed me his keys to use his airplane because he knew I only had the one plane. I don't think he'd have given me his keys if he thought it was 'pilot error.'"

"When I started flying, and for many years, women were suppose to stay home, tend to the babies and take care of the house. I was unable to have children because of cancer when I was a young woman, so it's hard for me to relate to women who have all this responsibility and manage to be pilots and career women. Things have changed. I admire them."

Ruth and Jim Hurst divorced in 1961. Diagnosed with diabetes, he could no longer fly, so they stayed partners in business with Ruth handling everything. Two years later, Hurst signed over his interest in International Air Taxi to Ruth. In 1971, she married longtime friend and well-known Alaska Bush pilot Jack Jefford. Ruth said, "Jack was the nicest man I ever knew." But with a chuckle, she recalls how before Jack retired from the FAA, he wanted her to fly a C-130 on a flight from Barrow, Alaska, to Fairbanks.

"I'd never flown one and we were in a whiteout all the way. Jack told me I'd have to land on instruments. I was sweating all over, just handling the big plane in a whiteout, and the thought of landing a plane I'd never flown had me ruffled, but I was determined to do it. He handed me the procedures to look over and when we were eight miles out of Fairbanks, it suddenly became *severely clear*! I should have known he was teasing me because he was on a different radio frequency than me all along and he knew the weather conditions in Fairbanks."

The Jeffords moved to the Matanuska-Susitna Valley, where they operated out of the Wasilla mid-town airstrip. Jack passed away in 1979, and once again Ruth carried on with flight operations. She never remarried.

About seven years ago, Ruth had to give up climbing in the cockpit and taking off for anywhere her heart desired, but she will not part with her airplane. "It's like a member of the family. I can't get rid of it."

Ruth has always loved playing the violin. With a handful of other musicians she helped found the Anchorage Symphony in 1942 with 7 members. Ruth was first violinist and concert master for 38 years. Inspired by her mother, a concert pianist, and her sister, a professional singer, Ruth studied at the American Conservatory in Chicago, the Cité Universitaire in Paris and the Mannes College of Music in New York City.

Internationally acclaimed violinist Paul Rosenthal of Juneau, Alaska, played in a string quartet with Ruth that he remembers she named "The Aurora String Quartet." When he spoke with me by phone, he said, "Ruth always gave a million percent. There's nobody I ever admired more."

When I asked Ruth which mattered more, flying or running her bow across the

33

strings of her violin, she sat erect on the couch and said, "Honey, I had the best of both worlds."

Other women came north before Ruth and tested their skills in the turbulent skies above the glaciers, but the person who stayed to fly across the glaciers and mountains, rivers and lakes of Alaska for six decades is a small powerhouse of a woman named Ruth Martin Jefford. She doesn't blow her own horn. She doesn't even accept that she's mentored other women, but she has. While she stroked her pet cat Tomboy's tawny-colored fur, she simply said, "I had to make a living, so that's what I did. I have no complaints. I can't think of anything I'd do differently."

7

No Place for a Woman:
PEARL LASKA CHAMBERLAIN

The noisy lunch crowd was jammed into Sam's Sourdough Cafe in Fairbanks, Alaska. Already seated at a table, patiently waiting for me, was white-haired Pearl Laska Chamberlain, who in 2010 will reach her centennial mark.

"I still have my commercial license and since I learned to fly in 1933, I've logged more than 3,900 hours," Pearl proudly boasted. Eager to talk about flying, Pearl continued after we placed our lunch order, ignoring the lunch-time noise.

"When I was kid, growing up in the Appalachian Mountains of West Virginia, I was the second oldest of eight children," Pearl explained. "Most people signed their name with an X back then and I didn't go to school till I was ten because there wasn't any school. After graduation from a one-room schoolhouse I became a teacher. In the winter of 1932, I had to walk a mile and half down Chestnut Mountain, across Brooks Creek and another mile and half up Tug Creek Mountain to the school where I taught. That's when I started dreaming of flying."

Pearl said, "I made $80 a month and helped two of my sisters in college, but I still managed to save a few dollars. After seven months, the school ran out of money and closed. I had saved $125 for flying lessons and that left me with $30 to live on."

The waitress asked if we'd be having dessert. Pearl shook her head to indicate

Pearl Chamberlain, age 10

no. I ordered chocolate creme pie. "You sure you wouldn't like a piece of pie, Pearl?"

"I never eat sweets," she said firmly. "I never have. I eat three regular meals a day."

Pearl opened a folder and handed me an article. "I think I'm one of maybe 20 women in the country who are members of the UFOs," she explained.

I scanned the article by Paul Harvey, dated July 3, 1994. "UFOs are United Flying Octogenarians, active licensed airplane pilots, over 80 years old," Harvey wrote. He added that at 88, John Miller of New York still logs 100 hours a year. Miller told Harvey they thought he was too old for combat in World War II.

It was apparent, as I observed 94-year old Pearl Laska Chamberlain, that she had never let age stand in her way either. As Pearl's son, attorney Louis Laska, had said, "My mother's the prototype for feminists! She was ahead of her time."

My chocolate pie arrived. Pearl handed her empty plate to the waitress, then she gave me a copy of *Heartland* magazine dated March 8, 1988. A photo of Pearl in 1933, right after she soloed in Bluefield, Virginia, in a Kinner Fleet open-cockpit biplane, graced the cover.

Pearl Chamberlain, 1933, Bluefield, Virginia, the day she soloed in a Kinner Fleet Biplane.

"You can have that," Pearl said. "I have another copy."

Pearl's zest for life and enthusiasm for aviation captivated me as I watched her eyes light up.

"In 1940 the college president suggested to me that I could get my instructor's rating if I qualified for the Civilian Pilot Training Program [CPTP] if I was quick to get my physical and apply, which I did, immediately," Pearl said. "They only allowed one woman out of ten students into the program, because the government didn't want it to seem like a sudden military build-up. But it was."

"What did your parents think about you flying?" I asked.

Pearl chuckled. "My mother wouldn't fly with me from Asheville, North Carolina, when I flew home with my first plane, a 1939 Piper J-4 that I bought for $1,500. She rode the Greyhound bus."

"And your father?"

"He had no interest in flying either. Said he hadn't lost anything up there."

It occurred to me that Pearl may have been the first woman to fly her own airplane from the Lower Forty-Eight to Alaska. She confirmed that as far as she knew, her trip from Asheville, North Carolina, to Nome, Alaska in 1946 was a first. "The women pilots I've met here had their planes shipped to Alaska and assembled in state," Pearl said.

In a story Pearl wrote in 1992 she described in detail her trip from Asheville to Nome. She began by "squirreling away every dollar possible" in 1944 and 1945. Then she flew to Seattle and went to the main office of the Northern Commercial Company, where she tried to convince them to sell her an Aeronca airplane.

"In President Volney Richmond's plush office I stated my case how on my way east for a short visit with my parents I would like to take delivery of an Aeronca Chief at the factory in Alliance, Ohio. I mentioned it would be good advertising for a woman to ferry an airplane to Nome. He deflated my ego by telling me he didn't need advertising, that he could sell anything in Alaska. He also told me the factory was on strike and the two aircraft available were already spoken for."

I remembered Pearl's son saying his mother was the original prototype feminist. He was right!

Pearl bought a 1936 Piper Cub coupe from the factory and flew home to visit and pick up her airplane. Her ego was deflated again when her mother insisted on riding the Greyhound bus. Ironically, when Pearl arrived in West Virginia a telegram arrived from Volney Richmond. He had reconsidered. But it was too late. Pearl had the Piper Cub and was ready to make her way north to Nome, Alaska.

When Pearl took off again, she had the company of a mouse running across her foot. She said, "Thank goodness I am not afraid of mice and got off in one piece!"

After stopping in Miles City, Montana, for a 100 hour check of her plane, and finding the mouse a new home, Pearl was on her way again.

"Merrily on my way north, I saw a harmless looking cloud and proceeded to fly through it. I had flown in West Virginia where thunder storms looked threatening and in Alaska where they were rare. I learned you don't trust dry thunder storms as I was buffeted from 2,000 feet down to 200 feet above ground."

Pearl continued on to Great Falls, customs, immigration, and into Edmonton, Alberta, where she landed to pick up required emergency gear and for a briefing. Two other aircraft joined in her adventure in the air over the newly constructed Alcan Highway. They flew north over Slave Lake and landed in a ballfield at Athabaska to purchase fuel. Their next stop was Grand Prairie, then on to Fort Nelson. With a longer gas range, Pearl had been able to pass up a landing at Dawson Creek.

Jean Glabov, a passenger in one of the other two aircrafts, pleaded with Pearl to let her continue north with her. She had little confidence in pilot Joe Barber's handling of an airplane. It proved to be a smart move. Barber crash-landed and was never found.

"Some 70 miles out of Fort Nelson we met the Rockies and a raging forest fire. I had heard how frightening forest fires could be but was not prepared for the balls of fire rolling from tree to tree. We could not see ahead. We navigated by looking down from our altitude of fifty feet. Jean helped by keeping a lookout on the right while I watched for trees on the left and prayed the pass was no more than 5,000 feet so I could get over it with my J4 airplane."

Pearl flew on to Smith River, Watson Lake, Teslin, Whitehorse, and when she reached Northway, she had put her foot back on Alaskan Territory in 1946. Jean continued by other means to her destination in Anchorage. When Pearl was ready to take off from Northway, her J4 engine sputtered and quit. She said, "I spent another day draining the tanks of more than half a gallon of rusty water." The following day she sputtered on to land at Weeks Field in Fairbanks, Alaska. From Fairbanks, Pearl flew on to Unalakleet.

"An Eskimo came to help me refuel my plane. He fell through the fabric wing. 'Oh no!'" Pearl remembered saying. "I found Wien Airlines had a can of dope [glue]

and with my nail scissors I cut out a square from my cotton *Gone with the Wind* skirt, patched the hole and flew on to Nome."

Pearl didn't bother to send a wire to Volney Richmond, president of Northern Commercial Company, when she arrived in Nome. She did what she set out to do, fly from the Lower Forty-Eight to Nome in 1946, on her own.

Pearl talked of teaching Navy cadets to fly after Pearl Harbor was attacked in 1941. "I got paid $2.50 an hour to teach cadets to fly seaplanes before I became a Women's Air Service Pilot (WASP). I'd been intrigued by the Army Air corp. and thought if I became a WASP maybe I could continue to fly. They sent us to Sweetwater, Texas, for flight training. One day I saw my name on the board, which meant they were washing me out. I was so mad I just walked out and decided I'd come to Alaska because I heard they desperately needed pilots and instructors."

"Why did they wash you out?" I asked. "You had been an instructor."

Pearl Laska Chamberlain, Women's Air Service Pilot (WASP), World War II, wearing the traditional "zootsuit" provided to women pilots, in Sweetwater, Texas.

With a shrug, Pearl said, "It was December 1943, and the program was winding down because the war was about to end. The men wanted their ferrying jobs back. I found out later that they had orders to drop a certain number of women every day, and I was just one of the unlucky ones," she said, as if it happened yesterday. "It had nothing to do with my ability as a pilot or instructor."

Before meeting Pearl, I read in Jean Haskell Cole's *Women Pilots of World War II* that women ferried planes all over the states and to Alaska for the lend-lease program with Russia till 1944. None of the women received recognition or acknowledgement of their service to their country. They were politely dismissed, or washed out. If one of the women died during active duty their classmates raised the money to bury them.

Women were not admitted into flight training in the Air Force again for thirty-two years after the WASP program disbanded, even though on December 20, 1944, General H. H. Arnold, Commanding General, announced, "Together with women fliers of our Allies, the WASP have proven that women have the ability and the capacity to perform the most difficult jobs in flying."

Pearl shook her head in disgust and said, "It was 1977 before Congress gave the WASPs honorary discharges and declared us veterans."

"Tell me about coming to Alaska after you washed out,'" I said.

Pearl's face relaxed. "I went to Alaska Star Airlines in Seattle to buy a ticket, but I needed permission from the defense command. The sergeant asked me why I wanted to go to Alaska. I said I wanted to fly, that I was a pilot." Frowning, she said, "He looked down his nose at me and asked what else I could do besides fly. I told him I was a teacher, but he wouldn't give me permission till I admitted I had worked as a waitress too."

"After you arrived in Fairbanks, did you find a job as a pilot?"

"I tried, but everyone was reluctant to hire a woman. Herb Hagar of Fairbanks Air Service at Weeks Field offered me a job in the office, and when I told him I wanted to fly he said Alaska was no place for a woman and he couldn't take a chance on me.

"I kept after him till he suggested I might find a job flying in Nome. So off to Nome I went and still no job, so I went to work as a waitress at the North Pole Bakery. Finally, Frank Whaley, who owned Rainbow Skyways, gave me a checkride but he didn't hire me till one of his pilots showed up drunk!"

"I spent the next two summers as a flight instructor, teaching construction workers, government employees and Eskimos with a yen to fly. I flew teachers and nurses to the villages, delivered mail and did flight-seeing."

"What'd you do in the winter months?"

"I went back to teaching school, after I quit working in the office for Alaska Airlines," Pearl said with a wry smile. "They didn't have money for fuel or money to pay the man with the honey truck back then." (In Alaskan villages without plumbing it is still necessary to use "honey" buckets.)

Pearl mentioned that she volunteered at the Pioneer Museum a couple days a week, and that she would be traveling out of state for the annual WASP reunion and a Powder Puff Derby reunion, then on to Tennessee to visit her son. Age could not keep Pearl earthbound in Fairbanks, Alaska.

Several days later, I phoned Randy Accord from the Aviation Museum in Fairbanks at Alaskaland and arranged for a personal tour because the museum was closed for the season. I invited Pearl and Phyllis Tate, another pilot, to tag along. We met Pearl at the Pioneer Museum, also located at Alaskaland. She was busy assisting visitors from China. I noticed a sizable gold nugget on a chain around Pearl's neck and commented, "Pearl, that's a beautiful gold piece you're wearing."

"Yes, it is," she replied. "This guy in Ophir [a mining district] gave it to me a long time ago, but he married someone else. I think I got the best deal."

Her directness and dry humor made me laugh. I believe this is what has helped Pearl through difficulties and disappointments in her long life. She married twice. Both husbands succumbed to cancer, leaving her a widow with a child to raise by herself.

Pearl said, "When I married Laska, I had to give up flying to help him run a trading post in McGrath. He came down with cancer three months after our son was born and I was soon left alone with the store to run, which I did for several years. Then I sold it, remarried in 1958 and taught school again, in Homer, eventually returning to Fairbanks to teach. I retired after 37 years of teaching.

"After I retired I went to the Lower Forty-Eight to help my aging parents, but I longed to return to Alaska, which I finally did in 1998." Pearl reached into her tote bag. "Here, I thought you might like to have this," she said, handing me one of her hand-stitched tote bags, complete with an Eskimo design, real fur ruff, and colorful cotton parka.

Before returning to my home in Eagle River, I invited Pearl to join several other women pilots for lunch at Sophie's Station, a quiet, subdued setting. In the lobby of the hotel, I reached to press the elevator button to go upstairs to the restaurant.

"I prefer the stairs," Pearl said. "I'll meet you upstairs."

Naturally! This is just one more way she stays active and healthy, and maintains a commercial pilot's license at 94.

8

One in Twelve:
VIRGINIA MERRILL CLAYTON

"I soloed the day the Japanese bombed Pearl Harbor, December 7, 1941," Virginia Clayton said. "They didn't call that a legal solo because all the aircraft were suppose to be grounded, but we didn't know what happened until we landed. They made me drive to Boise, Idaho, and get an Airman Identification Card. My official solo certificate was issued on December 15, 1941, in Boise."

No one I interviewed had the distinction of soloing on December 7, 1941, except for Virginia Clayton. She pursued her dream but she had to drive from Oregon to Idaho to fulfill that dream.

"I always used to look at airplanes and especially mail planes going over. Airplanes inspired me," Virginia said, "not any one person. I wanted to help my mom and dad. I'd tell them that 'when I learn to fly, I'll fly over Baker [Oregon] and drop you a bag of money to help you out.'"

Like many others, Virginia knew about the Civilian Pilot Training Program (CPTP) option if she went to college and was in the top one-third of her class. "I saved money for college, but the year I was going to start they took girls out of CPTP. I worked to earn money to pay for flight instruction at Martin Field in Walla Walla, Washington. My boss, Herman Martin, was a wonderful person. There was no control tower there so I flagged [guided or directed them on the ground] airplanes for the Navy cadets, in connection with Whitman College. That's where the cadets learned to fly. I flew Cubs and Kinner Fleets, a WACO, a UPS7 and a Meyers biplane. It was great fun."

"Herman told me, 'If you will stay and instruct for me, I'll give you your flying time up to your flight instructor's rating and your commercial rating.'" The fact that Virginia was the lone female among 12 male instructors at Martin Field didn't seem to matter.

"While I was working at Martin Field, instructing, I had my appendix removed. The guys got together and played cards for money," Virginia remembered as we talked on the phone. "Then they gave all their winnings to me to pay my hospital bill. They made me feel like a queen."

"The Navy program stopped when they sold some of the airplanes. After the war, the Piper Cubs were bought by a man in Fairbanks to start a flying school. The name of the school was Top of the World Flying School, the first one in Fairbanks. I inquired about it, then later on I received a telegram and a round-trip ticket. They said that if I would come up and instruct at this new school they would pay my return ticket if I didn't want to stay. They guaranteed me students day and night.

"Most of my students were men, of course, but I remember this one woman who came to take lessons and she had very fancy rings on her fingers. The other instructors told me she was a 'lady of the night' on 4th Avenue, but I figured that was none of my business. If she wanted to learn to fly, I would give her lessons."

Virginia laughed as she recalled an old-timer she took flying. "We had tandem seats back in those days and he was sitting behind me, but he kept banging something against the back of my seat. I turned around to find out why and there he was, leaning over taking off his heavy boots. He told me he wanted to feel the airplane without his boots on. From then on I called him 'Twinkle Toes.'"

With a smile in her voice, Virginia said, "I remember my first impression of Fairbanks. I thought there would be igloos and it would be cold here, but it was hot — my, was it hot! That was in June of 1944. I remember I got a letter from my mom and a package. She sent me a Jantzen turtleneck wool sweater and it was about 90 degrees in Fairbanks. Mom was thinking more of igloos, just like I was, so I learned a lot.

Virginia Clayton, 1944, only female instructor in the photograph, Martin Field near Walla Walla, Washington.

"I flew up until fall and made very good money, well over $600 a month. In 1944 when I came up here, that was real good money. I stayed with a family named Bragg and they only made me pay a few dollars to rent a room from them."

According to the Department of Labor the minimum wage was $1.15 in Alaska in 1944. I remembered making $1.15 at my first job as a retail clerk in 1957. A friend of mine said that she was paid 65 cents an hour in Salt Lake City, Utah, in the late 1940s. Virginia was right, $600 a month in 1944 was fabulous money!

"I don't know why I preferred instructing," Virginia said. "It was just what I wanted to do. I was real happy with instructing. And I did instruct women in Fairbanks, but I can't remember who they were.

"Flying at that time meant everything to me," Virginia said, "but after I met my prospective

Virginia Clayton, 1944

husband and began to date him, I began to think of getting married, and I thought that would be very wonderful. George Clayton was a mechanic for Pan American at the time. We were married in September 1944, three months after we met. So you see, I didn't wait too long after I met him till I got married.

"George was transferred to Seattle with Pan Am for a year and half and our son, Greg, was born down there," Virginia said. "I flew with George, helping him get his commercial and instrument rating, but after our son was born I always felt a mother should be home with her kids, if she could. I stopped flying and I spent my time with my son and flew with my husband.

"In spite of the fact I loved flying, I always had sort of an empty feeling, like there was something missing in my life and I didn't know what it was. Well many years later, in fact, not until I was 40 years old — I discovered what was missing. That was the spiritual side of my life. It isn't as if flying wasn't an important and delightful part of my life, but knowing our Creator — that part is vital for us to have a happy life. That really has brought me happiness all the rest of my life and continues to do so."

Women Pilots of Alaska

Virginia Clayton was reluctant to talk about herself at the start of our interview, although pilots in Fairbanks are quick to acknowledge her contributions to aviation in Alaska. It took the urging and encouragement of her daughter and her husband, George, to convince her to share her story about being the first woman flight instructor in Fairbanks, Alaska. Others that were interviewed for this book often remarked they felt flying was a spiritual experience. Virginia is living the feeling.

9

No Wheat Fields in Alaska: GINNY WOOD

"Flying is 90 percent boredom," Ginny Wood said, "but in Alaska, 10 percent is sheer terror! You may have to land dead stick on a sandbar or in the tundra. When I first came here there were no airfields, and definitely no wheat fields where you could put a plane down safely."

Ginny Hill Wood has lived in Fairbanks, Alaska, since 1946. She learned to fly, like many other women, through the Civilian Pilot Training Program (CPTP) in the Depression years when there was no money for lessons. Ginny was one of five women in a class of 50 at the University of Washington in Seattle.

"When World War II started all my boyfriends were drafted and there was limited gas for cars. If I hadn't learned to fly, I'd have been building airplanes. My father took me up flying with a barnstormer who came to Walla Walla, Washington. I was only four and I sat on my father's lap. Years later when I told my parents I was going to learn to fly, my father said to my mother, 'Edith, you know what that kid wants to do? She'll kill herself!' But my mother convinced him I should."

Ginny talked of her father being adventurous, climbing Mount Hood in Oregon and canoeing down the Willamette River, so it's no wonder his daughter would champion his outdoor spirit and lifestyle.

"After Pearl Harbor was hit, I began my official military training with the WASP after getting my commercial license and flight instructor rating. Then we spent five months learning to fly 'the Army way' all over again."

As Ginny talked, I tried to imagine her in the cockpit of a P-39 or a P-63 Cobra, or a P-51 Mustang or P-38 Lightning — airplanes the WASPs ferried during the war. She explained that the planes were made in Buffalo, New York, and ferried from Great Falls, Montana, to Alaska, then on to Russia for the lend-lease program, but neither she or her friend, Celia Hunter, were part of that effort. From all accounts it appears that the Russian pilots flew into Nome, Alaska, and ferried the planes on to their homeland, that none of the WASPs were allowed to ferry planes outside the United States or the Territory of Alaska.

Ginny Wood, wearing her WASP uniform, walking away from the P-61 Black Widow after a flight near the end of World War II. Alaska Aviation Heritage Museum, Anchorage, Alaska.

Ginny explained, "They sent us to Sweetwater, Texas, for five months and I opted for the Sixth Ferry Command in Long Beach, California, after I got my WASP Wings because they made more planes there than anywhere else. We weren't allowed to ferry planes out of the country but we flew fighter planes and bombers anywhere they were needed in the United States and to points of embarkation to be carried overseas. I flew planes from Long Beach to Newark, New Jersey, to be shipped overseas to the European Theater. When the war ended, WASPs did not get the GI Bill. We didn't receive any benefits.

"We flew as many as ten different planes, from fighters to puddle jumpers. We never knew where we'd be assigned from day to day. It depended on where the airplanes needed to be ferried. The men resented us because they felt we were taking their jobs, but that's not true because they wouldn't let any women pilots fly combat missions."

When I first phoned Ginny in the summer of 2002, she was caught up in a whirlwind of interviews and celebrations, commemorating the 50th anniversary of Camp Denali, which she and her husband "Woody" Woods and Celia Hunter established in 1952 in the rugged wilderness surrounding the highest peak in North America, Mount McKinley. There was no time to elaborate on the phone. Ginny was on her way out the door.

"I'm catching a plane for Anchorage in an hour," Ginny said. "And I still have to write the speech I'm giving tonight about Camp Denali."

People told me Ginny was reserved, a private person, "the visionary one," and that her friend and business partner, Celia Hunter, would have enjoyed the chance to share their adventures in the WASPs and later in Alaska. Unfortunately, Celia died in December of 2001, and now it was Ginny who navigated the minefield of nosy reporters, including me. Everyone wanted to know when and how Camp Denali became a reality, but I only wanted to talk with Ginny about her flying. She seemed relieved.

In our second conversation, Ginny talked about her flying following World War II. "After the war I went to work in Troutdale, Oregon, ferrying surplus planes for Reconstruction Finance Corporation. That's where I met Celia Hunter. We flew two Gull-wing Stinsons, war surplus planes, to Fairbanks during December of 1946, on the buddy system. There were always two planes traveling together. We flew into Fairbanks on New Year's Eve in a snowstorm. And I remember the first three weeks of 1947; it was 50 below and no commercial planes flew into Fairbanks, so we couldn't get a flight back to Oregon and our old jobs." Ginny laughed. "I'm still here! We got jobs hauling cargo by air from Fairbanks to Kotzebue with a guy who bought our airplanes. We weathered in at Galena, Selavik, and once for three weeks in Kotzebue. We spent a year flying to native villages and were often weathered in, which allowed us to know the Bush before Alaska cities."

I asked if she flew year-round.

"No, only that first winter. The next one, I took classes in the winter and then went to the University of Stockholm. After one semester we [Ginny and Celia] skied in Austria, then bought bicycles and spent a year pedaling around war-torn Europe. There were all kinds of youth bicycling across Europe after the war."

"Then you returned to Alaska?"

"Yes, on a freighter arriving here for Christmas 1949. Back in the Lower Forty-Eight, all I saw was opulence and affluence, and I wanted to return to Alaska. In the 1940s Fairbanks was the same as the '20s and '30s with log cabins and no running water. It was a very close-knit frontier community."

The next time I phoned Ginny with more questions, she said she was just going out the door, but to call her back at five because it would be dark by then and she'd be home. Her frankness and openness were refreshing. I could barely wait to talk with her again. At 5:05 Ginny was home.

"Sorry I couldn't talk with you earlier," she said when she answered. "I was headed out to ski. I used to cross-country ski about ten to 15 miles, but today I only went three miles in my neighborhood. There were lots of fallen branches on the trail so it took me a while to clear a path. I prefer to ski at the university on their groomed trails."

I could hardly believe what the blue-eyed woman in her mid–80s was telling me. Weather reports said it was five above in Fairbanks that day in mid–January 2003. I remembered Ginny had said it was 50 below when she first came to Alaska in December 1946, so five above would not deter her.

Ginny continued talking about her outdoor excursion. "I used to say if I wasn't on skis, I wasn't living."

I mentioned talking with aerial photographer Amy Lou Barney, who said she flew alone and took pictures through the open door of her plane.

Ginny replied, "I used to have to drop supplies to campers and climbers at Denali by opening the door of the plane. It wasn't easy with the wind pushing against the door."

I asked Ginny what plane she used to fly to and from Camp Denali.

She laughed a bit before answering. "My husband and I had a Cessna 170 and a three-place Piper that was souped up with a bigger engine, on floats."

As if it were yesterday, not six decades ago, Ginny shared her memories of her first flying experience.

"I remember when I soloed at Lake Union in Seattle where I landed on floats. I kept thinking, *I'm doing this all on my own!* I was full of glee. And the camaraderie and challenge during World War II was great, but I wanted to go on and do other things. That wasn't all there was. Now, I'd rather be hiking than flying, but I wouldn't have traded the experience for the world.

"When my husband and I owned a plane, I continued to do some commercial flying, but gave it up shortly after my daughter, Romany, was born. After 25 years of founding and operating Camp Denali in the Kantishna area of Denali National Park, I spent another 15 years guiding backpacking and paddling trips in the Brooks Range above the Arctic Circle in areas now called 'gates' of the Arctic National Park and the Arctic National Wildlife Refuge [ANWR]."

Ginny said, "I still live on the eight acres of woodland where we built our first log cabin in 1952, north of Fairbanks."

In her 2002 annual newsletter, "Wood Cuts," Ginny mentioned raising a "tolerable garden" and "splitting two cords of firewood" for her cook stove. Someone asked her if she was lonely, and she replied, "If you live alone and are lonely, then you are in poor company.... I still hike the many miles of trails that surround us, or ski them in winter with my retired sled dog, Kvejak."

Woody, a park ranger, left Alaska in the 1950s, but Ginny stayed and became well known across the state as an environmental activist and a WASP.

She shared her flying experiences in the military during World War II with me, why she came to Alaska, and her short-lived commercial aviation career to and from

Alaskan villages. I only wish our paths had crossed many years before. Maybe she could have taught me to cross-country ski.

Regarding flying, Ginny summed it up this way: "I guess I was the right age at the right time in the right plane. I loved the solitude and having the sky to myself when I was flying."

10

The Environmentalist:
CELIA HUNTER

Celia Hunter was honored by the Sierra Club in 1991 with their highest honor, the John Muir Award. In 2001 Celia and her lifelong friend Ginny Wood were given a lifetime achievement award by the Alaska Conservation Foundation. While flying an airplane was her passion during World War II, Celia pursued conservation and protection of Alaska's environment for the rest of her life. In an interview in 1986 Celia said, "I didn't set out when I came to Fairbanks to become a leader in the environmental movement. It just happened."

She was born on January 13, 1919, in Arlington, Washington. When she finished high school, Celia took a job as a clerk with Weyerhauser Timber Company for $50 a month to earn money to buy a car. Every day she drove past the airfield and one week after her 21st birthday she went for her first flight. From that time on she was hooked. Celia learned to fly at Everett Airport, Washington, earning her private license through the Civilian Pilot Training program in 1941.

Debbie Miller of Fairbanks remembers Celia describing her flying experiences:
"The viewpoint from on high is so different, and so much more comprehensive — just that whole feeling of being aloft. It gives you a feeling that birds must have. In fact, I think, if I wanted to be reincarnated, I'd like to be a bird of some sort."

Celia was accepted into the Women Air Service Pilots (WASP) in 1943 and trained to fly pursuit planes and to ferry P-47 Thunderbolts, P-51 Mustangs, P-63 Air Cobras and DC-3 transport airplanes across the U.S. and Canada. When the WASPs disbanded in December 1944, Celia continued flying commercially and worked as a flight instructor at Everett Airport.

Miller said, "Celia dreamed of flying to Alaska one day to see the vast wilderness that other pilots had described."

What Celia set out to do in December 1947 was ferry two gull-wing Stinson aircraft from Oregon to Alaska with fellow WASP Ginny Wood. Their 30-hour flight lasted 27 days because of winter conditions. Maybe it was fate that when they arrived

Celia Hunter, Women's Air Service Pilot (WASP), World War II. Kay Kennedy Collection, Alaska and Polar Region Archives, Rasmussen Library, University of Alaska Fairbanks.

in Fairbanks on New Year's Day in 1947 they were grounded for three weeks while temperatures remained at 50 below zero.

Celia and her friend Ginny found jobs with a travel agency in Fairbanks. In the summer they found flying jobs in Nome, Alaska. In the fall, as temperatures dropped again, the adventuresome young women pulled up stakes and went to study in Stockholm, Sweden. But Alaska offered something the two free-spirited young women couldn't resist: freedom and challenge.

Ginny returned first, soon followed by Celia. Together with Ginny's new husband, Morton "Woody" Woods, a Denali park ranger, the three staked out a wilderness camp known as Camp Denali in 1952 on public lands north of Mount McKinley in the Kantishna mining district near Wonder Lake. Today, each of the camp's sleeping cabins offers a wood stove, propane lights and a view of Mount McKinley, but no electricity or running water. The camp is designed for guests who prefer nature over television, room service and bar tabs. Naturalists, authors and scientists offer programs about nature and the environment. A bakery produces fresh bread, and a greenhouse dishes up fresh salads. There is a library and meeting hall stocked with plant and animal collections.

In the early years, Celia and Ginny flew people and supplies to the camp until road improvements to Wonder Lake were introduced. The three partners—Celia,

Ginny and Woody—felt people could see the wildlife and appreciate the wilderness experience if they drove rather than flew, and they never planned the camp as a destination resort with fancy trimmings.

Ginny, the visionary member of the duo, said, "We quarreled some. We laughed a lot. We did a lot of things together we couldn't have done separately. In physical things, she'd pick up that end and I'd pick up the other and without ever saying, 'You do this and I'll do that.'"

Celia had a slogan: "Anything Ginny thinks up, I can do."

Ginny had her own motto: "I can do anything Celia will help me do."

One can surmise that their team spirit was fostered when they were WASPs and when they originally flew under the buddy system to Alaska in 1946 and '47.

Woody departed for Seattle in 1962, leaving Celia and Ginny to run the camp, which they did until 1972, when, for the price of two handmade rocking chairs as a down payment, they turned Camp Denali over to Wally and Jerryne Cole, who continued in the spirit of the founders.

To have personally known Celia Hunter would have enriched my life, but Celia passed away at home in December 2001. The night before she died, Celia was on the phone compiling a list of senators who were on the fence regarding a vote in the U.S. Senate about drilling in the Arctic National Wildlife Refuge. The following day, then Governor Tony Knowles said, "Celia Hunter was a great Alaskan. She loved Alaska and was an articulate and passionate champion of our environment."

Former Governor Jay Hammond, who considered himself a close friend of Celia's, said, "We hit it off well and she had no reluctance in attempting to straighten me out when I had gone astray. I appreciated her counsel immensely and greatly encouraged her friendship. Celia was a terrific person and will be missed by all who loved her."

Others remember Celia for her ability to laugh, uncontrollably at times, and her dedication and perseverance. She was a formidable proponent of conservation causes, a fearless frontier spirit, considered unflappable when she pursued a challenge with the purpose and passion that made her life meaningful.

Ginny Wood, her friend of 56 years, said, "At 82 she had slowed down, but not in her zest for life or involvement in issues.... What a loss! ... What a graceful exit of a well-lived long life!"

As one of only a handful of early women pilots testing their mettle, or character, when they flew around Alaska in the 1940s, Celia had to have sheer guts and fortitude to carve a life in the wilderness. She was revered by environmentalists for her undying commitment to Mother Earth. Her legacy lives on. And who knows, she may be keeping watch from above as an eagle or raven, soaring through the air.

11

A Bird in the Air:
AMY LOU BARNEY

"I buckled up, opened the door and took pictures," Amy Lou Barney said. "It was seat-of-the-pants flying!"

In a phone conversation from her home in Juneau, Alaska, Amy Lou said that she flew a Piper Cub or a Taylorcraft (T-craft) by herself and took still pictures. Most aerial photographers hire a pilot or have a friend take them flying to photograph Alaska, but not Amy Lou.

"I wasn't a very good pilot," Amy Lou emphasized. "I never became a commercial pilot. I took lessons in Juneau and learned to land on the airfield back in 1947, then I learned to land on floats in the water so I could get around to more places." She paused. "That's the only way you can photograph most of Alaska."

I asked Amy Lou if she had a mentor or a family friend who inspired her to fly, but she said, "Oh no, Amelia Earhart was my inspiration."

Unable to speak without difficulty now because she's on oxygen, Amy Lou graciously sent me a copy of her recent book for background information about her life.

Amy Lou worked as a professional photographer in Juneau from 1937 to 1951. She "developed, printed, enlarged, tinted, retouched and framed pictures, first for Ordway's Photo Shop." Later, she and her brother Eckley bought the photo shop and renamed it Lu-Ek's. Amy Lou photographed weddings, dog teams, parades, the troops during World War II that passed through Juneau, territorial Governor Ernest Gruening signing Alaska's anti-discrimination bill in 1946, and thousands of other subjects. Aside from capturing history, Amy Lou is best remembered for taking aerial photographs.

In her book *Amy Lou's Alaska*, a pictorial history compiled by Amy Lou and her daughter, Renee Guerin, she describes her first camera:

"Beginning on May 1, 1930, George Eastman, founder and chairman of the board of the Eastman Kodak Company, commemorated the 50th anniversary of his business by giving away 500,000 cameras to any boy or girl in America whose twelfth birthday fell within that year. The only restriction was that the child must be accompanied by a parent or guardian."

1946 photograph of glaciers titled "God's Highway" provided by Amy Lou Barney.

"Lloyd Winter called my father to see if one of us kids was the right age. I remember Dad taking me by the hand down to Winter & Pond, a photographic studio, in order to pick up the camera. I was thrilled — it was a little Brownie box camera and came with a free roll of film."

Amy Lou's career was kick-started with one free roll of film and a Kodak Brownie. In 1937, the aspiring young photographer went to work for Ordway's Photo Shop, a friendly competitor of Winter & Pond.

"Amy Lou, mostly self-taught, worked with the more experienced photographers she encountered and never turned down an assignment she thought would be a learning opportunity," her daughter Renee wrote.

When photographer Fred Ordway was killed in an airplane accident, his wife, Laura, and Amy Lou continued operating the business. "Most of the photographs taken after 1942 that credit Ordway's were taken by Amy Lou," Renee wrote.

Amy Lou used either a 4 × 5 or a 2¼ × 3¼ Speed Graphic camera for commercial jobs, and she flew herself to take aerial shots. She said, "They were easier to handle in the air, because my favorite camera, a Folmer Graflex 3¼ × 4¼, was too cumbersome."

One black-and-white aerial photograph in Amy Lou's collection is titled "God's Highway" and even though it is a long expanse of glacial ice, it looks like a white painted highway wandering across the mountains. It seems nature plays tricks on our eyes when we're in the air.

Another aerial shot of Juneau in the 1940s provides a stunning view of the snow-capped mountains, with the territorial capital city claiming a foothold on a narrow strip of land at the base of the peaks, before the mountains disappear into the water. Even today, there is no roadway connecting Juneau, Alaska, to the rest of the state. Tourists visit the capital by air or ship, and that's how state legislators and supplies arrive too.

Once Amy Lou and Laura Ordway became business partners, they set out to participate in Juneau Chamber of Commerce meetings. Renee explained, "Although they were expected to pay their dues to the local Chamber of Commerce, they were not encouraged to attend the regular luncheons."

Unidentified boy, Fourth of July Parade, Juneau, Alaska, World War II, photograph by Amy Lou Barney.

One day Amy Lou convinced Laura to go with her to the Baranof Hotel where the luncheons were held. "When the two women walked into the hitherto male bastion, mortician Charlie Carter, then president of the chamber, stood and addressed the group: 'Well boys, we'll have to watch our language from now on.'" Amy Lou and Laura stayed and at subsequent meetings were joined by other women members.

In one photo, Amy Lou captured a photo of a young boy wearing a mock Navy uniform, riding in a miniature airplane, like a pedal car, in the Fourth of July Independence Day parade. The sign above him read, "Keep 'Em Flying." In contrast, on the same page of Amy Lou's book is a photo she took of a P-51 fighter plane at the Juneau Airport. A photo of Juneau children encouraging people to buy war bonds further depicts the era. The entire book is a wonderful trip down history lane. Amy Lou and Renee sorted through thousands of negatives and pictures to identify and date them for publication of the book in 1997. The Juneau-Douglas City Museum took pleasure in displaying part of Amy Lou's vast collection for a 50-year celebration.

Amy Lou Barney in 1947 using her Speed Graphic camera while standing on the bumper of a Plymouth.

Amy Lou's photos were not limited to the state capital. She took pictures at Ketchikan, Sitka, Angoon, Pelican, and Anchorage. She even captured a forest crew working to put a water line in Hoonah in 1938, when snow and ice covered the ground. She often photographed Mary Joyce, another Juneau pilot and dog musher, when she brought her dogs into the studio. Amy Lou photographed the village of Naknek and the Bristol Bay fishing fleet in the Bering Sea, providing a strange and rare sight of boats with sails. No powered boats were allowed in Bristol Bay when Amy Lou took the photo in 1947. Even today, boats in Bristol Bay cannot be longer than 32 feet, but they use engines, not sails. It is rare to find a vessel charting its course in Alaskan waters with a sail. Amy remembered arriving in Naknek. "I got out of the plane and was stuck in those mud flats—it was so deep I sank to my knees and dropped my 35-mm camera. It was the only camera I ever ruined."

One aerial shot of Anchorage Amy Lou took in 1947 shows Merrill Field airstrip surrounded by trees, unpaved, with only a sprinkling of buildings visible. It appears that Peggy's Airport Cafe, a favorite restaurant frequented by the Alaska Ninety-Nines and other pilots, had not yet opened its doors.

In 1951 Amy Lou went to work for the Territory of Alaska Employment Security Commission, which after statehood in 1959 was renamed the Department of Labor. When she retired in 1980 Amy Lou was the department's head administration law judge and the first woman in the 50 states to hold the position of chief appeal referee.

Whether she was flying "by the seat of her pants" taking aerial photographs, securing history on film, or filling the shoes of chief appeal referee, Amy Lou made a lasting impression in Alaska.

12

Ruby the Riveter:
RUBY PAPPAS

When Ruby Bennett made plans to come to Alaska to marry George Pappas in 1957, her mother said, "That's a jumping-off place — the melting pot of the world. It's not even a state! You're gonna freeze!"

"Ignoring my mother's concerns, I packed my bags," Ruby said.

Ruby met George on a blind date arranged by his cousin when he was home visiting relatives in western Nebraska. "It was the only blind date I ever had," she pointed out. George flew back from Alaska again in September to see her, which surprised even Ruby. He phoned her from Alaska, which cost about $35 a minute (a fortune) to use a radio phone. Soon George sent Ruby a one-way ticket. She made her way north. In Seattle her flight was delayed, but she was able to catch an earlier flight on another airline. When she arrived in that "jumping-off place," George wasn't there to meet her plane. With a mere $35 in her purse, she wondered if she'd taken the right step. Ruby sat down to contemplate her fate and a short time later saw George emerge from the Cloudhopper Bar and go into the men's room. When he exited, Ruby stood at the door. Ruby and George Pappas celebrated 47 years of marriage in 2004.

"It was February when I arrived and we had a little apartment on Deadman's Curve, in Spenard. I had a hard time figuring out direction, a common problem for *cheechakos* [newcomers], until I figured out the Chugach Mountains were to the east of town."

I smiled as Ruby shared this memory because when I moved to Anchorage in 1994, I was used to the sun rising in the east and setting in the west in Nevada. Not in Alaska! In the winter months the sun is only visible in Anchorage for five hours and it lazily rolls around the horizon causing great confusion to newcomers.

When Ruby arrived in 1957, Red Boy Sharp Cheese sold for 75 cents a pound, sugar cost $1.29 for ten pounds and a half gallon of ice cream cost 98 cents. Pot roast was 69 cents a pound, and a T-bone steak was $1.10 a pound. A 77-acre tract of land, on two creeks with a log home sitting on it, was offered for sale for $5,000. Alaska was still very much a frontier and would not become the 49th state until 1959.

Ruby Pappas with her Skyhawk on a round trip from Anchorage to Scottsbluff, Nebraska.
Star Herald, July 22, 1980, Scottsbluff, Nebraska.

Ruby and George bought a house in City View and when they sold it to move to College Village in Anchorage, they had to have a key made for the new owners. "That was the first key we ever had for that house," Ruby said.

In late 1959, George and a partner opened Aircraft Rebuilders at Merrill Field. But in 1964 the partner headed south and Ruby soon found herself doing the books, something she learned on the job. Ruby also had a mechanical aptitude because her father owned a garage back in Nebraska. When she started driving her dad told her, "You have to know what makes it tick too if you're gonna drive it." It wasn't long before Ruby was involved in riveting on airplane wings and fuselage. Even today, her husband George says Ruby could shoot a rivet better than most mechanics on Merrill Field.

Ruby learned to fly when mechanic John Rogers said he needed to renew his instructor rating. He'd teach Ruby to fly if she'd pay for gas and oil in his Ercoupe. She soloed on April 28, 1966. "I remember it well," Ruby said. "I was scared to death and my butt felt like it weighed a ton!" A 3" × 4" scrap of cloth with elastic on one edge lay on the table where we sat, with Ruby's name and a date scribbled in ink on the stretchy fabric. Ruby explained, "Oh, my husband grabbed me from the back, reached his hand in my jeans and clipped off this piece of my underwear with a pair of 12-inch sheet-metal shop shears and handed it to John, my instructor. It became a tradition whenever a woman soloed." Ruby's daughter Cynthia shopped for weeks for the right pair of undies for this ceremonial event before she went up to solo.

July 22, 1980, the *Star Herald* in Scottsbluff, Nebraska, ran a photo and story of Ruby when she and Cynthia flew a Cessna 172 home to visit her family. The story quoted Ruby: "Flying is the only way to go. In Alaska a lot of people have airplanes because there aren't many roads—so if you want to go—you've got to fly."

The Cessna had been wrecked in Kotzebue. With the proper FAA permits, George and Ruby repaired the plane for ferry and she flew it back to Anchorage. "After George repaired it, I had my own plane." I could go anywhere I wanted to go. It gave me a feeling of self-esteem, of complete independence and freedom."

She added, "People down south who have a private plane are usually doctors, lawyers, executives, but up here, people from all walks of life have planes because it's how you get around in Alaska."

A fun person to interview with a good sense of humor, Ruby shared a hangar story handed down over the years. "It's said if you wrote a bad check when you were out in Bush Alaska you could beat it back to town." There are still many remote villages in Alaska that receive mail and supplies infrequently, some as little as four times a year.

Anyone who lived in South Central Alaska in 1964 remembers the earthquake of Good Friday. Ruby's memories are vivid. "I was home with my kids and our dog when the quake hit. I gathered up the neighbor's kids and we sat outside in a snow bank for a while. To this day, I automatically push glass items to the back of a shelf—without thinking. When we went back into the house, I was cautiously optimistic and started to clean up before dark. Everything came out of the cupboards and spilled onto the floor and there was broken glass everywhere. We had a transistor radio that we listened to all night. Everyone was looking for family members and they'd announce names of people who were missing. 'If anyone knows where so and so is or has seen them have them call their family.' There was no electricity and our water tempering tank that fed the water heater fell down."

Ruby went on to explain that while recovery efforts continued, the following Friday about 5:30 P.M.—the same time the quake had jolted Alaskans with a magnitude of 9.2, the largest earthquake ever recorded in North America—one of the mechanics who worked at the shop said it was time to have a beer. Ruby said, "He planned to be sitting there with a beer when the next quake hit and that was the start of our weekly Quake-Wake Hangar Parties. George would make something he called 'North Platte Valley Greek Moose Stew,' which was pretty exotic." Joe Riley gave us a boat paddle to stir with. One time we flew to Homer and brought back live crab, which we kept iced in the snow under the planes. Then we made up a pot to steam them in the hangar. We always had lots of food, kegs of beer and entertainment, furnished by guests and hosts."

"One time I rode the hangar door with a line boy while George pushed the [open] switch. He was ready to jump down, but I told him George wouldn't crush his book-keeper. Dick Jensen grabbed the hose and sprayed us with water." It was obvious as

Ruby talked that pilots, and especially Alaskan pilots, know how to have fun. Ruby went on to say, "There was never an invitation to our Friday night Quake-Wake parties and we didn't have a guest book. But we needed a ton of friends to help. We'd go clam digging at Polly Creek, down by the inlet from Fire Island, and come back and make clam chowder. When it was time to go home, George began turning out all the lights. The parties continued every week for a long time, then we went to monthly and finally, annually, but it wasn't the same, so we stopped having them."

Ruby was a member of the Alaska Ninety-Nines. "There were five of us at my first meeting and when we met the following month I became the chair. One of the things I'm very proud of is a survival course we put on, usually held in the winter." Ruby always took along a survival kit when she flew, with every imaginable item that might be necessary in Bush Alaska. She kept a set of file cards, recording the entire list of items, making note of the weight of each item too.

Ruby could be described as obsessed with organization — a person who can juggle several tasks at one time. No doubt she learned early on, when she took over the office responsibilities in her husband's new business, that it was easier to put your hand on an invoice or receipt if it was filed in the right place. She kept the books by hand before computer automation. A trip downstairs into her sewing room is evidence of her penchant for organization. Every scissor and measuring tool has its place, every fabric neatly folded in marked plastic containers. Spools of thread arranged like a color wheel in a paint store — absolutely nothing out of place, and Ruby knows where to find every item she needs, the same as if it were her cross-country survival flight kit.

The entire time we sat and talked, Ruby fidgeted in her chair, her mind constantly engaged, anticipating my next question. One leg rested on the corner of the table from time to time. She was in her own home and she was clearly relaxed. Ruby is not pretentious. She's fun-loving.

Ruby said flying has been so much a part of her life, their life, that it will be hard to give up someday. I remembered she said learning to fly was the greatest thing that ever happened to her — being able to go anywhere, giving her a feeling of self-esteem, of complete independence and freedom. It's no wonder she was restless. Ruby would rather be in the air!

13

Flying Doctor:
Dr. Nancy Sydnam

"There were no heroes for women when I was growing up until Amelia Earhart came along. When I was a teenager, I saved up to buy a $75 U.S. savings bond so I could have a free ride in a float plane where I grew up in Lynden, Washington," Dr. Nancy Sydnam said. "That was my motivation to buy a war bond. One trip around the Puget Sound and I knew that someday I'd get my wings. In 1944 I didn't have the money to pay for lessons."

Nancy became a family physician. She eventually received her private pilot's license in 1958 at Merrill Field in Anchorage, Alaska, and her float plane rating in 1965. The first time we talked on the telephone, she said, "I only fly to pick berries and hunt ducks now." I couldn't suppress a laugh and asked how low she flew when she picked berries. Nancy laughed too.

Before arriving in Alaska, Nancy pursued post-graduate education in Philadelphia, Pennsylvania, at the Women's Medical College. In the early days of the college, she said, "The nice boys of Philadelphia would throw fruit in the path of the young women as they walked to school. They taunted them and scoffed at their ambition. When I began attending the women's college, it was 100 years old ... very well established, yet no woman had been admitted to the Philadelphia Medical Society. I remember when the first woman was admitted to membership in the elite Philadelphia Medical Society in 1950. I felt very proud."

Marriage to her high school boyfriend when he returned from the Korean War was Nancy's ticket to Alaska, a place she had dreamed of while growing up in Lynden, Washington. Her husband was employed by Pacific Northern Airlines (PNA), but not as a pilot.

"There were no roads here so that's why I decided to learn to fly," Nancy said. "My husband never enjoyed flying before or after he got his license. He always said it was just a way to get from one point to another. We flew to remote areas to hunt moose and ducks. We fed the family on moose meat." (When Nancy said "remote," she was referring to landing on lakes and river banks, a common practice in Alaska.)

Dr. Nancy Sydnam

In the 1950s, Dr. Milo Fritz recruited Nancy to fly with him in their own airplanes to the outlying villages along the Yukon River, primarily to do tonsillectomies and remove adenoids to help reduce the high incidence of other medical and hearing problems. In addition, the team provided free medical examinations, eye care, and even pulled a few teeth for their Native Alaskan patients. "We paid all our own expenses, except for one 30-day trip when the American Cancer Society gave me a $300 stipend so I could offer pap tests and breast exams," Nancy said.

She remembered using her vacation time at the clinic in Anchorage where she worked to make the trips to the Bush communities of Alaska. "When we flew to the villages along the Yukon River, I loved the sights, the smells, the people, the relaxed manner they went about their daily life, indifferent to city life that I was accustomed to in Anchorage. I liked being on 'Bush time'— where time stood still. People lived in log houses and had a subsistence lifestyle. There was typically no running water except in villages with a central city well."

On a trip to a small village in the Brooks Range, Nancy recalled, "We had finished our work for the day and some of the Native children — teenagers—challenged us to a game of volleyball. I was young and fit and said, 'Sure,' and in no time they whipped our butts! They were quick and fast, and there was no grass to play on, only pounded

Dr. Nancy Sudnam with her dog Tigger in her Super Cub going duck hunting.

63

dirt that was very well worn, which we had failed to notice." Nancy laughed out loud. "They really snookered us, but it was great fun."

Nancy looked across the frozen lake outside her dining room window, her red and white Super Cub standing ready. "I had to stop flying for a while because the stick kept hitting the kid — I had to quit till the baby was born," she remembered.

She also recalled some harrowing times in the Alaskan skies and some humorous ones too.

"One time my son Ben wanted to bring his new girlfriend with us to fly across Cook Inlet to check our beaver traps. I had no idea he'd told this young lady that the plane we'd fly from Merrill Field across the inlet had wheel skis and that it was okay for touch-and-go landings, but not to stop because we might sink through the ice! We made a safe landing, with no difficulty, and it wasn't till then she told me how she'd been set up by my mischievous son." Nancy shook her head and smiled. "She was much more relaxed on our return trip."

Another time, Nancy had been asked to give a visiting priest a flight-seeing trip down Turnagain Arm to Prince William Sound and back to Anchorage. "I was using a friend's plane and on the return flight, as we flew over the golf course, my friend's wife pointed skyward to show her golfing partner her husband's plane flying overhead. At that same moment, the engine quit. In an instant, I switched to the alternate gas tank and the engine kicked over again, much to my passenger's and my relief."

Reliving a tense flight, Nancy admitted to using bad judgment while flying over the mountains to Aniak in bad weather instead of following the river. "I had an emergency tank with ten gallons of fuel when I got lost. Weather came in, and I had no more than two minutes of fuel left. Luckily, I recognized some trees and landed in the village of Sleetmute. My husband had gotten word that we were lost and hadn't arrived at our destination, but I had no way to contact him from the village. What he didn't know was that I had a gas can with extra fuel in the backseat of the Tripacer. Since there were no radios in Sleetmute, and knowing my husband would be worried, I decided to continue on our trip — even in poor weather conditions. This time I flew low over the riverbed at 50 feet. When we arrived in Aniak, there was a terrible cross-wind. After landing, fighting the crosswind, we slowed to a crawl. People ran out and grabbed the wings to keep us on the ground."

Nancy breathed a deep sigh. "I was sure glad to get there. There was no Global Positioning System [GPS] or radar back then. You had to follow directional radio beacons to find your way."

I watched Nancy's expression and studied her hands while she talked. Her hands were relaxed, neither small nor large, soft, well manicured, her fingernails unpolished. I tried to imagine her using medical instruments while she treated her patients. She gave me her full attention when I had a question, no doubt the same way she listened to her patients. She looked peaceful as she talked about caring for Alaskans over the past forty years.

"Having a family medical practice is as much about teaching patients as teaching students in school," she said. "I never minded because I can look back on 40 years of treating several generations. I first saw my patients when they were children. They came in for school exams, then college exams, when they married, and when their children needed care. It was very rewarding for me to provide continuity of care."

I asked if she ever accepted barters in lieu of payment? Nancy replied, "Oh yes, I had this lady from Girdwood who always brought me brown eggs as payment and that was fine with me. In medical school we were taught that patients were more than a disease or a condition, like diabetes or appendicitis.... Patients were human beings, and it was our responsibility to give to the community where we practiced medicine."

In 1967, Nancy's husband's job as a state trooper took the family of five to Juneau, the state capital, where she took a much-needed break. "But I filled in a day and a half every week for a local doctor when I needed extra money, or the weather was bad and the kids and I couldn't go fishing or Dungeness crabbing. We went fishing, hiking, mountain climbing, and I learned to ice climb before we moved back to Anchorage. I was renewed and ready to open my own medical practice, and divorced, after 22 years of marriage."

Retired now, Nancy enjoys every moment to the fullest and still flies to the Pribilof Islands three times a year as an itinerant physician to provide family medical care. "Weather and winds are too tricky to take my own plane there. Icing up is a serious problem. I remember one eerie flight with ice on the wings of the De Haviland Beaver before we even left the ground in Aniak, but the undaunted male pilot refused to consider the risk, keeping me on the edge of the right-hand seat all the way back to Anchorage. He said this was nothing compared to what he normally experienced."

In retirement, the trim brunette continues to stretch her wings. "I only fly for recreation now," she said. I noticed a cello resting against the piano and asked if she played either one. "I bought the cello for one of my sons, but he pursued other interests, and there it sat all those years, so I decided to learn."

Like everything Nancy Sydnam undertakes, perfection comes naturally. She plays cello in the local civic orchestra and recently had the honor of playing with the internationally acclaimed violinist Paul Rosenthal.

With little time to spare in her retirement years, Nancy continues to develop new skills and has become a masterful woodworker, creating several high-quality pieces of furniture, including a desk she built for one of her sons. She has a garage full of lathe saws, band saws, jointers and planers. Using a variety of exotic woods from as far away as Africa, she designs, cuts and finishes unique pieces of art. It's fair to say Nancy uses the same gentle, caring touch while woodworking that she used with patients while practicing medicine.

Another interest was field training competition with her black Labrador, Tigger. Numerous trophies are proudly displayed in her home that recognize their hard-earned accomplishments. During quiet times, Nancy composes prose. She has also had several poems published in *Ice Floe*, a collection of poetry of the far north.

Reflecting on her career, and her desire to become a pilot when she was very young, she said, "Life is what you make it, and there are many more choices now than when I was growing up in Lynden, Washington. Be a participant, not an observer!"

14

Still Smiling:
ANN WILBUR

Ann Boardman Wilbur lives in Girdwood, Alaska, where skiers from all over the world come to test their abilities at Alyeska, within walking distance of Ann's home. When I pulled into the driveway of her light-blue two-story home, I saw stairs that seemed to reach all the way to the stars. Ann came walking outside to greet me. "I'm sort of having a yard sale," she said. "Give me just a minute."

I followed Ann into her storeroom, which was chock full of aviation photos and family mementos. I stood there in awe of the priceless history filling my eyes and my senses. It was like a mini-shrine, attesting to a lifetime of memories and achievements of the Wilbur family.

I was willing to camp on the bottom stair of Ann's home to do the interview so she could continue with her yard sale, but she didn't seem concerned about missing a potential buyer. Before we went up the steep stairs to her living room, Joe Wilbur appeared. I asked if the school bus parked nearby was his and Joe explained that he had a mobile repair shop inside the bus and planned to sell it lock, stock and barrel. Ann smiled.

Ann told me she learned to fly and soloed at Merrill Field in Anchorage after she met Joe, who became her instructor, then her husband. "Joe came north to make his fortune," she said. "He was making $2.60 an hour working as an aircraft mechanic in Las Vegas, Nevada, then someone told him he could make at least $16.00 an hour in Alaska. That was in 1953! You had to join a union, which required a local sponsor, and they wouldn't let Joe in, so he settled for $2.90 an hour, a 30-cent raise! For several years he worked out of a mobile repair school bus, traveling from Seward to Big Lake until 1960." This explained the bus in their driveway.

Upstairs, Ann and her mother, Elizabeth Boardman, sat with me at the table where I took notes. Ann seemed comfortable in jeans and a blouse. Her mother, however, was dressed in a navy-blue skirt and crisp white blouse, her white hair perfectly groomed, as if she were going to work in Anchorage. Ann explained that her mother had been a cartographer with the FAA. The Anchorage basin is home to a large number of the estimated 10,572 aircraft in Alaska, and boasts of the world's largest float plane population based at Lake Hood, near Ted Stevens International Airport (formerly Anchorage International)

"My mother worked in the Anchorage Center, designing traffic patterns and maps for pilots including private planes, military, helicopter and seaplanes. My mother enjoyed her work very much. She did all the mapping by hand before computers," Ann explained because her mother can no longer remember her role with the FAA.

Ann then spoke of how she and Joe married and together forged Wilbur's Flight Operation & Repair Service, later known simply as "Wilbur's." Tongue in cheek, Ann said that in some circles the successful 42-year business at Merrill Field was called Wilbur's College of Aeronautical Knowledge. They also operated a flight school, where pilots like Patty Wagstaff trained before competing in La Havre, France, in international aerobatics.

"We owned Wilbur's and operated Flight Safety Alaska," Ann said. "We were the local Piper and Cessna dealers. In the mid-eighties we also added airline service to in-state locations including Valdez, McGrath and Cordova. All of this sounds like instant success," Ann said with a big sigh, "but it wasn't. We lived aviation! From

Ann and Joe Wilbur, 1984, Merrill Field, Anchorage, Alaska, in front of their business, Wilbur's Flight Operation & Repair Service. *Anchorage Daily News* Archives photograph.

the time our feet hit the floor in the morning till we climbed back into bed at night, all we did was talk about aviation. Our daughter Meg used to tell us to stop talking shop at the dinner table. Now she works one job during the week and spends all her weekends at Merrill Field. Kind of ironic, wouldn't you say?"

As the story unfolded, I learned that Joe was the "hands on" partner. Ann was the business partner. Someone had to keep the train on the track, and that someone was Ann Wilbur. They were a unique husband-and-wife team.

"We lived over the store, so to speak, with our seven children," Ann said. "There was no job too big or small. Before I married Joe I had worked at a florist shop and did some clerical work at another job, but I learned to do our books, the general ledgers. I handled the counter, the phones, the money, and paid the bills. Joe thought I was better at dealing with banks to get financing so I did that too." Continuing, Ann said, "I had to learn from scratch. When we added the airline business, I didn't even know where to buy baggage tags, but I asked around and quickly found a source."

I watched Ann quietly and lovingly respond to her mother's needs. It was evident that Ann was good at multitasking. She laughed softly. "They used to say that if there was a Wilbur around they'd run circles around anyone else."

In 1964, Alaska was shaken to its core by a 9.2 earthquake, the largest shaker ever recorded in North America. Ann remembers it well. "I had been home, baking cookies for Easter and coloring Easter eggs for the kids. I needed something at the store. My mother had just gotten off work, and we ran into each other at the store. I decided it might be a good time to take her over to Merrill Field and look at the place where I wanted to move our family. We spent all our time there anyway.

"The kitchen was done but the rest of the place needed finishing. There was a bed standing up against one wall. Mother and I were standing by the kitchen counter when the big quake hit. We both grabbed the counter, then we held onto each other. We couldn't get out of the building because the bed had fallen across the doorway.

"Later, Joe told me he was in the hangar when the quake hit, and the wings on the planes started flapping. He ran outside in time to see Merrill Field runway rolling like ocean waves. No one in our family was harmed, but we aided in the recovery for several months following the

Elizabeth Boardman (Ann Wilbur's mother) FAA Cartographer, Anchorage, Alaska.

event by ferrying people and emergency supplies from the port at Whittier to Anchorage, Seward, and Valdez."

In 1969, Wilbur's business and hangar burned to the ground. Someone else might have called it quits, but not Ann and Joe. "We built a 5,400-square-foot hangar at a cost of $80,000 — pennies on the dollar for what it would cost today for the same facility," Ann said. "When I was a member of the Seven Star Flying Club it cost $7.00 an hour to use the Super Cub and around 40 cents a gallon for aviation fuel. That's less than it costs to go to the movies today," she said. Later, I asked around and found out that renting a plane for an hour today runs $150 to $200 and fuel costs about $2.50 a gallon. In Bush Alaska, it's $5.00.

With some gentle nudging, I convinced Ann to talk more about herself and flying.

"I've made eight or nine trips up the highway," she said, referring to the Alaska-Canadian Highway known as the Alcan. "I ferried Pipers, Cessnas, and Maules from their factories in Florida, Kansas, Michigan, and Georgia, to sell in Alaska. The first Maule we bought we put on floats. It was finally certified in December after landing on Twin Islands Lake, with an FAA inspector approving the plane's airworthiness. My role was to work with the FAA inspectors to have the paperwork signed off on

Left to right: Bruce, Ann, Rich, Joe and Ken Wilbur (not pictured: Steve Wilbur, who was on a flight across Cook Inlet the day this photograph was taken), Merrill Field, Anchorage, Alaska. *Anchorage Daily News* photograph.

different planes. Joe returned to Merrill Field for a safe landing in the Maule, on floats, without skis!" Ann added, "In December!" I assumed this meant the floats had wheels too.

Most waterways in Alaska are frozen in the winter months, but Ann and Joe had a motto, "Never give up." In order to bring in airplanes to sell in the spring, they had to have FAA approval or lose out on potential sales. "When the Maule was certified, we all celebrated and I made a video, which we took back to the factory to share with Mr. and Mrs. Maule. It was quite a triumph."

Safety has been a key factor in the way Ann and Joe did business the past 42 years. It was Ann, not Joe, who taught hazardous material (haz-mat) classes to their staff and pilots. While she talked, I imagined Ann with grease under her fingernails, but she made it clear that was Joe's area of expertise, not hers.

Like the famous Flying Wallendas of circus fame, the Wilburs are a force to be reckoned with in Alaskan aviation.

"Our oldest son, Steve, is a pilot and mechanic. He is director of maintenance at Mather Aviation in Sacramento, California," Ann said. "He acts as liaison between the company and the FAA too." Not unlike what Ann did at Wilbur's for so many years.

"Son Richard is an airline pilot flying 737s. He had the misfortune to be working for companies that went out of business a few years ago. He is a skilled instructor and A & P mechanic (like his father). He lives in Colorado Springs, Colorado.

"Our son Ken took flying lessons, soloed and did some cross-country flying," Ann said. "He worked in our parts department and was my assistant in the accounting office. He later worked for Peninsula Airways before he died.

"Our son Bruce was killed in an airplane crash on Mount Torbert, across Cook Inlet near Beluga. He was returning from a maintenance mission with one of our pilots. He was also a pilot in both airplanes and helicopters and an A & P mechanic, and accomplished skier," Ann said. "Bruce was just 25 when he was killed.

"Our two daughters worked in the company for us too. Anna departed for Seattle when she was 18, later returning as a single mother with two children. She worked for us in accounting and at the counter. She left again for college in Fairbanks and later remarried. She soloed when she was 16 but didn't continue. She married one of our flight instructors."

Ann fondly titled the next part of the Wilbur story "As the Prop Turns." "Daughter Meg worked for us in our parts department, 'chasing parts,' fueling planes. Her earliest work was fueling planes for a penny a gallon. Sometimes the pilots would gas up planes and have her write the gallons on her pay sheet." Meg later became manager of the airline counter at Wilbur's and stayed with the airline during the sale and transition to the new owners in 1991. Meg works weekends at Take Flight Alaska at Merrill Field, the flight school started by Ann and Joe.

"Our son Paul has lived in Honolulu, Hawaii, for 19 years and doesn't fly because he gets airsick," Ann said. "He joined the Army and returned to Honolulu to attend college, never coming back to Alaska. Today he is 'Mr. Goodwrench' selling car parts," Ann said with a mother's proud smile.

If you were counting, the children number seven. It's mind boggling to envision Ann fixing meals for nine every night, handling the company books and financing, teaching haz-mat classes, and staying married to the same man and business partner for 44 years. The business environment alone, on a day-to-day basis, could have taken its toll on their relationship. Not many husband-wife teams work well together, but the Wilburs are unique.

A few minutes before our interview concluded, Joe came upstairs and sat down in his favorite chair to read the paper. I asked him when he learned to fly. Straight faced, he simply said, "The last day I flew." Then he nonchalantly went back to reading the paper.

Ann rolled her eyes and shook her head. "All these years and I've never heard him say that."

Some months after our interview it occurred to me that I forgot to ask Ann what it felt like the day she soloed. In an email she replied that it was hard to remember exactly, but she did recall making sure her pilot's log book was sticking out of her pocket for all to see because she was very proud of herself for taking the step to learn to fly.

In October of 2002, Ann was in a car accident in Arizona, suffering major damage to her back, neck and pelvis. Thankful she survived the crash, Ann was required to wear a halo for several months that rested on her shoulders while her neck healed. Ann admitted that she didn't like the confinement or the limitations of the halo because she's an active person.

When we first met in Girdwood, the day she was casually having a yard sale, Ann was talking about renewing her pilot's license. She did, because she's a Wilbur! It's no surprise that Ann and Joe Wilbur were successful, in spite of earthquakes and fires and family tragedies. They have the Alaskan spirit: Never, never, never give up.

15

A Test of Endurance:
INGRID PEDERSEN

I walked up the plywood ramp to Ingrid Pedersen's front door. Einar, Ingrid's Norwegian husband, and two large long-haired family dogs met me at the door. The dogs sniffed and licked my hand, then retreated to a sunny place by the sliding door in the dining room. In a heavy Norwegian accent, Einar explained that Ingrid would be along in a few minutes, that she had gone on a last-minute errand. I gazed around the comfortable living room and dining room, filled with artifacts and photographs the Pedersens have collected on their many arctic trips.

Ingrid arrived, her wispy strawberry-blond hair signaling she had rushed home for our interview. "I went to the store for custard pie, strawberries and chocolate ice cream," she explained in a soft Swedish accent. "Would you care for a cup of coffee … or tea? Whatever you like. What could I get for you?"

I accepted a glass of ice water and we sat down together at Ingrid's lace-covered dining room table. A photo of Ingrid, standing in front of an airplane, hung on the wall over my left shoulder. She leaned forward, her vivid blue eyes intent on me and my questions, a warm smile on her face. She explained that the ramp leading up to the front door is there to accommodate their wheelchair-bound son, who was in a head-on car accident near Fairbanks 20 years ago.

"Einar and I met when we worked for Scandinavian Airlines [SAS] Flight and Training School," Ingrid said. "The Polar Professor, as he was fondly called by his colleagues, taught polar navigation to pilots and navigators from SAS and a number of foreign airlines. I was a secretary. Einar was the chief navigator at SAS. He barely noticed me. I was impressed with him because he was a very kind soul and very shy also. When I told him I wanted to become a stewardess, he said, 'Why not a pilot?'

"I had a feeling he really didn't expect me to go through with that, so of course, I had to do it! From the beginning, I enjoyed flying immensely. The course was relatively easy, and I started flying in a J-3 in March of 1957, soloed on the 13th of May and received my private license in June, when I was 24." Beaming, Ingrid said, "I was the only female in a class of 20."

She talked of marriage to Einar in 1958 in Stockholm, Sweden, a son being born, and staying home to raise her stepson, who was then eleven. Einar made sure Ingrid had enough to do by making her a gift of a "beautiful, but very hairy, white female Alaskan husky" when he returned from a polar trip. "When Einar left on a trip, I stood in the exit door, vacuuming clean his uniform from top to toe!"

Eyeing the sleepy dogs by the sunny sliding door, I saw clearly that not much had changed in 44 years in the Pedersen home. I noted a photograph on a nearby wall, showing one of their fearless huskies trying to make friends with a polar bear.

Einar was given a position with SAS in Anchorage, Alaska, in 1962 for a year and a half. Ingrid had completed her commercial written test while still in Stockholm, but after she arrived in Anchorage, she obtained her private, commercial, and instrument ratings according to U.S. Federal Aviation standards.

"We loved Alaska," Ingrid said. "It looked so much like Norway, but on a much greater scale. When we moved here, we never locked our house or our car. It wasn't necessary."

Ingrid Pedersen on a trip from Fairbanks to Scandinavia in a Cessna 206, 1968.

Ingrid is vibrant and radiant, so it was easy to get caught up in her story and forget to keep notes. And she did something that really distracted me. She gave me dessert. And I managed to drizzle chocolate down the front of my blouse. "Not to worry," Ingrid said, handing me a napkin. "It's nothing, really, nothing." She would have made a wonderful flight attendant if she'd hadn't become a pilot, I thought.

There was one burning question I had yet to ask my hostess. "What made you fly over the North Pole in 1963 in a single-engine airplane?"

Ingrid smiled and leaned forward, anxious to share her adventure. "Einar had for many years wanted to fly over the North Pole in a small plane at a low altitude. He is not a pilot, and none of his colleagues would agree to make the trip with him. They told him it

74

would be a perilous and foolhardy adventure. I said yes, of course, but looking at that polar map with the large ocean of ice and cold, the black water seemed endless, all 2800 miles of it!"

Not since 1926, when Richard E. Byrd and pilot Floyd Bennett first flew over the North Pole, had anyone — least of all a woman pilot — repeated the daring feat in a small airplane. That is, not until 1963.

"We had gone to Wichita, Kansas, and bought a Cessna 205 and had extra tanks installed. We christened the plane *Snowgoose*. I trained with Max Johnson in Anchorage," Ingrid said. "He thought Einar was a brave but very foolhardy person leaving the flying to his wife. Our departure point was Fairbanks, where a crowd of FAA people, friends, and other onlookers had gathered. Sig and Noel Wien gave me lots of advice for taking off with an overloaded plane. The FAA people checked everything!" She paused.

"There was even a fire engine parked at the end of the runway."

"*Snowgoose* carried 175 gallons of fuel, life vests, a raft, several radios and transmitters, a tent, sleeping bags, rain gear, heavy clothing, a rifle, cooking utensils, fishing gear, a flashlight, and pemmican for a month," Ingrid said. "We taxied to the takeoff position and the plane felt heavy, like an overfed goose. After an extended takeoff run, the stall warning came on and continued for almost an hour. I could only make the plane climb a 100 feet per minute in the beginning. It was an enormous relief when the stall warning stopped."

Ingrid Pedersen on a polar flight in the Cessna 205 that she nicknamed *Snowgoose* when she flew over the North Pole in 1963.

Several pilots who have had a stall warning screaming in their ear later told me it's nerve wracking and *very* irritating.

Ingrid continued with her story. "Seventeen hours after takeoff, we were over the North Pole. We had given our position report on the hour, every hour, and 'Operation Normal' every half hour. We were in contact with Alaska, Seattle, Vancouver, Dundas on Greenland, and Norway. There were lots of Russian voices on the airways, which were impossible for us to understand. I reported 90 degrees north, circled and threw out the Alaskan flag and three Scandinavian flags. Then we celebrated with coffee and sandwiches."

Ingrid is quick to remind me that Einar was the navigator. "He was the polar expert and the expedition leader. He had flown over these regions so many times, he found the way to our destination. At that time, there were no automatic navigation aids available. Einar took sun shots with his sextant. A drift sight was mounted in the window on his side of the plane, enabling him to get drift and ground speed, and he used navigational tables. I flew the plane, took care of the radio and transferred fuel to the wing tank. We never had any disagreements. Einar didn't interfere in my flying. Technically, I was the captain of the airplane, but a green arctic pilot like me didn't question anything a polar navigator did, who had flown this route hundreds of times already." Smiling again, Ingrid said, "We just had a great time!

"After we circled the North Pole, we turned south. Of course, everything is south at the North Pole. We had four more hours to go to Greenland. At the pole we had lost a little time due to headwinds; now we were getting tail winds. It was just marvelous to finally have the deep fjords, snowy mountains, large glaciers of Greenland in sight. We landed on Station Nord 21 hours after departure, five minutes ahead of schedule!

"There was a big welcome by 30 Danes manning the station in Nord. Our bodies were stiff. We could hardly straighten out and we were almost deaf due to the engine noise. There were telegrams waiting from all over the northern hemisphere."

Newspapers heralded Ingrid's accomplishment: "Pilot Sets New Polar Record, September, 1963." Ingrid was awarded the prestigious Amelia Earhart Medal, the highest honor given by the International Women Pilots, the Ninety-Nines. A dinner was held in her honor in Anchorage and renowned Alaskan pilots Bob Reeve and Jack Jefford were on hand to congratulate Ingrid and Einar.

Ingrid made other trips across the Arctic Circle in the following years, ferrying planes from the Lower Forty-Eight across Canada to Norway, Sweden, Greenland, and Iceland. She said, "I landed on moving ice floes and flew over the ice cap at 13,000 feet. The ice cap is deceiving. It is so immense that it looks like clouds, but it's not. Quite a few planes have gone down there. Black mountain tops rise up from the ice cap, and it's fascinating. On one trip I heard the noise of a volcano and saw rocks as large as our house spewing out."

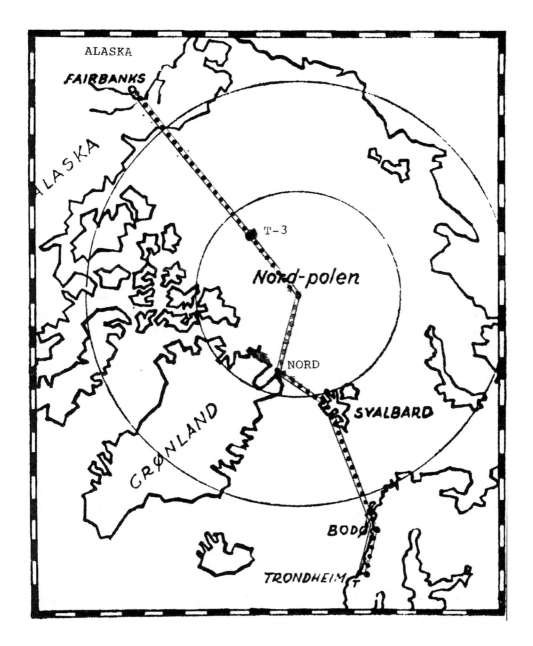

Over-the-Pole route taken by Ingrid and her navigator husband, Einar Pedersen.

I asked Ingrid if the record-setting flight she made in a single-engine plane changed her life in some way.

"The polar flight did indeed change my life," she said. "It never occurred to me when I learned to fly, back in Sweden, that someday I'd make aviation history. I had flown 2,400 miles and remember telling the reporters that the flight was a test of endurance as much as anything else."

16

An Exceptional Girl:
DOROTHY MAGOFFIN

When I telephoned Dorothy "Dottie" Riddle Magoffin to request an interview, she explained that she was going through chemotherapy treatments for cancer. But she wanted to meet me and talk about her life in Alaska, if at all possible. We set a date to meet in September when the aspen trees along the one-lane dirt road leading to her home in Fairbanks were beginning to shed their golden leaves.

Dottie met me at the screen door leading into her kitchen, a warm smile on her face, and invited me into her comfortable home. We sat down at her dining room table, which overlooks the community of Fairbanks, and she offered me some tea. I learned that Dottie's husband, Jim Magoffin, had politely gone before I arrived, leaving the two of us to get acquainted.

"Two years ago, when I got the news that I had cancer, I couldn't think," Dottie said. "I didn't want to talk to anyone. I didn't know how to react. It was the first time since Jim and I were married in 1946 that I didn't send out Christmas cards. But then I realized you can't put your knees up under your chin and quit." Dottie's green eyes shimmered as she added, "I might even start flying airplanes again."

Flying and Alaska were what I wanted to hear more about, and Dottie was happy to share her experiences. "We met at Maxwell Field in Alabama where I was a secretary, and Jim was a flight instructor in the Air Corps. I would hear his footsteps coming down the stairs, and I'd run into the hall to the water fountain. He'd stop and hold the handle for me while I took a drink … every time.

"When the war ended, Jim got a job at a placer mine in Ester, Alaska, about ten miles from Fairbanks, because he had a degree in mining. His father had come north for the Klondike Gold Rush of 1898 and told magnificent stories of Alaska. I'm sure he influenced our decision to come here.

"Jim and I were married on April 11, 1946, and we made our way up the Alcan Highway, camping along the way, arriving in Alaska on the 20th of that month. My

Dottie Magoffin standing on the floats of a Cessna 185 in a camoflage shirt and hip waders at Walker Lake, above the Arctic Circle.

friends back in Alabama were appalled at the thought of me moving to the wilds of Alaska, but I thought we had it made.

"When we got to Fairbanks it was hot and dusty, and I was shocked because of all the daylight. It never got dark! We stayed at the Cheechako Hotel till we moved out to Ester."

The smile left Dottie's face as she continued. "Jim was hired as a supervisor at the mine, but he worked right alongside the other men doing heavy manual labor, shoveling for hours on end. His shoulder bothered him from all the shoveling. I'd throw myself across our bed and cry because I felt so bad for him, but I never let him see me cry."

"Did the mine in Ester provide company housing?" I asked.

"Oh no, nothing like that," Dottie said with a chuckle. "We had a small cabin with no plumbing or running water ... no electricity or telephone ... not even a radio. We had a wood-burning stove for heat, a gasoline stove for cooking, and we used lanterns for light. Jim was making $272 a month. Three months after we arrived, I got pregnant, and all I had to wear were Jim's GI coveralls, but that was okay.

"We both enjoyed hunting and kept ourselves from starving by shooting ducks, rabbits, grouse, ptarmigan, moose and caribou," Dottie said. "One time, I hunted alone at the dredge pond near our cabin. I managed to get to the middle of the pond on a huge hydraulic pipe and sat there, patiently waiting, my 12-gauge Winchester shotgun ready. When I fired, I lost my balance and landed in the pond — my husband calls it 'that awful gumbo.' Some of the men from the mine site saw me and told my husband I was covered in mud from head to toe."

Observing the attractive, well-groomed woman across the table from me, I couldn't help but say, "Dottie, I find it hard to imagine you with a shotgun or covered in mud. You could have been a professional model."

Dottie had no comment, although a slight smile crossed her face.

In Jim Magoffin's book *Triumph Over Turbulence* he wrote about his wife: "Dot was not the typical soft spoken Southern belle. She seemed so happy all the time I nicknamed her 'Sunshine.' She was always a snappy dresser with a pretty, slim, little figure that accentuated the clothes she made or bought — always in good taste." He also said Dottie was "an exceptional girl," no doubt reflecting on her willingness to make a life with him in a bare-bones cabin in Ester, Alaska, in 1946.

Dottie said, "After I got pregnant it was awkward to handle a gun and get around on snowshoes in the winter. Our son Jim Jr. was born April 19, one day shy of a year after we came to Alaska. We found a house in town, in Fairbanks, and the day we moved was when Jim Jr. was born. We felt ensconced in an oasis of convenience and ease.

"Jim had found a second job as a flight instructor at Fairbanks Air Service before we moved from Ester. He worked there at night after his job at the mine in the daytime. Each evening, as a flight instructor, he made more than he did in a whole day at the mine, working seven days a week.

"We used our war bonds to buy our first airplane, a Taylorcraft. We used every cent we had — $3250 — to buy the plane," Dottie said. "The mine tailings had been bulldozed flat for a roadway and since it was near the cabin in Ester, we used it as a landing strip. But when we moved into Fairbanks, Jim quickly brought the airplane into Weeks Field."

"Do you think those early experiences gave you the courage you need now to help regain your health?" I inquired.

Dottie nodded. "Would you care for some more tea?"

I followed her into the kitchen. "Friends of ours from Alabama surprised us last night," Dottie said, opening a large box of sugared pecans. "They brought them all the way from their place in Alabama. They're very good."

Dottie's thoughtful, gracious manner spoke volumes to me as we returned to the dining room and gazed across the Tanana valley. "How many acres do you have here?"

"We still have the original 160 acres we bought in 1957," Dottie replied.

"Any plans to develop it — subdivide, or sell off some of the land?"

Reflecting as she gazed outside, Dottie said, "Oh no."

Dottie and Jim Magoffin in 1990 at their cabin at Magoffin Lake in Alaska. Photograph by Judy Jordan.

"Tell me what happened after you moved into Fairbanks in 1947 and had running water, electricity, and heat!"

"My husband started his own flying business," Dottie said. "Our house was only a block from the airport, and he didn't have a phone, so if a call for a charter came in, I'd hang a red flag on the pole outside to let him know he had a customer."

"Had you learned to fly yet?"

"No, not until 1955. We bought a flying school in 1950, but with two sons to raise and helping my husband with the business, there wasn't time for me to learn. Jim would take me up in the Taylorcraft for a little dual instruction, but I'd go home crying. You just can't take your husband seriously," Dottie said, rolling her eyes.

"I wanted to be able to fly on my own," she added, "because once the plane was loaded for a charter, there was never enough room for me. I had several instructors and I soloed in a Cessna 140 tail dragger, built up my hours in a Tri-pacer and a Supercub, and got my seaplane rating in a Supercub. I'd go out and gas it up and go!

"In 1957, I went to Fort Worth, Texas, and got my commercial pilot's license and my instrument and multi-engine ratings," Dottie said. "I was the only woman in ground school. Then I did a lot of VIP flying for our business. I'd take them out

81

Dottie Magoffin in the cockpit of a Cessna 180 near Kodiak, Alaska.

to Walker Lake for fishing trips, and I did charter flights and flew many of our scheduled flights to Clear Air Force Station."

"Ever have an unruly passenger?" I asked.

"You know, it's funny, but the only time I remember having to get serious was
with a guy who kept talking about his dog and puppies, and I was on final approach
to land. He kept talking, so I finally said, 'You've just got to shut up. I'm going to
land now.'"

"Ever have anyone refuse to fly with you because you're a woman?"

"It's amazing to me," Dottie said, "but the only time I remember was some
women who didn't believe I was the pilot. When I reached over and closed the door,
they asked me when the pilot was going to board. Women asked lots of questions
while we were in the air, but the men seldom asked any questions."

Two hours had passed like it had been 15 minutes when Jim Magoffin returned
home. I invited him to join us and he said, "I don't want to interfere."

"Dottie, I've been here for a couple hours," I said. "I don't want to tire you out."

She smiled. "I'm fine."

Jim spoke up. "You know, she's been cured for a year, but she's such an entertaining patient they keep giving her appointments so she'll bring them a tray of cook-

ies and fresh fruit every time she goes in for treatment." From where Jim Magoffin sat on the edge of a chair in the living room, he reached over and gently patted Dottie on the back. She looked at him with the same affection she must have felt at the water fountain at Maxwell Field, Alabama, in the 1940s. They are a loving couple and clearly a strong team.

In his book, Jim explained about the early years as a non-scheduled airline and the trouble he and Dottie had getting a foothold in Alaska because of competition and grandfather rights. The Civil Aeronautics Board and the Civil Aviation Administration (now the Federal Aviation Administration), came down hard on non-scheduled airlines, once ordering the Magoffins out of business on the grounds that nobody in Alaska needed their services. But Dottie and Jim persevered, gradually growing and expanding the business to cover much of the world. They sold their company and retired in 1982.

While they owned the airlines, it was Dottie that saw to it the passengers were top priority. She personally inspected the planes for cleanliness and instructed the stewardess to pay particular attention to the needs of the children. It was not uncommon for the airlines to serve special desserts with festive napkins, not typical of commercial airlines. No doubt they had an occasional treat of Alabama pecans.

Jim and Dottie and I talked briefly about the upcoming gubernatorial race, other women pilots in Alaska, and airplanes the Magoffins donated to museums in Fairbanks and Anchorage. As I was leaving, I asked if I could take a picture of them and, at first, Dottie was hesitant. Jim and I assured her she looked fine, and if she'd been covered in mud, holding a shotgun, she would still have been very photogenic. Jim ran back inside to get his camera, insisting on taking a picture of me with Dottie. "We have your address, I hope," he said, planning to send me a copy.

It was time to drive back down the tree-lined dirt road to civilization, and I was sad to leave. Dottie gave me a warm hug and looked into my eyes. "When you came in the house this afternoon, I felt like I'd always known you." I blushed and felt touched by an angel. I knew that anyone who ever crosses Dottie Magoffin's doorstep feels the same. She is an "exceptional" woman and pilot.

Dorothy Riddle Magoffin
March 19, 1925–March 1, 2004

"During the night before she died, as I sped back to her bedside, I drove in the glow of one of the most fantastic displays of Northern Lights I had ever seen. Now, I know the scientists say it has something to do with sunspots and the ionosphere, but I prefer to believe it was angels dancing in celebration."—*From the eulogy by Dottie's son, Jim Magoffin.*

17

Perseverance:
Darlene Dubay

Darlene Dubay was relaxed, comfortable in her sweat clothes, sipping from a water bottle. She had been outside working in the garden of her home in Anchorage when I arrived. The soft spoken 5'3" strawberry blond spoke with confidence as she talked about her desire to belong to an exclusive club ever since she learned to fly in 1973. Darlene aspired to become an airline pilot. She was hired at age 50 by Northwest Airlines. Only 5 percent of 5,000 pilots at Northwest are women. Darlene is very proud to wear the Northwest uniform and fly an Airbus 320. She achieved her life-long goal with patience and determination.

Not long after she signed on to fly with Northwest, Darlene described walking through an airport in her dark-blue uniform, cap on her head, stroller suitcase and flight bag in tow, when two men sidled up to her and said, "Are you a pilot?"

"I told them I just borrowed the uniform so I could parade through airports. The first man caught my humor, but the second still may not believe I'm an airline pilot."

Darlene grew up on a farm in northern Michigan, the youngest of eight. "I learned to do my part because we all had to help. That gave me a good work ethic. At five years old, my brothers had me drive the tractor while they loaded hay bales onto the trailer." Darlene held her arms out to form a large circle, to show how big the steering wheel had seemed when she was just five.

"That was the start of learning to be confident. I loved the fresh air, and that's where I got my appreciation of nature." The prolific flower gardens at her home in Anchorage, where there is a very short summer growing season, attest to her love of plants and nature. Bud, her husband, is also an avid gardener.

After finishing high school, Darlene left home to go to college at the University of Michigan, but married during the first semester and soon had two children. "In 1971, when my husband finished dental school, we moved to Alaska, where he had accepted a commission to serve as a dental officer in the U.S. Public Health Service [PHS]. Bud served for two years, which fulfilled his military obligations. As the

Darlene Dubay, with her Piper PA-18 at Knik Glacier, Lake George, Alaska.

itinerant dentist based at the Alaska Native Medical Center in Anchorage, he traveled to remote villages in southwestern Alaska, including Kodiak Island, the Pribilofs, the Aleutians and the Dillingham and King Salmon areas. Darlene said, "The children and I frequently traveled with him. All of us fell in love with Alaska, and we couldn't leave after two years. We loved it here."

It wasn't long before Darlene pursued flight lessons. "It's the only way to get around Alaska and really enjoy it," she said. "I got my license before my husband got his. I soloed at Merrill Field in Anchorage in May 1973. I absolutely love flying!"

Between 1973 and 1980 Darlene worked as a dental assistant with her husband on trips to several villages along the Yukon River Delta. "The people were so friendly. They invited us into their homes for dinner, and after several years, we were almost like family."

While raising a son and daughter, continuing her education, and assisting her husband in his dental practice, Darlene said she really got hooked on flying after she took a few aerobatic lessons at Merrill Field, doing maneuvers such as loops, rolls, Immelman turns and Cuban eights.

"It took me a long time to build up my courage for that first lesson," she said. "It seemed so dangerous. My instructor's name was Ken Johansen, who had been a

Swedish Air Force pilot. He was so relaxed in the backseat of his Bellanca Decathlon 8KCB that I had an image of him sitting in his living room having a beer. That put me at ease. During the first lesson, he showed me how to strap into the parachute and fasten all of the safety belts. He said, 'If we have to get out of the plane in an emergency, pull this pin to release the door, rotate this buckle to release your harness and then *yoost yump.*'

"In spite of my apprehension, I loved aerobatics. I loved the visual images of a kaleidoscopic earth and the physicality of it. Initially, I took aerobatic lessons to build my confidence and competence in an airplane, but I got hooked. I bought my own Decathlon and performed in air shows around Alaska … Soldotna, Gulkana and Fairbanks. Later, when I was instructing at the Fort Richardson Flying Club, I leased my plane to the club and wrote an aerobatic course syllabus for which I obtained FAA approval."

Darlene also gave Patty Wagstaff her first ten aerobatic lessons when Patty was first learning in Alaska.

"Aerobatics taught me how to handle planes better," Darlene said. "It improved my physical and technical skills. In aerobatics you use both the right and left brain. The technical, analytical skills necessary for controlling the plane and being aware of a myriad of data are complemented by an intuitive sense of what makes a routine artistic. The right being intuitive and the left being analytical, I was always analyzing clues. I had to focus on the task and take in other extraneous data — prioritize and analyze, all at the same time."

As Darlene explained the complexity of learning aerobatics, I thought back to my interview with early Alaskan Bush pilot Ruth Jefford, who said her first husband, an early-day barnstormer, tried to teach her aerobatics. Ruth had laughed as she described her experience: "I was all over the damn sky! I prefer straight and level."

Nothing deterred Darlene. Next she obtained her instrument rating, commercial license, and sometime along the way she obtained a float plane rating too, followed by instructor, airline transport and multi-engine rating. Darlene did it all.

"I landed my first commercial job hauling fish from Kaltag to Unalakleet, and while I was in the air I spent all my time looking for places where I could make an emergency landing. There was an incident when I was taking off from Kaltag with a load of fish. I knew something didn't feel right even though the instruments seemed okay. I decided to abort and return before taking off fully loaded with fish. A mechanic checked out the plane and couldn't find anything wrong with it so I planned to return to Anchorage without the load to have the plane checked by my own mechanic. As I lifted off, with only one other person on board, I knew that something still was not right. The plane would barely climb above the trees. I made a wide turn and came back. When the mechanic checked the plane again, he found one of the cylinders was totally destroyed. It only had 60 percent power."

It appeared that everything just fell into place for Darlene, one, two, three, but she said 1981 was the low point of her career. "I flew a Twin Otter for Alaska Aeronautical Industries to build time. I flew to Homer, Kenai, Cordova, Kodiak, Valdez and Iliamna. I was paid $600 a month and if I flew over 75 hours a month, they paid me $12 per flight hour. I flew 25 days straight with no time off. They didn't maintain the planes well and had lots of co-pilot turnover. Fifteen men were hired before me even though I had more experience than any of them."

"On my first trip in the right seat to Valdez, the pilot wouldn't let me do anything. I kept trying to work with him as a crew member by asking if he wanted me to read the checklist or make radio calls or handle the weight and balance calculations. He would say, 'No, I can handle it.' By the time we got to Valdez I was steaming and I told him that I would not fly back with him. He didn't believe me and told me I had to return with him. I did, but not till he agreed to let me fly the return leg."

Darlene smiled when she said, "We flew together frequently after that, and once I earned his respect we became good friends and enjoyed working together.

"In the early '80s I decided to get a flight engineer certificate to improve my chances at getting an airline job. However, no one was hiring regardless of your abilities or qualifications. I quit flying for about a year. During that time, I interviewed with Alaska Airlines but was not offered a job. I didn't consider other airlines because they would have wanted me to commute to Newark, Chicago, or Los Angeles. I wanted to stay in Alaska.

"Then I met a guy who flew Twin Otters for ARCO, the oil company, and he said they needed temporary pilots out of Kuparuk up on the North Slope. I applied and got the job. Through another friend, a few months later, I heard that ERA was hiring in Anchorage. They hired me to fly a Twin Otter in their commuter operation for about a year. Then I was checked out in the right seat of the Convair 580, which means I could fly as a co-pilot. ERA was well run and the planes were well maintained," Darlene said.

Darlene flew in the right seat in the Convair with an "old school" pilot who didn't think women belonged in the cockpit. "I always had to prove myself with every other pilot more so than the men did. I had to be extra professional. I was ready to upgrade to captain, not for the money, but for the responsibility. The chief pilot groomed his friends and they went on to be pilots for major airlines."

Darlene's progress was slow, frustrating, but steady and consistent. She was determined to succeed. After three years with ERA she took a job with the FAA Flight Standards District Office in Fairbanks doing aviation safety inspections. "In 1989, I transferred to the office in Anchorage. Working with the FAA was fun. I loved my job with flight check, flying low level, doing what other pilots didn't get to do. I checked navigation facilities in a Convair 580 and delivered logistical support to the Bush stations."

Darlene also flew a Sabreliner and a Lear 60 all over Alaska while she was with the FAA until the Sabreliner was retired. They transferred their pilots to Sacramento,

California, where Darlene worked two weeks checking navigation facilities in the western states. Then she returned to Anchorage and sat behind a desk for two weeks, which she said was very boring.

"When I got wind that Oklahoma City planned to close the Anchorage office and move all of us to Sacramento, I pursued my ultimate goal. I was hired in '97 at age 50 by Northwest Airlines, and it's the best job in the world. People are still surprised to see a woman in the airport in uniform. I'm the first officer because of seniority. There's no favoritism, with very strict union rules. Being hired by Northwest means I finally made it to the pros. It's a difficult lifestyle but trade-offs and benefits are great!

"I was nervous and excited about being interviewed at Northwest and went through some counseling to prepare how to put myself in the best light. The hiring process is lengthy. It begins with a battery of tests, including aptitude, intelligence and psychological tests. Each test lasts seven minutes, and we were to answer as many questions as we could in that time. The entire battery lasted six hours and there were 100 applicants. This was in Egan, Minnesota, and I really didn't expect to get to the next step when they sent all of us home after one day of exams.

Darlene Dubay in cockpit of Northern Airlines 747 at Ted Stevens International Airport, Anchorage, Alaska.

"They called me in a week and asked me to come back to Egan for the next level, which was using a 747 simulator to check my basic flying skills. I felt really good about that. That part was easy for me. Then they invited me to interview with three people, including the chief pilot and the director of personnel. I wore a dark-blue suit with a soft white tie-style blouse. The interview was non-threatening. At this point in the process, they assume that you are technically proficient and they mainly want to see how you get along in the work setting.

"At the end of the interview they asked me to tell them three things about myself that I would like them to remember as they considered my application. I remember saying I was a quick learner and I really, *really* wanted to work for Northwest, but can't recall the third thing I said.

"They had me wait in the foyer. It was a rainy day. I watched the droplets run down the windows and in a short while the director of personnel appeared and at that same instant, so did the sun. The woman said, 'We want to offer you a job, contingent on your flight physical.' I refrained from jumping up and giving her a hug.

"The following day I took the physical and passed, came home and we took a short vacation to Oregon. Every day I checked for phone messages at our home and finally there was a message giving me a class date. That's when I knew it was for real.

"So, on November 10, 1997, I began basic indoctrination with 20 other pilots. We studied regulations and Northwest policies and procedures. Then we were assigned to one of three positions, first officer in a DC-9, first officer in a Boeing 727, or second officer in a 727. Positions are chosen according to seniority—from the oldest in the class to the youngest. I was the second oldest in my class and chose the DC-9.

"It was the most difficult training I've ever experienced. Kind of like drinking out of two fire hoses at the same time. I was at school ten hours a day, studying aircraft systems, learning procedures and responding to questions. By the second week of training we spent the afternoon in the simulator in addition to the classroom study in the morning. At night I continued to study for four or five more hours. It was very stressful.

"I kept thinking, *What if I wash out? What if I miss my big chance?* I studied every waking moment — while eating, while driving to school, while brushing my teeth! That's all I did. School lasted six weeks."

Darlene had the stamina and desire to succeed, perhaps because in her early 30s she started running. "I didn't want to gain weight as my metabolism slowed down. I love to eat. So I joined several running groups and ran many races from 10Ks to marathons. I like the challenge of racing. It gave me added energy to push myself harder. I competed in marathons in Anchorage, New York City, Minneapolis, Boston, Lake Placid, Tucson, and in the desert sun of Las Vegas. My greatest challenge was the Iron Man Triathlon in Lake Placid — a 2.4 mile swim, 112-mile bike ride and a full 26.2 mile marathon."

When asked how she handles the responsibility of piloting a large passenger plane, Darlene confidently replied, "I'm technically proficient, so my passengers are safe. I just concentrate on my job at the time, and I don't worry about the passengers. That's what I'm paid to do.

"As the first officer in the righthand seat, I do the same tasks as the captain. On most trips the captain flies the first leg and then we trade off. As the non-flying pilot, I handle the radios, read the checklist, make public announcements and help the captain to watch for traffic. When I'm flying the aircraft I call for checklists and make decisions about the maneuvering of the aircraft. Basically, we both do the exact same job except that I have less seniority and don't have the ultimate responsibility."

Darlene smiled as she said, "We both received the same training and abide by the same standards, but the captain has the responsibility and consequently makes more money! With any of the major airlines there's not much turnover unless someone retires or loses their medical, so you have to stay to achieve seniority.

"In some cases, when I was hired, I was more experienced than the pilots I flew with, but I was new with Northwest. I have to retire at age 60 because of FAA regulations, but I wouldn't trade the variety of experiences I've had for the money or the prestige." Still relaxed, Darlene beamed as she said, "I can't believe they pay me to do it!"

18

Monday's My Day Off:
HEIDI RUESS

Heidi Ruess has logged more than 27,000 hours of flight time since she learned to fly in 1965. Most of those hours have been in the skies over Alaska where she instructs other people at Arctic Flyers, based at Lake Hood in Anchorage. She is busy teaching year-round and likes to say, "Monday's my only day off!"

The short-haired Swiss woman met me with a warm smile at the airstrip just north of Lake Hood on a very cold, blustery February day. I followed her to a ten-foot log cabin that serves as her base of operations. Heidi said, "It took me 20 years to get approval to have an office on a finger of Lake Hood where my airplane was parked. I sort of cheated because I got so tired of waiting for official approval. I had a guy construct the cabin exactly in the middle of my lot and my husband's lot. By the time the inspector arrived the cabin was finished. He wasn't pleased, but he didn't make me tear it down. It allows us to park a plane on either side of the office."

The spunky, petite brown-eyed woman described herself as "strong willed and determined … and a little bit sneaky." She said, "I had to be!"

Heidi met her husband, Hermann, when they were still in Zurich, Switzerland, their homeland. She was 16. "When I met him he was wearing a Swiss uniform. When I married him he was wearing an American uniform. We kept in touch through letters and became engaged to marry when I was 19. We married in South Carolina when I was 20, and our honeymoon took us to Alamogordo in New Mexico where Hermann was stationed in the Air Force. He had been drafted and because he wasn't a U.S. citizen, he either had to sign up or return to Switzerland. That's what brought us to Alaska in 1957 for two years."

Heidi recalled their first flight together when her husband was stationed at Elmendorf Air Force Base near Anchorage. "He took me flying with a plane he rented from the Seven Star Flying Club for $5.00. We were low on gas and there was no radio. He told me the plane was held together with baling wire! He was right. We had to buzz the tower at Merrill Field, and when they flashed the green light we got the go ahead to land.

Heidi Ruess, summertime on floats at Lake Hood, ready to take off and land on water in her Taylorcraft.

"After Hermann served his tour of duty we returned to Seattle, Washington, so he could finish his education. He worked full time and went to school full time." Heidi laughed as she remembered, "I spent a lot of time taking our two kids on long walks so Hermann could study. Very long walks. Once my husband got his mechanical engineering degree we moved to Los Alamos, New Mexico, where we both had to have top-security approval. Hermann worked at the Los Alamos laboratory as an engineer; I worked part time as a secretary.

"I got tired of waiting at home when Hermann was out flying. I began to think there has to be something to this, so I took a pinch-hitter course, which is for the passenger, such as a spouse like me. That way, if we were flying together with our children, I'd have some idea what to do. I enjoyed learning to fly, more and more, and overcame my fear of heights and air sickness. I learned to eat apples, which kept me from getting sick. There was another woman taking classes at the same time, and I decided to solo first. I felt very competitive at the time."

Heidi didn't just solo, she pursued numerous ratings. "Between 1965 and 1973, I obtained an instrument rating, a commercial rating, instructor rating, instrument instructor, single-engine sea ticket, multi-engine and multi-sea ticket. Eventually, I added my airline transport rating," Heidi said.

She never mentioned feeling frustrated or overwhelmed with paperwork and checkrides as she progressed from one level to the next. Heidi's face was animated as she recalled all the steps she took to obtain advanced ratings, obviously pleased with herself.

"In the afternoons, I began giving flight instruction, and I loved it. Most of the people I trained in New Mexico had PhDs, with degrees in physics, chemistry and math. They did great on the written part, but they drove me nuts with technical questions. I'd always say, 'Just fly the plane.'"

"Young people are the easiest to instruct because they listen," Heidi said. "Older people have their mind set and don't like it when I question their motives. An important part of teaching people to fly is getting to know them. I call it 'psyching them out.' I find out their strengths and weaknesses so I can help them become good pilots."

Had any of her pilots become commercial airline pilots, I inquired.

"Oh yes. Several have gone on to fly with the airlines, and we had one young man who became a test pilot for Lear Jet."

The Ruess family made a choice to relocate to Alaska when the division Hermann worked for was shut down in New Mexico. He was hired by the U.S. Fish and Wildlife Department in Anchorage. Heidi went to work as a flight instructor with a former student of hers at Pat's Flying Service when they relocated to Anchorage.

"Hermann worked in a hangar at Lake Hood reconfiguring the 'Aleutian Goose,' a Grumman Goose. He made do with the corks off champagne bottles to replace missing knobs in the cockpit," Heidi said with pride. "He flew it too! He loved his job. They used the plane for long-distance surveys of bowhead whales, walrus, seals and birds."

"It was named for the endangered Aleutian Goose," Hermann explained.

Heidi, her son, Richard, and her husband are all experienced pilots. The men fly Citations and her daughter, Heidi Ruess Jr.—a tag she coined in high school—also learned to fly but gave it up to train dogs. "She makes more training dogs than I do teaching people to fly!" Heidi said.

The friendly, personable woman relaxed into her captain's chair and reflected on teaching people to fly. "I enjoy the confidence my students gain—every one of them—when they solo. It's like they're saying to the world, 'I am somebody. I'm doing something others don't know how to do.'"

Heidi was chief flight instructor at Northwestern Air Service, where she flew a Cherokee low wing that she didn't like. "I also flew a Super Cub that I did like."

Petco offered Heidi a job and she taught students there, flying a twin-engine Baron, Citabria, 7ECA and a GCB (a bigger plane, Heidi noted). She also flew a Cessna 150 and 172 and a Mooney. Opportunity for advancement knocked again.

Heidi Ruess, wintertime at Lake Hood, ready to take off and land on wheel skis, in her Taylorcraft.

Heidi left to fly for Ketchum Air Service at Lake Hood, doing summer charter work.

"We only flew when the tourists were around, so I started instructing part time in my Cessna 150. Then I took a short-lived nine-month job with the FAA, learning to fly a C123. It was like driving a truck!" Heidi said, holding her arms in a large circle in front of her. "We flew cargo to the flight service stations—cars, trucks, household goods. I didn't like it very much and lacked the basic mechanical knowledge to gain the respect of the men. It just wasn't the plane for me.

"In 1978, I decided to start my own business at Lake Hood. I'm still doing the same thing because that's what I love doing: instructing. I've logged more than 22,500 hours instructing, and I do it year-round. I find that if the person learning to fly is paying all or part of the cost to learn, they are more motivated and they learn faster."

The Ruess family own two Cessna 150s and two Taylorcrafts that they put on skis in the winter and floats in the summer. They also own a Cessna 172. Four of their planes are blue-and-white and one is red-and-white.

"We enjoy flying to our cabins on Donkey Lake near Skwentna," Heidi said, "and we fly our students in our planes and theirs to remote areas to fish and camp. It's a lot of fun. One time we landed five planes on the road between Talkeetna and Mount

McKinley, then pushed them off the road. We went fishing on boats on the Chulitna River. It's a good way to give students an introduction to flying in Alaska." Heidi laughed again. "It's really the only way to get around here."

The phone interrupted us. It was time for Heidi to meet a student at Lake Hood for a lesson … and it was her day off. It was Monday.

19

A Survivor:
ELLEN PANEOK

Ellen Paneok could easily have slipped into the bottomless crevasse of a frozen glacier and disappeared. Born in Kotzebue, Alaska, Ellen was in the fifth grade when her parents divorced. Her Inupiaq Eskimo heritage — her dark eyes and straight black hair — came from her mother. Her strong-willed determination came from her father, a man of German descent who was in the United States Air Force stationed in Alaska.

Following the end of her parents' marriage, Ellen and her two sisters came with their mother to live in Anchorage where Native Alaskans were not always accepted as equals.

Ellen said, "I was a stringy-haired girl wearing Salvation Army hand-me-downs. My classmates taunted me, beat me up and called me crude Eskimo nicknames, like 'Skeemo.' I didn't have much confidence, so it didn't take much to hurt me. I learned to run fast and hide!

"From nine to 12, I took on the role of parent because my mother was never around. My mother told us that my father was a deadbeat dad who didn't pay child support. But what money we did have my mother spent. One time I remember going to the grocery store and filling the cart to the top and marching right out the door, without paying, to feed us." Ellen leaned back in her antique oak dining room chair to reflect. "My childhood was one of survival.

"Somehow, I managed to care for my two sisters until a state social service agency knocked on our door when I was about 12. I fought them every step of the way, kicking and screaming, determined to keep our family together. I didn't want us to be split up," she said, slamming her hand down on the oak dining table. "My youngest sister was adopted and my other sister and I were sent to two different foster homes. I was very angry and rebellious," Ellen said. "I ran away from several foster homes because I was very unhappy."

I was surprised by Ellen's openness about her painful childhood. In an effort to lighten the mood, I asked about a collection of ceramic, glass and silver horses carefully placed on a nearby antique sideboard. Ellen picked up a small hand-painted

Ellen Paneok at the Alaska Aviation Heritage Museum, standing on the tire of a 1934 Stinson Gull-wing aircraft, 2002.

horse. "This collection belonged to my grandmother, and when my middle sister died in 2002, it was passed on to me." She said that she was able to locate her other sister, Tina, who had been adopted and lives in the south. But it was apparent as I studied her face that Ellen's tragic childhood cannot be erased.

Ellen changed the subject. "Can I refill your glass with soda?"

"I got bounced from one foster home to another before I landed in girls' lock-down at 14. I didn't care about anything, especially school. I didn't have anything to do in lock-down so I walked up to a magazine rack and found one with an airplane on the cover. It could have just as well been a magazine about boating at that time in my life. I didn't care. But, by the time I finished looking at the one with airplanes, I said to myself, 'This is going to save my life.'"

The counselors at the lock-down facility and Ellen's teachers thought she was obsessed with airplanes and made her go to counseling. "There's no denying it," Ellen said with a chuckle. "I was obsessed with airplanes! I wrote poems about airplanes, drew pictures or painted pictures of airplanes. Fortunately, my last foster home was a loving environment that helped me turn my life around.

"When I received my first native corporation dividend from CIRI [Cook Inlet Regional Corporation], I was 16," Ellen said. "Wearing second-hand clothes, I took the $1,500 check, hopped on a city bus and went to Merrill Field in Anchorage and signed up for flying lessons."

Ellen Paneok on fuselage of a Cessna 180. Photograph by Randi Hirschmann.

Ellen's dark, native eyes lit up. "I skipped history and English classes to take flying lessons. Before long, the money ran out so I taught myself to do pen-and-ink drawings, which I sold for $10 apiece. And I taught myself to do ivory carvings—scrimshaw — and I sold them to the tourists.

"In my sophomore year of high school, I had an English teacher who told me I was lazy and shiftless. I told myself, 'Too bad. Watch me do it!' When I turned 20, I received my GED and my private pilot's license."

Ellen's mother nicknamed her "Paneok," which means "fish's tail," and Ellen changed her surname to Paneok when she became an adult. Listening to Ellen relate the heights and depths of her life struggles, I imagined a whale thrashing in shallow water, desperate to survive and prove that she could do whatever she set her mind on. Flying was the key. In a quick glance around her home, I counted five airplane propellers that dominate the colorful decor, every wall proudly displaying photos or paintings of airplanes, and endless aviation memorabilia … even in the bathroom. It was very clear what makes Ellen's heart sing.

Ellen recited a favorite quote by Leonardo da Vinci: "Once you have tasted flight you will walk this earth with your eyes turned skyward. For there you have been and there you long to return." She added, "I've always liked that quote. Come on, I'll show you around my home."

We walked through the hall and down a few steps. "This is my exercise room." Life-size posters of *Star Trek* characters Spock and Kirk hung near her treadmill.

Ellen encouraged me to follow her up another short flight of stairs to her computer room, with more aviation memorabilia on the walls and on shelves and above her computer. "I cleaned this up just so I could show you," she said with a chuckle.

A comical photo of a small plane perched on huge farm-tractor-size tires hangs above her printer. A calendar on the other wall with a photo of an open-cockpit airplane — airborne with the pilot desperately clinging to the tail of the plane, his white neck scarf dancing in the wind — made Ellen giggle. "Isn't that funny?" she said.

A surrealist 12" × 14" black-and-white photo of Ellen drew me to it like a magnet. The image, photographed by Carolyn Russo from the Smithsonian Air & Space Museum in Washington, D.C., captures the essence of Ellen's heritage. The white ruff of an Eskimo parka surrounds her face, strands of her long black hair the only contrast in the stark image.

"Oh, that was taken by the photographer from the Smithsonian," Ellen said in a matter-of-fact tone as she led me to a balcony overlooking the living room.

The balcony wall was full of bookshelves and more treasures. Ellen reached for Bob Reeve's book *Glacier Pilot*, and showed me where he penned these words to her: "To an air charmer. Have an ever-sparkling life."

Ellen said, "I liked to drop by his office at Reeve Aleutian Airways in downtown Anchorage, where we'd talk about flying. I told him I was thinking of becoming a stunt pilot and that I wanted to do air shows."

Ellen lowered her voice, pretending to speak like Reeve. "He told me, 'Ellen, that's too much work.'" Carefully, with respect, almost reverence, for the well known Alaskan pilot, Ellen returned the book to its place on the shelf among other books on aviation history. "Bob Reeve was definitely one of my early mentors."

A complex person, a woman with a heart-breaking childhood, emerged during the interview. A dark-eyed Eskimo woman with a passion for life and airplanes and a sense of humor that carried her through personal tragedy, surfaced frequently during our three-hour talk. Her stories were limitless, never boring. What she told me could have been a fast-paced action-adventure movie, yet true to life.

In 1980, Ellen was ferrying a plane from Kotzebue to Anchorage with another pilot, whom she eventually married. He sat in the right-hand seat, entertaining himself by singing out loud, "You picked a fine time to leave me, Lucille," when the Piper Tri-Pacer Ellen was flying quit somewhere between McGrath and Farewell, Alaska.

"It was July 10, 1980, at 3:10 P.M., the last day I ever had a cigarette!" Ellen said, wide eyed. "Boy, when the engine quits in that plane, it's like a homesick brick, heading for the ground! I managed to crash land in some trees and Jerry and I scrambled through the only door to get out of the plane ... in case the engine caught on fire. I didn't know I had three cracks in one vertebrae from the crash. I just wanted out of that airplane in case it burst into flames!"

Ellen remembers that fateful afternoon almost too well. "It was mid–July and the worst part was the swarm of mosquitoes that engulfed us. I took some spruce tree boughs and engine oil and made a smoke fire. The fire also called attention to the missing plane, which was green like the trees, but it was a day and a half before we were rescued. If I hadn't made that smoke fire, they never would have found us."

Ellen flipped her long black hair over her left shoulder and continued. "A C-130 pinpointed our emergency transmitter [ELT], then they saw the smoke fire and dropped a radio and hand-written messages about the planned rescue. I still have all three hand-written messages as a reminder of that experience," she said. The three rescue notes are in pencil, neatly framed, hanging on the wall near her front door.

"It's a day I will never forget," Ellen said, fighting back tears. "I'm sorry, I always tear up when I remember the concern on the faces of the guys that rescued us. They didn't know how bad we were injured, or how many of us there were."

The subsequent marriage to Jerry ended four years later when he became abusive, but before he died in a plane crash in Cambodia, they became friends again. Even though he asked, Ellen was unwilling to chance marriage to him again.

Ellen Paneok hand propping the 1939 L-1 Stinson Vigilant (painted on the nose of the aircraft is *Vigilant Virgin*) at the Alaska Aviation Heritage Museum, 2003.

Ellen's fascination with aerobatic flying never waned. In 1983 she traveled to Texas to learn "from the best" — Duane Cole, who also trained champion aerobatic pilot Patty Wagstaff, a close friend of Ellen's. "I flew aerobatics a few days with Duane Cole, then I practiced for a full year. I'd practice two and three hours a day. I'd get out of the plane with bruises on my upper legs and shoulders where the parachute straps rubbed. My left hand would be bruised from shoving the stick around and it would hit the airframe. But I loved aerobatics!

"Then my dreams were dashed in 1984 when I blacked out in a 45-degree downhill dive because of high blood pressure. I cried and was very angry when the doctors told me I couldn't continue. I thought that was the end of my dreams."

After this disappointment, Ellen said, "I bounced back and decided to specialize in 'off-airport' work, which is the epitome of challenge — to land where no one else lands." As if she was in the cockpit, surveying the ground below, checking the direction of the wind, both hands guiding her fantasy flight, Ellen said, "I land on beaches, mountain knobs, sand bars and in gravel pits. I've landed at Point Possession and Montague Island, where they say beaches have a reputation as airplane eaters!" Ellen's expression was electrified as she talked of flying. "I've landed in dozens of places on the west side of the Alaska range.

"In 1984, I bought my first plane, an Aeronca Chief, which had a 75-horsepower engine that sounded like a John Deere tractor. I put big tundra tires on it and named it *Rags*. The other pilots teased me about Rags … about the tires, the color of the plane — which was bright orange — and the speed. Nothing deterred me, though," Ellen said.

"My training ground with my new plane was the Knik River sandbar, right up to the Matanuska Glacier, but I discovered my limitations when I learned that you can't power your way out of everything. I had about 400 feet on one side of the river to land and take off, but one day I put Rags down and thought, oops, we're sinking into the soft, damp sand. I climbed out of the aircraft onto the sandbar, dug the Aeronca out, and dragged it backwards by the tail." Ellen used her long arms and hands to show how she tugged on the tail of the plane. "It was no easy task — till I was almost in the water. Then I had to hand prop the engine. I powered up, kept on going — with everything Rags had — till I had to yank back on the yoke to miss the trees."

Ellen leaned back in her chair again, her eyebrows raised as she admitted, "There were green streaks on the prop and leaf stains on the windshield when I landed at Philo's Airstrip in Wasilla. All the guys came running out to see why I had a five-foot tree hanging off the landing gear, which I didn't know about till I climbed out of the plane!"

The intrepid young woman also flew hunters and fishermen, and dynamite, to remote places. She ferried mine workers to and from their villages and back to Aniak, Alaska.

"Life at the mine site, in a crude quonset hut tent for a year and a half, amidst a cluster of tents, was like living in a M.A.S.H. unit. The men in camp were ready to shoot me several times because I'd put vases and flowers on the tables in the mess hall," Ellen snickered. "They couldn't care less what was on the tables—as long as there was food!"

Ellen told yet another story while the ceiling fan overhead maintained a room temperature of 60 degrees. Any warmer and Ellen would feel it's too hot. I pulled my sweater around my shoulders to ward off the chilly air and suggested she should live in Barrow, Alaska. This led to a story about the northernmost tip of the American continent.

"I was working for an air taxi operator in Barrow. I'd been flying a Cessna 185 from Wainright and Atqusuq and could typically off-load 800 pounds of mail in a few minutes. But that day, I had to sit down and let someone else unload, which really surprised them. On my return flight to Barrow the temperature outside the cabin was minus-27 degrees. I had the heater on full blast but the windshield kept icing up inside, and suddenly I realized I couldn't feel my face or arms or legs. I kept wondering, 'What the heck is this?' I took a credit card and scraped the ice on the windows inside the cabin. It didn't help."

Ellen's face flushed red as she spoke, even with the fan circling overhead. "On final approach into Barrow, I was losing my vision and could only focus on what seemed like a tunnel on the runway. When I landed, I climbed out, fell on the ski and passed out. In a while, when the cold air brought me to, I managed to stagger inside and collapsed again." Her voice quickened. "I was gasping for air, like a heart attack victim, while two firemen transported me to the local hospital.

"A gray-haired male doctor told me I was just hyperventilating, and he sent me home. The same day another pilot flew the same airplane to Deadhorse—a forty-minute flight—and was admitted to the hospital. He phoned to say he was diagnosed with 30 percent carbon monoxide poisoning in his lungs and they immediately put him in a hyperbaric chamber.

"My flight in the same aircraft, earlier that day, had lasted for two hours, and the director of maintenance suspected all along that I was suffering from the same problem, but he couldn't convince the gray-haired doctor at the hospital. I spent the next four or five days on my couch, trying to recover, but I was so weak I couldn't even lift a magazine. I felt like a pool of liquid. I returned to the hospital where a woman doctor determined that I had a severe potassium deficiency, brought on by CO poisoning. Immediately, she put me on oxygen, which didn't help much, then I was rushed to Intensive Care and plugged into monitors, with tubes running everywhere."

The color left Ellen's face. Her eyes narrowed as she recalled watching the heart monitor beside her bed. "It would go bleep ... bleep ... bleep, bleep, bleep. It was all over the place. Then I saw a straight line. I was flat lining! Dying! Lying there feeling totally helpless, I couldn't even yell for help, but in my mind, I knew I didn't want to die."

Ellen was quiet for a moment after retelling her near-death experience, then a warm smile crossed her face. "Obviously, I made it. I'm here to talk about it. But it was scary as hell."

Shortly after Ellen's harrowing incident, the muffler manufacturer recalled the parts that were causing carbon monoxide problems, and detectors were installed in the cockpits. Ellen lost her medical right to fly. She spent three months recovering from the incident, then the FAA medical examiner gave her the go-ahead to fly again.

Her experience reminded me of another female pilot. In 1929, during the Powder Puff Derby, there was speculation that Alaska pilot Marvel Crosson lost her life to carbon monoxide poisoning. The winner of the cross-country race, Louise Thaden, also experienced CO poisoning and breathed through a special air tube (in an open-cockpit airplane) after experiencing the same symptoms Ellen experienced.

Ellen loves nothing more than to talk about flying. She relaxes and is happiest when she's talking about her favorite thing to do: fly. One of the propellers she owns belonged to a 1938 Fairchild 24 that she wrecked "big time" going into the strip at the headwaters of the Talkeetna River near Wells Mountain. "I had to take two mechanics to the site of the wrecked plane several times to make the plane airworthy, even though it wasn't perfect. Flying that jerry-rigged plane back to Wasilla was the longest hour of my life! I felt sure it would come apart in pieces, mid-air. I had to fight lots of wind turbulence on the way back and go around twice before I landed. I imagined slamming into the ground and the landing gear coming off."

With her left hand flat, Ellen gestured to show how the Fairchild touched down. "Kiss, kiss … smooth as I could have made it. Then I climbed out, sat down on the tire and breathed a big gulp of air. The mechanics drove up, rolled down the window of their truck and handed me a beer. While I waited for the plane to be repaired for two weeks, I shot a caribou, which was the reason I'd gone to Talkeetna in the first place. That caribou cost me $13,000," Ellen said with a wide grin. The head and antlers of the majestic animal are proudly displayed on a nearby wall in her home.

When Ellen turned 24, her long-absent father contacted her. He flew from San Diego, California, to the village of St. Mary's, Alaska, where Ellen was working, to renew their father-daughter relationship. "Eventually we grew close again," she said. "It's amazing how much alike we are even though we didn't spend much time together when I was a kid. He's strong willed, just like me." Ellen also reconciled with her mother before she died in 2001.

In 1997, Ellen's father traveled to Washington, D.C. to see his daughter give a presentation before 300 people at the Smithsonian Air and Space Museum. The former stringy-haired rebellious teen recalled the formal private dinner at the museum, hosted by the curator. "There were twelve people, including my father, the curator, congressmen and senators. I looked over the elegant table, covered with white linens, fine china, crystal and sterling silverware. Then I looked up, and there was the Wright Flyer directly overhead!" Ellen gazed upward, as if seeing the image in her own dining room. "I was absolutely awe struck when I saw that plane overhead — the plane the Wright brothers flew in 1903!"

Friend and pilot Patty Wagstaff said, "I think of Ellen as a renaissance woman because she is so talented at so many different things. She is an artist, a pilot, a writer, a businesswoman. She is a cook, a traveler, a fun person to be with, and a good friend. As a woman her accomplishments are noteworthy. As an Eskimo woman they are even more so."

Ellen has given presentations across the country at museums and boys and girls clubs and particularly likes to speak to youth groups. "I tell them I was in the same boat, and I didn't get any encouragement. Everyone pooh-poohed my learning to fly. When you decide to do something, don't let anyone or anything discourage you. It's up to you."

Ellen is truly a survivor, a role model and mentor, an inspiration and friend to me now, who enriches the lives of everyone who meets her or hears her talk of her flying experiences across Alaska. Surely Ellen Paneok is one of the brightest stars among the Northern Lights.

20

Turned On by Learning:
CAREN DELLA CIOPPA

The drive to Caren della Cioppa's hand-hewn log cabin leads up and around hairpin turns on Lazy Mountain, northeast of Anchorage, Alaska. Caren's cabin is tucked back in the woods, with summer flowers surrounding a rock garden and pond that she built. A cylindrical glass bird feeder hangs outside her kitchen window where small sparrows busily feed.

The first meeting, face to face, after two months of e-mails between us, is a chance to confirm what Caren shared with me. I remember her last e-mail when she left Barrow, Alaska. She wrote, "I'm not very interesting, now that I'm no longer flying on the North Slope."

The dark-haired woman, whose 55 years don't show, greeted me at the front door as if I were coming to stay a few days, not just for a two-hour interview. I glanced around her cozy cabin, thinking what a wonderful retreat this would be for an artist or writer. Classical music floated through the cabin from the overhead loft.

Caren slid a dark-blue certificate holder across her plum-colored kitchen counter while she took two cold water bottles from the refrigerator. "It just came today," she said, beaming. "After six years of study, I finally received a BA in Language from UAA in Japanese, with Russian as an option. Sheepishly, Caren explained, "I'm a language freak. I studied Latin for four years in high school and firmly believe my interest in languages was inspired by my grandfather, who spoke and taught Latin, Italian, Greek, English, and French. Before I received this degree," Caren added, "I obtained a Bachelor of Science in Electrical Engineering [BSEE] at Northrup Institute of Technology in Los Angeles. I was one of few women in the engineering program in the 1960s. I had received a scholarship in order to pursue this goal, but by the time I obtained my BSEE, the industry was in a slump and jobs were not plentiful.

"In 1976, I was working on the ski patrol at Mount Shasta in northern California, where I decided that saving lives was much more fulfilling than engineering. I moved to San Diego in southern California, where I was hired as the first woman

Caren della Cioppa, FS Air Service Superstar 700, Anchorage, Alaska.

ambulance driver and EMT by Hartson's Ambulance." Caren pointed to the window, where we could see a sparrow that had stopped to refuel at the glass bird feeder.

"Last night, there was a moose and one of her babies lying outside on the grass," Caren said, pointing to the grassy area near the front of her cabin. "There were two babies a couple of days ago. I'm afraid one of them didn't survive. A bear probably got it."

Caren invited me upstairs to show me a photo of the moose and baby calves on her web site. "I'm sort of a computer nut," she said, "and I love to take photos wherever I go." She paged down the web site to show me vivid scenes she photographed on trips to Tibet, Thailand, Japan, Greece, Turkey and Italy, among other places.

By now, Caren was read to talk flying.

"While I lived in San Diego, I encouraged my boyfriend to take flying lessons because that's all he talked about! The day he got his license he took me up flying and let me touch the controls for a minute or so, and that was all it took. I realized that if he could learn, so could I. I only took a few lessons in 1983, but after I moved to Anchorage…. Well, I should explain that my mother and I came here on vacation, and when the plane was circling to land in Anchorage, I turned to her and said, 'I'm going home, selling everything I own, and moving here.' And immediately after we got back, I did exactly that because I was tired of the Southern California rat race, and I was so thrilled with all those mountains I saw in Alaska.

Caren della Cioppa in fur parka, standing beside her Cessna 140, Palmer, Alaska.

"Soon after, I made another trip to Anchorage to take the paramedic test for Anchorage Fire Department. I didn't have a guaranteed job with them, but I was number one on their hire list. Then in April 1984, I quit my paramedic job in San Diego and moved into my VW bus and drove up to Anchorage. I got hired by Soldotna Fire, but quit six months later when Anchorage hired me."

I listened and thought about Caren's comment, "I'm not very interesting," as she shared another facet of her life.

"Mountaineering is one of my favorite passions. I enjoy climbing and hiking in the gorgeous mountains of Alaska. I've done two expeditions on Mount McKinley, but still have not made the summit. I'm hoping for success on the third try, soon."

Caren seems a little shy, but she has certainly not been shy about pursuing what she wants, whether it be a job as a firefighter, or attempting to scale 20,320' Mount McKinley, popularly called "Denali" by Alaskans. These are not things most people do, let alone most women. I teased her about not being "interesting" as she continued.

"With a good job with Anchorage Fire Department I finally had enough income to continue flying lessons. I did my first solo at Merrill Field in Anchorage through Aerotech in 1984 and I was totally thrilled. I think the first solo is always a turning point for most people. I was actually kind of slow to solo and a little slow to learn, initially. But once I soloed, I was really excited and nothing could stop me."

I thought of how Caren had emailed me prior to our interview that her father was a pilot in World War II, but he didn't live long enough to see her become a pilot and fly with her in her 1946 Cessna 140. I'm sure he would have been proud.

"I got my private license, then went on to get my commercial, instrument, instructor, instrument instructor, airline transport license, multi-engine land and sea ratings, and single-engine sea rating," Caren explain, matter-of-factly. "Then I decided that I should also have my A & P so I went to the UAA Aviation Maintenance school and got an associate degree in Aircraft Maintenance."

I glanced at her small, delicate hands and had a hard time picturing her with grease under her fingernails. Caren not only flies airplanes, she knows what's under the cowling and what makes the engine purr. I remembered the outdoor pond and rock garden she built and realized she enjoys getting her hands dirty if the need arises. Caren is "turned on by learning" ... everything!

"Meanwhile, I was working full time for the fire department as well as flying multi-engine charters and instructing for Wilbur's, based at Merrill Field in Anchorage. I left Wilbur's and flew for a while for FS Air Service doing multi-engine charters. All of my flying experience — 3,800 hours — was part-time while working for the fire department. When I retired, I started looking for flying jobs again and flew for Aeromap for several months."

Had she ever had a close call while she was flying, I asked, and, if so, how did it affect her.

"We were flying along Lake Iliamna when my engine quit because a valve broke off. I ended up having to land in the flattest spot I could find, a shallow swamp. When that happens, you don't have time to think about dying. You concentrate on landing ... somewhere, anywhere. The plane flipped over and my dog, Foxtrot, came flying forward and peed on me." Caren took a deep breath. "The owners of a lodge in the Pile Pass area rescued us in their boat. We flew to the Iliamna airport, and I brought a different engine back a week later with two engine mechanics in Supercubs. We found a sandbar nearby and landed the Cubs, pushed my plane to the sandbar that had unfortunately been too far away for me to reach when the engine quit. They changed the engine, and made a clear runway on the sand bar, then I took off and flew home to Palmer."

Caren took a moment to reflect. "It was an interesting adventure, for sure."

In the spring of 2002, Caren applied via fax for a job with Cape Smythe Air in Barrow, Alaska, to fly their Navajo. "I faxed my resume and they hired me the next day right over the phone. During the brief period I worked for Smythe, I flew a 207 to Wainright, Atqasuk, Point Lay, Nuiqsut and Deadhorse above the Arctic Circle. In the Beech 99 I flew right-seat to Kotzebue, Point Hope, Point Lay, and Deadhorse. People, cargo and mail all fly together in Bush Alaska, and it's the pilot's responsibility to off-load everything, which may mean handling 2,000 pounds of cargo and supplies, plus refueling in all kinds of inclement weather. This is no-frills work, and I earned every dime."

Alaskan pilot Ellen Paneok, who also worked in Barrow, described offloading as "Everything from soda pop and Pampers to live wolverines!"

I reminded Caren that when she was in Barrow, a community of mostly Eskimos, with a population of 3,000, I had asked her to go downtown with a friend and a camera. I asked her to have her photo taken in front of the arched whalebones, a local landmark similar to the famous St. Louis arch, though not as large. I also requested a photo by the skeletal carcass of a bowhead whale placed in front of the North Slope Borough Administration office. Caren agreed to do both photos. But the request that elicited a surprise response was when I asked her to stand in the doorway of a plane she flew in Barrow, in her uniform, and wave at the camera.

Laughing, Caren pointed out, "My uniform was a pair of blue jeans, wind pants and my pink jacket, all of which smelled of aviation fuel all the time. And in the summer when the ice and snow disappear, my 'uniform' was covered with mud too. In the winter, I would have been wearing Carhartts, bunny boots and a parka. Whatever I needed to stay warm in the frigid cold!"

Caren's quiet persona and exotic appearance attract men. "But sometimes they feel threatened by my brains," she said. "All my life I've worked in traditional men's jobs. I put two husbands through college, and later we divorced. One ex-husband is a dentist, the other is an oceanographer. Currently, I'm weighing the possibility of pursuing a PhD in Computer Science and have no plans to remarry."

Caren leaned across her kitchen counter as she reflected. "I need intellectual stimulation. I'm easily bored and need to use my mind. I've been weighing the possibility of a trip across the Mongolian Steppe. Flying in the bush in an odd place like Mongolia, or maybe Africa or Australia, might be very intriguing to me. Making a flight into Russia and on to Mongolia involves getting special permits and since there are no small planes there, there's no aviation fuel. My plane could fly with vehicle fuel, but there are no airstrips or mechanical help, or parts, if something needs repair or replacement."

Unintentionally, Caren had just described the early days in Alaska aviation where there were no airports and no fuel, and certainly no replacement parts or mechanics.

"I like dreaming about doing things like a trip across the Mongolian Steppe ... or going to Africa," Caren said. "I don't plan to leave any stones unturned."

It's hard for me to believe Caren thinks of herself as "not very interesting." How many men or women have a degree in electrical engineering, a second degree in language, have saved lives as an EMT and firefighter, have climbed Mount McKinley, and fly in Bush Alaska! The answer to the question? Only one, and her name is Caren della Cioppa.

21

Pancho Flies Again:
LOUISE GETTMAN

Louise Gettman was late for our interview when she appeared in the lobby of the Millennium Hotel in Anchorage, barefoot. She had just come from a morning run around Lake Hood, where the float planes are based. The suntanned, long-legged young woman suggested we hike next door to her cabin and enjoy the warm sunshine. We settled at the picnic table on the grassy point, near water's edge and watched float planes land and take off. More than once, Louise pointed skyward as a commercial aircraft passed overhead, and said, "That's what I fly" or "I'd sure like to take that one for a spin."

Louise talked about when she was young. "I always rearranged the furniture in the shape of an airplane, put my younger brother in the backseat, and pretended I was teaching him how to fly. I had six brothers. I'm the only girl, and my mother tried to keep me in dresses, but I was always climbing trees and playing outside, getting dirty. I didn't understand why I had to wear a blouse. I would rather die than be a little girl!"

"I made airplanes out of Legos and Tinker Toys. And my eyes were always glued to the sky when a plane went over. I guess my dad was my biggest influence because he was a fighter pilot in World War II." Louise has photos of her father when he was a pilot in the war above the stone fireplace in her cabin, his goggles and leather cap nearby.

In her younger years, Louise's family lived in upstate New York, then moved to Daytona Beach, Florida, which she said was not a good environment for teenagers. "At 13 I was hanging out at the Boothill Saloon, but my parents didn't know it. My mother had spent 14 years in a convent and tried to raise me like a nun, which I hated. But my dad took me in tow, talked to me about my plans for the future and paid for flying lessons. I soloed when I was 16 at Ormond Beach, Florida, in a 150 Aerobat and thought maybe I'd become a stewardess someday.

"After I got my license, I asked the instructor, who had also been a World War II pilot, to show me what the plane could really do. That wasn't a very smart thing

Louise Gettman standing on the tail of a C-130 with a Neptune P2B approaching, Wenatchee, Canada.

to ask right after I got my license, but we did loops, rolls and spins, and I loved every minute of it!"

Louise asked her dad about joining the military but he didn't like that idea because he lost so many of his friends in the war. At 18, she moved to California and worked as a waitress while getting her associate degree in Aviation at Foothill Community College in Los Altos, California. By 1993, with the help of well-known aviatrix Amelia Reid in San Jose, California, Louise pursued additional flight ratings.

Louise was so fascinated with Amelia Reid, who logged more than 55,000 hours during a career that spanned 60 years, that I failed to ask her which ratings and licenses she obtained in San Jose. What seemed important was listening to Louise talk about her mentor, a woman who made a significant difference in her life.

"Amelia was known for her low-level routine called 'Butterfly' for its graceful, slow maneuvering," Louise said. "Even at the age of 76, she continued to fly in air shows. She instructed over 4,000 students in the art of stick-and-rudder flying and aerobatics."

Soon after, with a credit card and a car, Louise opted to drive to Colorado Springs and try to get a job flying. She went to one hangar, showed the owner her log book and he said, "If I really get desperate, I'll hire you as a line person." Louise was willing to mow the grass and pull weeds around the hangar just for a chance to fly. She returned the following day and was hired. She flew scenic trips, short errands around the Rockies and handled the duties of office manager, which she said she hated.

"But I lived in the hangar and loved it," Louise said. "I wanted to work on engines, and I didn't care if I was covered in grease.

"One of the highlights of my career was a chance to fly War Birds to air shows during the 50th anniversary of the end of World War II. One hundred fifty planes flew from Long Beach, California, to Long Beach, New York. I got to fly two T-6s, two BT-13s, a TBM, and a DC-3, which is when I fell for the DC-3. I had to find a job where I could fly the DC-3. It's the best airplane in the world ... graceful ... sweet. It sucks up all the lift under the wings as it flies. It's the most graceful plane in the air.

"After that experience, I went to Michigan because I heard there might be a chance I could get into DC-3 Ground School, but the guy who promised me I could took a different job and I was left out. I waitressed at the airport and did some mechanical work, and sometimes I jump-seated in a DC-3 till school started. When

Louise Gettman, first officer, in cockpit of a 747.

I completed my schooling I heard about an opening during fire season in Missoula, Montana, and off I went. I thought this was a good way to help out and give something back. I flew a P2 Neptune that has two radial engines and two jet engines and holds 22,050 pounds of fire retardant. This job took me to New Mexico, Arizona, Washington, and Oregon, but never Alaska."

In 1998, Louise obtained her A & P mechanics license and worked as a fire bomber in Wyoming, living in a tent till the short-lived contract ended. "We'd swoop down on a fire and dump our load, which acts as a tourniquet and chokes the fire. I like flying low in smoke and flames."

Watching Louise's enthusiasm reminded me of another pilot I'd read about. Early-day pilot Pancho Barnes loved the deep-throated roar of mighty engines, just like Louise. Pancho is described as a woman who embraced perilous challenges, well beyond the tenacity of other daring pilots, forever defined by her brazen disregard for personal danger. Pancho bought an alfalfa ranch in the Mojave desert east of Los Angeles during the depression of the thirties, naming it The Happy Bottom Riding Club. After World War II, test pilots at Edwards Air Force Base made the riding club their second home.

"Pancho's outrageous vocabulary, airplane stories of the early years, free booze, and her uninhibited ways were a natural magnet for the free spirits of the early years of experimental rocket ship flying," according to Gene Nora Jessen in *The Powder Puff Derby of 1929*. Chuck Yeager, the first test pilot to break the sound barrier, was best man at Pancho's fourth wedding in 1952.

If you yearn for adventure and challenge like Louise and Pancho, Alaska is the place to be. Louise soon found herself in the frozen north, a place she always dreamed of, flying for Brooks Fuel in a DC-4 out of Fairbanks, Alaska. She flew six days a week delivering diesel fuel, propane and aviation fuel to remote sites in Alaska. "My boss said we flew a smorgasbord of fuel. He was right." Louise added, "I'm a good freight dog because I'm a night owl."

"My first day on the job I flew to Barter Island in the Beaufort Sea above the Arctic Circle. When I flew into Tobin Creek Mine I saw crashed planes on either side of the runway, which increased the *pucker factor,*" Louise said with a laugh. "I flew to other places like Gains Creek and Indian Mountain. All of these locations have short landing strips, no pavement, and not much else."

Louise's experiences are akin to the early Bush pilots who made flying in all kinds of weather conditions and landing where there was no airstrip a way of life in Alaska. Like most Alaskan Bush pilots, Louise did all the loading and off-loading too. It never mattered that she was a woman; it's just part of the job.

"In the summer it was typical to fly 100 hours a month, but everything slows down in Fairbanks in wintertime, and I was lucky to fly 20 hours a month. In January 1999, I went to work for FS Air, flying a Beech 18 to Kodiak Island five nights a week from 9:00 P.M. to 3:00 A.M." With a shrug, Louise ran her hand through her long, wavy brown hair. "I remember the ink in my pen would freeze, and my microphone would frost over from moisture in the cockpit."

One night when Louise was out with friends in downtown Anchorage she met a pilot with Polar Air and they talked. The following day he tracked her down and phoned to say if she wanted to fly for his company to be in Long Beach, California, the following day for an interview.

"I dropped whatever I was doing, flew south and interviewed successfully. I went through seven weeks of training to fly right-seat in a 747 starting in the spring of 2000. At age 29, I became one of four women pilots with Polar Air." (There are currently 400 pilots flying for the company.)

Louise flies two weeks on, two weeks off, to places like Kyrgyzstan, a former Soviet Republic member that borders Afghanistan. "We fly what we call one-night stands—six hours in, five on the ground and six on the return. One trip I took pizza to the U.S. troops stationed there because they begged for pizza. I felt sorry for them." She also delivered military supplies and ordinance.

Other jaunts with Polar Air include Australia, New Zealand, Japan, Russia, Hong Kong, India, Singapore, Cairo, South Africa, Fiji, Sicily, and Guam. Louise has flown to places her beloved father never had the chance to fly. She has flown over 80 different aircraft, including helicopters, ultralights, and a trip aloft in a hot-air balloon. "It's more than I ever dreamed of," she said, her eyes misty.

As we spoke, an occasional bird hopped across the grass and lifted off, competing for airspace with float planes, while a duck paddled around in the water. A float plane landed or took off every few minutes on Lake Hood and high-wing Cessnas and Pipers took to the air from a nearby landing strip, while we watched. Louise said, "I absolutely love living here. It's the best."

Even though Louise travels worldwide, she said, "I wouldn't live anywhere else but right here. In Alaska, nothing can replace the intimacy of the relationship between yourself and a radial engine, and the millions of acres of uninhabited wilderness. It equals heaven. It was as I always dreamed — the beauty of Alaska is in its peacefulness. Only a place so remote and devoid of people could share secrets that are like hidden treasures. Search long enough through the fog, and you will find your reward in a herd of caribou running through Anaktuvuk Pass or a golden grizzly staring back at you with the same surprised expression."

The olive-skinned, reflective young woman skis in the winter in Resurrection Pass in Alaska, which is known for its extreme skiing. She hikes in the Chugach Mountains in the summer months, where she may encounter a moose or bear and she's probably at more risk than when she sets a plane down in the Middle East.

While we talked, a plain white parcel rested on the table. Louise said, "I know what it is because I know who it's from." Finally, she opened the gift, a replica model Grumman TBF-1C "Avenger" and a book about World War II sent by an admirer in Southern California. The model plane was complete with a four-bay bomber belly —

another replica for her ever-growing collection of aviation memorabilia. Every wall and shelf in her small rustic cottage on Lake Hood screams out "I love to fly!"

Louise also paints watercolors of airplanes. An image of a fire bomber she flew in the Lower Forty-Eight stands against the wall of her bedroom, ready to be hung near her baby grand piano. To relax, Louise writes poems and invites her friends to come over for Key Lime pie. She told me to stop by anytime even if she wasn't home: "Enjoy the fresh air and watch airplanes take off and land, or come on in and relax."

The intrepid brunette has ridden on the back of an elephant in Thailand and hiked across the Alps. She's been to Hitler's Eagle's Nest in Bavaria and walked through 4.5 kilometers of bunkers underneath the old hotel where she stayed, but her heart belongs in Alaska where she plans to stay forever.

Like a wide-eyed, bashful girl of 14 going to her first prom, Louise said, "I certainly never dreamed I'd be flying all over the world, doing what I do."

Resurrection Pass
by Louise Gettmann

Sun's fingers brush the snow
Gently off her mountain hair
My skis are only witness
To the resurrection there.

On a Corcavado sunrise
Lensticulars hug the pass
And blow their wings out laughing
At my foiled trail-break dash

Sundogs in pink & green
Chasing their own tails
Bark down the white rabbit
Who kindly broke my trail

And wrought with iron flowers
Wrung from sub-zero's night
Steely balls of frozen bells
Peeling out of sight.

They're laughing with my childlike joy
Laughing as I fall
Through geometric pine trees
Wonderland's checkered hall

I laugh back, for I am not cold
And no mountain is too high

Women Pilots of Alaska

My skis have wings, & my voice sings
With the wind, the stars, the sky

And the distant, glowing mountains
Under oceans running deep
I slide down her snowy, sun-laced face
To the life I choose to keep.

(Used by permission)

22

Sheer Energy:
DEE RICE

"I've been on the run," Dee Rice said, sounding out of breath on the phone. "I'd really like to meet with you, but I'm director of ops at Larry's Flying Service so I'm basically on call all the time."

I offered to meet with Dee whenever it was convenient for her.

"We could meet at the office ... but it's always busy and we couldn't really talk without interruption," she said, thinking out loud. "What if you came here to my place? I have a late flight tonight, but how about tomorrow morning. Not too early though."

Dee gave me directions and I could almost see her motioning left and right with her hands as she explained. The following morning I tapped on her apartment door and could hear a small, yappy dog on the other side. Dee, wrapped in a bath towel, invited me inside and pointed to the coffee carafe on the kitchen counter. "Make yourself comfortable while I finish getting dressed."

The little black Shih Tzu she called Bare returned to her post on a pillow in her favorite chair, curled up and kept one eye on me. A fresh bouquet of red-and-white carnations on the white tile table called my attention to a book of anthropology beside the vase. Nearby was Dee's laptop computer. An artificial pine tree stood in one corner, turned upside down and sprinkled with blinking white lights. It looked like a rare type of palm tree, but it was September in Fairbanks, Alaska. In a couple minutes, Dee reappeared wearing a summer dress, barefoot with wet hair. She poured herself a cup of coffee and settled onto a chair at the table for our interview.

"I don't have too much time," she said. "We have two new pilots I have to meet with today, but we should be fine for a while. I don't know what you want to know, but I'll try to answer your questions the best I can."

I started by asking if she was originally from Alaska.

"I was born here but after I married we went to live in Wisconsin. I really missed Alaska while I was raising my family. I have two sons."

"Did you learn to fly in Fairbanks?"

Dee's large blue eyes sparkled as she talked: "My dad was a pilot, and I liked

Dee Rice in the cockpit of a Navajo flying to the Arctic Circle into Venetie at the base of the Brooks Range, Alaska.

flying with him so when I learned at age 26 in Wisconsin, I said, 'Dad, can I borrow your keys?' I think he was surprised. He had a Lance and it was fun to fly. After I got a divorce and came back here to live, he bought me a Cessna 150. Both of my sons fly, too."

"Thinking back, do you remember how you felt when you soloed?"

Dee rolled her eyes around as she thought, but a telephone call interrupted her train of thought.

"All right," Dee said. "They're there now? I didn't expect them till later today. I'm in the middle of an interview. Okay, I'll be there by ten-thirty." She sat down at the table again.

"Let's see, you ask about when I soloed." She glanced at the wall clock, nervous energy and coffee fueling her day. "I have to get over to Larry's by 10:30. The new pilots showed up. Anyway, it was pretty scary learning to fly, but I had to overcome my fear. Once I learned about flying I loved it. I always dreamed of being a pilot. I got my commercial and instrument ratings, airline transport and certified flight instructor ratings here in Fairbanks."

The phone interrupted us again.

"But I flew last night," she said to the caller. "I don't think I should…. How many hours do I have this month? Okay. I'll do it. I'll be there at 10:30." Dee hung up, threw her hands in the air and went to the kitchen to refill her cup. "I swear, they'd have me going 24 hours a day if I was willing ... and it was legal! Have some more coffee if you want," she suggested.

Dee explained that when she was very young if she was afraid of something she could overcome it by learning more about it. "My mother knew I loved water and she was afraid that I would drown so she gave me swimming lessons every summer until I was sixteen. By the time I entered Lathrop High School here in Fairbanks, my physical education teacher had me teach the class how to swim.

"The summer after I earned my private license, I told my Dad that I was afraid of stalls. Stalling the airplane is mostly about landing, because you don't want the airplane to be flying as you are touching the ground. You want it to completely become a ground vehicle, or that's when accidents happen. Anyway, he told me to gas up the Cessna 150 and told me a real good, fun way to do one stall after the other. When the wing would stop flying and stall, I was to just let the nose fall and relax all the pressures—that is, stop pulling back on the control yoke and see that the airplane will start flying again all by itself. I could even just let go and it would fly again all by itself. Whew! That was relief!

"Oh yes, I had to do this practice until the plane was almost out of gas, so I practiced for over two and a half hours. I overcame the fear of flying at that point and I could feel and understand much better how the wing really works and trusted that the airflow over the wing really does keep the airplane in the sky."

Dee's exuberance spilled over as she said, "Alaska's all about Bush flying. That's why I'm here. But I do have a life too. I cross-country ski in the winter. Take classes." She held up the anthropology book. "I play on a volleyball team, and take country western dance classes two nights a week." She giggled. "Sometimes I have to put the brakes on myself."

"How did you become director of operations at Larry's?"

"My dad had me fly the C46, the biggest tail dragger ever built. It's a World War II Big Bird," Dee said. "That plane shook and so did I when my seat flew back because it wasn't latched properly. I couldn't reach the rudder pedals. I don't know what shook worse, the C46 or me. I decided there had to be something in between a Cessna 150 and a C46 so I decided to get more experience with big stuff and bigger airplanes some other way.

"I became a certified weather observer, a ticket agent for Air North, sold aviation fuel, drove a school bus and flew as a flight attendant. All of these jobs I held at the same time. By doing each of these jobs I gained more experience and learned how to fly my dad's PA32R300 Cherokee Lance. It wasn't until after my father died that I went on to get my other ratings in order to get a job flying."

"When you got more hours did you get a commercial job?"

With hands waving in the air, Dee said, "My house burned down in Nenana, the company I worked for as a flight attendant went bankrupt, I was going through a second divorce, and my Dad had just died. I went to Larry's to get a job as a ticket agent so I could be around airplanes, but the lady didn't hire me. Figuring I didn't really have much left to lose, I went back the following week and talked to the chief pilot, Paul Haagland, who knew my Dad. I told him that even though I only had 500 hours that I was willing to take it slow and be helpful. I was hired that week as a pilot for the same company that I tried to get a ticket agent job with the week before!

"I worked for LFS for eight years, but I quit and went to work for a family that owned Umiat Enterprises, flying a Super Cub and a Cessna 185. I worked there four years, flying all over the North Slope. I flew supplies into camp and flew hunters and biologists all around the Slope. A large part of my job was to fly with a biologist to count moose, caribou and musk ox. But the problem was I didn't make much money."

It was 10:15. Dee should have been saying goodbye and heading off to work any minute. I pointed to the clock, but she was too involved in our interview to notice.

"About the time I was getting discouraged at Umiat, Larry phoned and asked if I'd like the job as chief pilot. My friend Paul Haagland had moved on from there before I left, and Larry had just fired the new chief pilot. So anyway, that's when I became director of ops. I've been back at Larry's now for four years."

"What does your job entail?"

Dee chuckled. "My biggest prerequisite for my job is my background as a mother of two sons. A lot of my job is organizing, mediating and guiding new pilots. I train and encourage new pilots, all of whom are either younger or about the same age that my sons are now."

"Are you the only female pilot at LFS?"

"I had been for the eight years prior, but during the last four years we hired two more women pilots. They're no longer with us so I'm still the only female pilot at LFS. Year-round we have 17 pilots. We're always busy and during the summer months we hire a couple more pilots for the even busier season."

Dee smiled and pointed to a nearby photograph. "That's my friend, Ed Camasi. I'm teaching him to fly right now. Teaching is what I enjoy doing most." Dee's words flowed as fast an Irish jig. "We've known each other for several years, as friends and enjoy the same things. We're going slow. Other men tried to keep me from the interests I have and my need for learning, which is very important to me. But not Ed. That's what makes us good friends."

Dee ran her fingers through her tousled red hair. "I fly scheduled charters from Koyakuk to Hughes, Ruby, Galena, downriver to Nulato, Huslia. That's where I pick up mail, and yesterday I hauled three moose and their racks back to Galena. I also have scheduled trips between Ruby and Fairbanks."

"Do you ever have any problems with the passengers because you're a woman pilot?"

Dee nodded. "Yes, once in a while. If I notice liquor on their breath before they board, I won't let them ride with me. I had one guy who tried to get amorous with me, and I gave him a little feel for aerobatics, then he settled down. I told him to sit down and be quiet or I'd off-load him!"

"Ever have an accident or near-accident?"

"December 21, 2001, is the closest I've ever come." Dee walked across the room to her makeshift office and pulled out a newspaper clipping from the *Daily News-Miner* in Fairbanks. "There's the whole story. I was between Huslia and Galena when an engine caught on fire in the Navajo I was flying. I have a strong survival instinct, so I just kept flying it till I got it on the ground in Galena — about twenty minutes. I was shaking, but I was determined to try to land safely. I thought about my sons, my dog, and the eight passengers on board." Dee stopped to catch her breath. "It was a catastrophic engine failure, which is very unusual. The inspection that takes place after an incident like this determined that the engine actually came apart and that's what caused the fire.

"When I had that incident and the fire, my father's words and presence seemed to be guiding me. 'Just fly the airplane, Dee. There is nothing you can do with that engine. Secure it the best you can with what you've got and wait for the fire to go out. Concentrate on what you have, one engine and electrical equipment to fly with. Don't concentrate on the emergency, fly the plane!'"

Dee smiled. "That's exactly what I did and we landed safely."

Her father was Bob Rice, chief pilot for Wien Airlines for a number of years. He also flew for Alaska Interior Airways (AIA). Dee said, "My dad learned to fly in Wenachee, Washington, and he came to Alaska so he could get paid for flying. Back in those days they just told you to take off and fly. There was no training."

That evening when I had a chance to read the news article Dee gave me, I understood. She told the reporter, "I feel there were definitely some miracles going on in that airplane last night."

Fred Huntington, who was in the right-hand seat beside Dee, said that when he heard the bang he thought something had hit the plane from outside and a second later the engine was ablaze. "The whole airplane was kind of out of control. We weren't nose down but we were weaving around and losing altitude. The pilot — she was pretty well shaken up — she did her job calmly even though she was shaking. The flame was only about a foot from where she was sitting. Everybody was praying to the top of their lungs. You could hear the fire just torching out there — wwhh-hoooossshhh — like that."

After reading the article, I paused to recall my brief but enlightening face-to-face meeting with Dee Rice. I could almost imagine her on ice skates, juggling a handful of apples. She would defy gravity, pirouette into a graceful spin and glide across the rink, with a big, satisfied smile on her face, ready for the next challenge she would face.

23

Sky Dancer:
PATTY WAGSTAFF

In the cockpit of her aerobatic plane, slim, fit, suntanned Patty Wagstaff grasps the stick, sometimes with both hands, her body thrown left, right, forward, backward, even though she is secured by a five-point harness. Her green eyes are hidden from the camera lens by dark glasses, her blond hair whipping around her headset with every change of direction, while she performs arduous aerobatic routines. Patty adjusts her headset microphone and nudges her sunglasses back up the bridge of her nose, as the airplane puts her through negative or positive G forces. This is Patty's office, her workplace, like no other in the world.

In 1980 Patty obtained her private pilot's license at Merrill Field in Anchorage, Alaska, just as Irene Ryan and Mary Barow did back in 1932. Ryan spun a career in Alaska politics, Barrow leveled off to be an educator for the rest of her life, and Wagstaff took to the air, returning to earth only to refuel.

Patty's father was a commercial pilot with Japan Airlines, her uncle was a World War II fighter pilot, and her sister is currently an airline pilot with Continental. Patty's former husband, Bob Wagstaff, an Anchorage attorney, was her first flight instructor. When she learned to fly, Patty was satisfied to fly straight and level, but yearned for more of a challenge than going from point A to point B.

When Anchorage pilot Darlene Dubay gave Patty her first ten aerobatic lessons, the fun of it for Patty was doing barrel rolls, spins, loops, pulling Gs. Flying became a way of life for Patty—"an intoxication" as she wrote in her book *Fire and Ice*. In a telephone interview she said, "My wild side took to flying. Aerobatics brought purpose to my life. I found ecstasy. I found a new world."

In late December 2002, actress Meryl Streep was being interviewed about her latest movie. She said, "I can't believe that I'm in my life sometimes." When Patty became the first woman to win the U.S. National Aerobatic championship in 1991—a contest she would win again in 1992 and 1993—this might have been something Patty would have said too.

Patty's sleek red, white and blue single-seater Extra 260 that she competed with

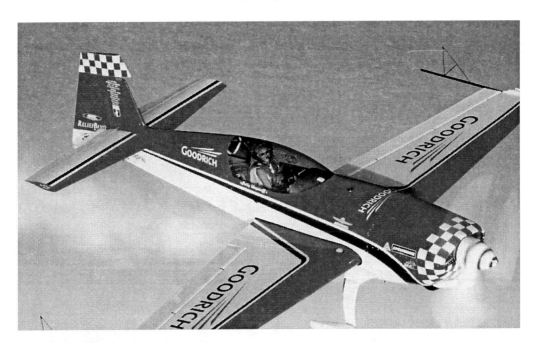

Top: Patty Wagstaff flying her Extra 300L competition air-show airplane, with a roll rate of 420 degrees per second. *Bottom:* Patty Wagstaff (left) and Darlene Dubay, her first aerobatic instructor, 1980, Stillwater, Oklahoma. The airplane is Wagstaff's Extra 260, now on display in the Smithsonian Air and Space Museum, Washington, D.C.

in 1991 is housed in the Smithsonian's National Air and Space Museum in Washington, D.C., in the Pioneers of Flight gallery in commemoration of her accomplishments. Her Extra 260 is showcased beside aircrafts flown by Amelia Earhart, Jimmy Doolittle, and Charles and Anne Lindbergh. Most pilots become attached to these inanimate objects, as if they are a member of their family, and Patty is no exception. "I wish I

5/20/84
Performers Schedule

11:30	Briefing at FSS
12:30	Opening Remarks
12:35	Golden Nugget Sky divers
12:50	U.S. Air Force F-15 Fly-by
1:00	Fred Keller - Rutan Defiant
1:15	Ultralight Demo - Mike Jacober
1:30	Mike Barbarick - Bellanca 7ECA
1:45	Richard McAdoo - Starduster
2:00	Radio Control Models -
2:20	Bush X-Modified Fly-off
	Lee Thompson vs Kirk Ellis
2:30	Intermission (Wx Brfg.)
3:00	Super Challenge Match
	John Schandelmeier, Lee Thompson,
	Kirk Ellis
3:15	Patty Beck - Bellanca Decathlon
3:30	Golden Nugget Skydivers
3:45	Lee Watne - Pitts S-1
4:00	Doug Geeting - Pitts S-1
4:15	T-28 Fly-by - Alaska Division
	of Forestry
4:25	Airport Reopens for Departures

First-time air-show performance schedule of Patty Beck Wagstaff, Gulkana, Alaska, May 20, 1984.

still had that plane," she said on the phone. "I'd like to take it up for a spin or two. Maybe I'd fly across the country, inverted."

It's this kind of gutsy attitude that has always made Patty stand out among her peers, along with her drive and confidence. Early on she made it clear that she not only wanted to be the best woman pilot, she wanted to be the best pilot. But Patty credits early women pilots for inspiration and is a member of the Alaska chapter of Ninety-Nines. She is also a member of Women in Aviation International, based in Florida. Patty has received the coveted Betty Skelton "First Lady of Aerobatics" trophy six times between 1988 and 1994.

Neither of Patty's parents every imagined their daughters would become pilots. Toni Combs, Patty's sister, is a captain with Continental Airlines, and based in Guam. Toni began lessons at Merrill Field in Anchorage at age 16 and soloed in the summer of 1977—"the year Elvis died," Toni said. "I had always wanted to become a pilot since I was very young. My father would bring home model airplanes and I would sleep with these things instead of dolls or teddy bears. Crazy, but true."

Toni obtained her commercial and instrument ratings while attending the University of Alaska and driving school buses. "I'd get up at 5:00 A.M. before anyone was out on the roads and be home late at night after school, with flying in between. Once I built up 500 hours, I pursued my Airline Transport Rating [ATP] and got a job in Puerto Rico." Since then Toni's career has taken her around the world.

She said, "I haven't met an airplane I didn't like."

When I asked Patty if learning to fly in Alaska was somehow different than, say, Phoenix, Arizona, she said, "Oh yes, definitely. You have to prepare for emergencies to fly in Alaska. You don't wear sandals when you take off because you may have to walk back and no one's going to bail you out if you get in trouble. You're on your own. And if you're not instrument rated in Alaska, it's like skydiving without a parachute!" Patty was telling me this from her home in Florida when she added, "I miss flying up there."

There are no shortcuts to the achievements Patty, a member of the U.S. Aerobatic Team from 1986 to 1996, has logged. There are no quick, easy methods to becoming a top competitor or a top air-show performer. Patty is committed and works incessantly with complete dedication to her sport. She compares it to the Olympics, yet she's harnessed into a high-performance airplane, executing what she calls "hardcore aerobatics" at the lowest levels allowed, executing her routine with precision and complexity.

Patty truly fits the description "*Sky Dancer.*" She was a National Aerobatic Champion in 1991, 1992, and 1993.

Patty told me a bit about her aerobatics shows. The demands of an air show performer keep them busy from the initial preflight briefing by the air-show boss first thing in the morning. The announcer and the organizer go over the sequence of events and decide on radio frequencies. After the briefing there are interviews with

Patty Wagstaff, preparing for her first air-show performance, May 20, 1984, at Gulkana, Alaska, flying a Bellanca Decathlon airplane.

the media and interaction with the crowd attending the air show. Each performer is expected to spend time in their sponsor's booth or chalet too, but as Patty explained, she's always watching the weather to see what the conditions of the day might be — clouds, wind, incoming weather. Safety is her motto at air shows.

"About an hour before my flight I start mentally preparing, walking through my routine, visualizing my flight," Patty said. "After my performance I spend time signing autographs and talking to the fans. When the show ends, we all make sure our airplanes are put to bed and serviced for the next day. If there are maintenance problems we need to take care of those. Then it's back to the hotel to get ready for a social event planned by the air-show committee, which I always attend." With a laugh, Patty added, "I usually sleep on Monday."

When she's performing, Patty said, "I feel electrically alive from the top of my head to the balls of my feet when I am close to the earth — tumbling, gyrating, rotating, dancing in space, and yanked or pushed by positive and negative Gs."

Patty's awards are endless. In addition to those already mentioned, her significant achievements includes National Air & Space Museum Award for Current Achievement (1994); International Council of Air Show Sword of Excellence (ICAS) in 1995; Top-Scoring U.S. Pilot at World Aerobatic Championships (1995); and inductee into Women in Aviation International Hall of Fame (1997). In 2001 she was named a presidential appointee to the First Flight Centennial Federal Advisory Board to plan the 2003 Centennial of Flight. Patty was a member of the National Air & Space Museum and on the advisory committee for the Evolution of Flight Campaign at the Ameri-

can Institute of Aeronautics and Astronautics in 2000 and 2001. She can also brag of the Rolly Cole Memorial Award for contributions to Sport Aerobatics (1987), the EAA (Experimental Aircraft Association) Major Achievement Award (1993), the NAA Certificate of Honor (1994), the CAN & Flyers Readers' Choice Award for Favorite Female Performer (1996), the Charlie Hillard Trophy (1996), the NAA Paul Tissiander Diploma (1997), and the Bill Barber Award for Showmanship (1998). She was also the Western Flyer Readers' Choice Favorite Airshow Performer (1991) and International Aerobatic Clun Champion (1993). (Details of Patty's numerous awards and her air show schedule may be found on her web site: www. pattywagstaff.com.)

Patty said she has dedicated herself to excellence and when you're the winner, you may as well have a bull's-eye painted in the middle of your back. "You become the one that everyone else wants to beat!"

There really is no off-season for Patty. She keeps a flock of seven exotic birds because she loves everything that flies, and she also has three dogs. She swims, rides horses, cares for her birds and dogs, paints and writes, and almost daily handles a raft of

Top: Patty Wagstaff pictured with a list of her numerous awards on the tail of her aircraft. *Bottom:* Patty Wagstaff, 2003.

paperwork, telephone calls and emails. Then she escapes to the airport and practices aerobatics—what she was born to do.

Patty does stunt flying and coordination for the movie and television industry. She is a member of the Screen Actors Guild, the Motion Picture Pilots Association and the United Stuntwomen's Association. She has narrated and been in several documentary videos and has done several television commercials.

In her spare time, Patty trains young, less-experienced pilots in Kenya, Africa, at the request of the Kenya Wildlife Service. "They felt that they might lose fewer pilots and planes if they learned some aerobatics," Patty said. She described Kenya as bush country not unlike Alaska, with dirt and gravel runways. "There's a paved airport in Nairobi, but all the other airports are very rough."

When I viewed the television special about Patty's role with the Kenya Wildlife Service, I was appalled at the senseless killing of wild game, like elephants, rhinoceroses and leopards. Poachers kill elephants for their ivory tusks and the rhinoceros horn is rare and sells on the black market for thousands of dollars. The offspring of the animals are usually left to die of starvation. Pilots with the KWS risk their lives every day to locate poachers from the air, while they are fired on from the ground. Patty teaches uncommon diversionary flight maneuvers to the KWS pilots that may save their lives and the animals they protect. The pilots are quick to acknowledge her willingness to travel around the world to work with them, and they are very impressed with Patty's aerobatic skill and knowledge.

Patty is a member of an elite group. In 2000, Women in Aviation International compiled statistics that indicate the total licensed pilots (student, recreational, private, commercial, airline transport and flight instructor) in the United States numbered 625,581. Only 36,757, or 5.88 percent of those were women. Of the 137,642 licensed airline transport pilots, like Patty's sister Toni Combs, there were 4,411 women pilots, or 3.12 percent. Patty is one of only five or six women who perform aerobatics for a living in the United States, an elite minority.

Puzzled why so few women take to the air, even 100 years after the Wright Brothers first powered flight in 1903, Patty gave me her take: "I think there is a lack of confidence in many women in their ability to handle machinery. I believe that this is, in large part, due to the upbringing and society's expectations of them. I believe that women make wonderful, safe and thoughtful pilots and wish more of them would take it up."

Patty's reflection on "lack of confidence" brought to mind interviews with women aged 31 to 94 who said their confidence soared when they made their first solo flight, in spite of sweaty palms and butterflies in their stomachs, in spite of parents or spouses who scoffed at their ability or "crazy ideas" to climb in the cockpit of an airplane and fly away, to be free. Amelia Earhart said she did it "for the fun of it" and so did a host of women who followed her lead.

There's no doubt being in the public eye and receiving endless awards, has given

Patty a chance to mentor young people. "I encourage everyone to pursue what they think they might be good at, what they might enjoy, and what draws them in. You can't do it all when you're 16 or 20.... I couldn't. But stay hungry for experience, for growth, for new roads, for new journeys. And don't get too comfortable where you are."

Will Patty ever sit back and sip Piña Coladas on her Florida veranda and let the world go by?

She said, "I can see a time when I'm not on the road doing air shows every weekend, but the best thing about what I do is that one never stops learning. The challenge never goes away. I retired from competition in 1996 after doing it full time for 12 years, but have thought about competing again. I'm just not sure. Competition at the international unlimited level takes a huge physical and emotional toll, and takes a great deal of time and dedication to stay competitive at the top levels."

Patty said she enjoys doing interviews, but added, "Public speaking makes me nervous. The best part is that I'm able to set my own schedule, and I have a wonderful sponsor—the Goodrich Corporation. It's a good life. I never know what's coming my way next and I don't worry about it. I just keep doing what I'm doing and for now, I'm happy with this routine."

There was a long silence before Patty said, "Something will reveal itself, when it's time."

Like she said earlier, her wild side took to flying and aerobatics brought purpose to her life. It doesn't get any better than that.

Patty was inducted into the National Aviation Hall of Fame in Dayton, Ohio, in 2004.

24

To Hell and Back:
MEGAN RUST

"I went up to solo in a Cessna 152 and when I turned on base there was a Piper on the runway so the tower told me to go around. I flew between the tower and the runway within 500 feet," Megan Rust said with a laugh. "I could see the whites of their eyes in the tower! Rich Wilbur, my instructor, was standing on the ground tearing his hair out. I chose a path that was not the best available, and my move was not expected. An experienced pilot would not have flown where I did. It wasn't a deadly mistake, just a bit reckless. A beginner's mistake. But I made an impressive first landing. It was exhilarating and I proved I could handle it!"

This is the first clue of how gutsy Megan Rust can be when she was under pressure. She planned on becoming a corporate pilot. But first she set out to get a degree in biomedical engineering at Washington State University. After her first year Megan decided it was "too hard." She said, "It wasn't cool or unique so I took a year off and returned to Alaska. That's when I took flying lessons."

Rich Wilbur of Wilbur's Flight Service instructed Megan in 1977. "I guess he figured that since my family owned Rust Flight Service, I should be able to solo after 5.4 hours of instruction." (Megan noted that most people solo with an average of 12 hours in the cockpit.) "The truth is I never had any training because when your family owns a flight business they never take you flying.

Megan returned to school, in Florida at Embry-Riddle Aeronautical University (ERAU). In 1979 she earned a BS in Aeronautical Science. She obtained her commercial pilot's license with single and multi-engine ratings and was a certified flight instructor. After college, it never occurred to Megan to fly with Rust's Flying Service at Lake Hood in Anchorage, a business started by her father. "I wanted to do more than fly float planes, even though I did get my float-plane rating," Megan explained.

Megan and I are both members of Sisters in Crime, a national organization open to both readers and writers of mysteries. Our paths crossed at meetings in Anchorage from month to month, but we never got acquainted. When I would see her at a

Megan Rust (standing on a 10 foot ladder for the photograph), with Rust Flying Service De Havilland Single Otter, Lake Hood, Anchorage.

meeting or conference, I'd notice a scar slightly visible near her mouth and realize her speech was sometimes labored. I knew her family owned a flying service so it seemed likely to me she had been in an airplane accident. Megan seemed reserved, somewhat unapproachable. When I began to interview women for this book, one of her classmates at Embry-Riddle suggested I contact her because her story was unique.

I emailed Megan (pronounced "Meegan") and for the next two days she responded with great enthusiasm. We set up a convenient time to talk on the phone. She had moved from Alaska to Port Townsend, Washington. I admit I was uneasy because I didn't want to offend Megan with biting questions about an airplane accident. All my fears immediately went away when Megan picked up the phone. She started asking me questions about my reasons for writing about women pilots of Alaska.

"That's simple," I replied. "No one has written about the women in aviation in Alaska. They need to be recognized for their accomplishments!"

Megan agreed and the interview began.

"I needed to build up hours so I gave flight instructions at Fort Richardson Flying Club. There was no way I could get a corporate flying job with only 200 hours, which is what I had when I graduated from ERAU. Then I went to work at Evergreen

Helicopters, flying Twin Otters to Bethel, Kotzebue and Nome, Alaska. They hired me with just under 1,000 hours of flight time, which was their minimum requirement. They talked of sending me to the Middle East to fly but decided that wasn't realistic because I was a woman. In six months their contract with Wien Airlines would end, and I would be out of a job."

I taped our phone interview, with Megan's permission, and I took notes from time to time just in case my recorder failed me. The last thing I wanted to do was ask Megan to repeat her story.

"What I'm going to tell you, I don't remember," Megan said. "It had to be retold to me after I recovered. Anyway, I flew into St. Mary's on the Yukon River in 1984 in a Cessna 402 twin engine, which was a step up towards the corporate job I wanted. I'd flown from Bethel to St. Mary's and was walking on the ramp towards the old Wien terminal. There was a forklift unloading a DC-6. The forklift didn't have a backup warning system and it hit me, knocked me down and rolled over me. Immediately, they put me in the Twin Otter and flew me to Bethel Hospital to stabilize me. The two-ton machine crushed my pelvis and, more importantly, my head."

Megan's ERAU classmate, Berta Degenhardt, told me it was absolutely amazing her friend survived. Megan told me, "I'm lucky I'm not a vegetable." This answered the questions I had about the scar on her chin and her slightly labored speech.

"Once I was stabilized they transferred me on Alaska Airlines to Providence Hospital in Anchorage. I was in a coma for one month, then spent the next two months in the 'coma arousal' stage, in and out of consciousness, not particularly lucid. Fortunately, when I started to come around, the decision was made to transfer me to Craig Hospital in Denver, Colorado, which is one of the ten best head and spinal rehab hospitals in the nation. I couldn't have gone to Craig if I hadn't been covered by workman's compensation insurance. I was there for five and a half months."

Megan's voice began to fluctuate, as if retelling her experience brought back the pain. "I had to learn to walk and talk all over again, as if I were a baby. It was hell because when I started to fully grasp what happened to me, I was completely frustrated."

Shivers ran up my spin while 5'4" Megan shared her story and I swallowed back tears, my voice no doubt wavering as she drew a picture of her private hell.

"I'm lucky my mind wasn't all that focused," Megan said, "because I would have become more frustrated. I can't handle pressure and stress now because of my injuries.

"Even though I would like to fly again, the FAA won't give me a first-class medical certificate to be a commercial pilot, and I've accepted that," Megan explained. "Sometimes I miss flying when I'm at SEA-TAC in Seattle and see a jet take off. But fortunately, I stumbled into writing, which is maybe even more fun." She laughed. "No doubt you've heard the old saying: Flying is 98 percent boredom and 2 percent sheer terror."

Megan's perspective and positive outlook awed me. The fact her injuries were not because of an airplane accident, or a car accident, but a disastrous error on the part of a forklift operator, angered me. But I found it encouraging when Megan said she "stumbled into writing" because she has had three mysteries published. Her main character, or protagonist, is a medevac pilot named Taylor Morgan, probably Megan's alter ego. Her books include *Dead Stick* published in 1998, *Red Line* which came out in 1999, and *Coffin Corner*, which was released in 2000. To avoid the dreaded deadline and the pressure, Megan has two more mysteries completed, ready for publication.

"When trying to find another career — after I could no longer fly — I purchased a book called *What Color Is Your Parachute*," Megan said. "Using it, I discovered that advertising might be a good field for me. Creative problem solving was right up my alley so I enrolled in Journalism and Public Communication at the University of Alaska Anchorage. I took screenwriting as an elective. That's where I found how much I enjoyed writing. When I graduated at the end of '91, I decided to write a novel, not pursue an advertising career. I had no idea how hard it would be to get something published and by the time I figured that out, I was hooked on the writing, so I plowed on."

I thought of how Megan ends every e-mail with a quote from Gene Fowler: "Writing is easy. All you do is stare at a blank piece of paper until drops of blood form on your forehead." Most writers use their own experiences and turn them into fiction. The same is true of Megan's work. What follows may have made its way into one of her mysteries:

"I was landing out by Hooper Bay at Tununak. The main runway that runs east and west had a crosswind of 25 to 30 knots. I knew I couldn't land a Cessna 207 in that strong a crosswind, so I decided to put it down on the taxiway, which was really crazy. I had four men with me and I was determined to show them I wouldn't have to turn back. I made two passes and the winds didn't let up. Tununak is an uncontrolled airstrip, or I never would have gotten away with it. The taxiway was about 750 feet long and maybe 25 feet wide and full of ruts, but I slammed it down on the very end of the taxiway and brought the plane to a full stop after about 150 feet." Megan paused. "Women are always under pressure to prove themselves. That landing was really stupid of me. The worst part is I had to push that plane backwards after I landed, by hand, because of the winds."

Whether it's piloting a plane with plans for a lifetime career as a corporate pilot, or writing mysteries, Megan's unfortunate trip to hell and back can inspire anyone to keep trying, to climb the mountain to see what's on the other side, no matter what the odds.

25

A Wild Hair:
CHARLOTTE LUCKETT

It was 10 below zero when I phoned to ask Charlotte Luckett if she was flying during the winter months. To my delight, Charlotte replied that yes, she was flying because she was instructing during the off-season. I asked if I could take a flight with her.

"You bet!" Charlotte replied, full of enthusiasm. "How about Tuesday at 11:00 A.M.? Meet me at Thunderbird Air at Birchwood Airport, and we'll go fly."

I asked her how I should dress for winter flying.

"Just dress comfortable," Charlotte said.

Tuesday arrived. I was ready by 10:00 even though it's only a five-minute drive from my house to Birchwood Airport. Jeans, a red fleece pullover to keep me warm in five-below-zero weather, and my snow boots seemed like the best choice, plus a pair of gloves, and a heavy down jacket with furry hood. I almost forgot my camera.

When I pulled up to Charlotte's office, I noticed a long extension cord leading from the building to the engine of a 1965 blue-and-white Cessna 206. Red wing covers and an engine cover made of rip-stop vinyl were still in place to protect the airplane.

Charlotte greeted me with a hug. Refusing my help she went outside and for the next half hour diligently worked to ready the Cessna for our winter flight. First she removed the wing covers. She checked every inch of the blue-and-white bird, making sure it would be free of ice and frost. She came back inside and got a long-handled broom to clean the hard-to-reach areas of the plane. The last thing she did was remove the engine cover as I watched from the warmth of her office with a cup of hot cider cupped in my hand. With her gloved hands, Charlotte carefully wiped both sides of each blade of the propeller. I could see small amounts of frost fall onto the snow beneath the Cessna. Then she motioned for me to join her. It was time to go.

The morning fog had cleared off but the nippy cold air caught in my throat when I stepped outside. As I climbed into the 206 from the left side, Charlotte began her passenger safety check by explaining how to lock and unlock doors on both sides of the airplane in case of emergency. She pointed to a fire extinguisher beneath her seat. Once we were seat belted, headsets covering our ears, Charlotte began her regular pre-flight checklist. When she turned the key, the prop slowly labored to turn, as if saying, "Not today, it's too cold!" Charlotte apologized, but she was determined to take advantage of the clear blue skies. With the help of the mechanic from Thunderbird Air, and a set of jumper cables, we were soon airborne.

At first it was hard to see because the windshield of the cockpit was still a little frosty. Charlotte took off heading west towards Anchorage, then made a wide circle across Cook Inlet,

Charlotte Luckett receiving the FAA Alaska Flight Instructor of the Year Award, 2002. Photograph by Joette Storm, FAA Alaskan Region Community Relations Director.

which is five miles wide. Most of the inlet was frozen with huge chunks of ice, reminding me of Rocky Road ice cream. Frost covered all the vegetation below, including the trees and nearby snow-covered peaks. A few houses dotted the tundra below.

Denali, or Mount McKinley as visitors to Alaska know it, was in full view to the north. The 20,320' peak can be very elusive, but today it was smiling at the sun and us.

We flew along, the cabin warm and cozy, the windows free of frost, all alone, in a valley with snow-capped mountains reaching for the sky on both sides of the airplane. The 206 hummed along, as if traveling an eight-lane freeway.

Charlotte said we were at 2,000 feet off the deck, but while she circled close enough to the edge of the expansive glacier where it "calves," or breaks off, we were within 100 feet of the iridescent blue ice. From my window the edge of the glacier looked to be about 12 feet high, but if I were on the ground, I knew it would be more like 50 to 100 feet.

I quickly used up a roll of film, and as fast as my fingers would move yanked the second roll out of my pocket and inserted it in the camera. It was all happening too fast! As we flew across the top of the glacier, I saw long ripples of ice, like waves, but I knew that between those ripples were bottomless crevasses too.

Traveling downriver, Charlotte explained, "Lots of people land here on the sand bars in the warmer months, and there, on the river."

I flashed back to my interview with Ellen Paneok and how she talked about practice landings on the sand bars at Knik River. Now I could see for myself, and it seemed very bold and intimidating, almost surreal.

"This way is Friday Creek," Charlotte said, pointing to the left side of the plane. "There are lots of good hunting areas in there. On our right is Hunter Valley, and up ahead are Meadow Creek and Grasshopper Valley."

I felt like a tourist on a summer flight-seeing excursion, but it was January and it was below zero outside the cabin of the aircraft. While I snapped more pictures, Charlotte responded to Jeni Hunter at Flight Service in Palmer, Alaska, about air traffic. She showed me which button to press, and I said hello to Jeni, whom I had already met. No doubt Jeni was caught off guard when I told her my name. In her usually upbeat tone Jeni said, "Are you having a good time?" My answer was obvious.

Our afternoon delight ended after a little more than an hour. When we taxied back to Thunderbird Air, Charlotte and I looked at each other and grinned like two teenagers who had just gone joyriding in their father's car. She said, "You want to go up again ... right now?" I was sure tempted.

Later Charlotte told me about her start in aviation. At sixteen, she set out from Kentucky with four friends in two vans for the Last Frontier. She said, "I just got a wild hair. I was raised on a farm and learned to hold my own with three brothers. We'd have corncob fights and pink belly matches—that's where you hold someone down and slap their belly till it turns pink. We lived in the city before we got the farm, but it wasn't for me."

Charlotte's first job in Alaska was flipping hamburgers at McDonald's in Anchorage, a short-lived career. In 1979 she was hired by the U.S. Forest Service to help transplant salmon eggs, cut trails, and establish bridges across swampland to Nancy Lake and Troublesome Creek in the Matanuska-Susitna Valley. She got her first taste of flying when she rode in a Forestry float plane to Whittier from Lake Lucille.

At the end of the day, the men would head off to fish, while Charlotte and a girl-friend stayed behind in camp. "One evening, while there was plenty of sunshine, we peeled off our clothes to sunbathe. In a short while, we spied a black bear headed our way. My friend jumped up and ran off. I reached for a nearby rifle and fired a shot near the bear to scare him. He raced back into the woods. My friend had grabbed a chainsaw. I wasn't sure what she planned to do with the chainsaw, but she thought the sound might scare him away."

Charlotte returned to Kentucky for a short while, but Kenny Luckett, who was also from there, followed and asked her to marry him and return to Alaska. Charlotte laughed. "We returned on April Fool's Day 1980, and found a place with no running water or electricity—a one-room cabin on Lazy Mountain, a few miles out of Palmer, Alaska. When our first child was born, we needed a larger place and found one with electricity, but still no running water."

In 1982, after obtaining her General Education Diploma (GED), Charlotte began to drive school buses. She drove the Chickaloon route, which meant getting up at 3:30 A.M., but she said, "I liked it. I enjoyed the peace and quiet on the way to round up the kids, plus I got to see the northern lights." Charlotte continued to drive school buses for 16 years and became an instructor for the bus companies, which she really enjoyed.

But by 1992 she was hungry to learn something new and decided that aviation ground school would be interesting. "I promised myself that if I scored well on the written tests, I'd reward myself with flying lessons. Carla Larson gave me my first lesson. She showed me the instruments while we flew around, and on that first flight, it occurred to me that I could become an instructor. I taught people how to handle a school bus, so why shouldn't I teach people to fly."

Charlotte had dreamed of flying when she was about ten. "I pictured myself with arms spread out like wings. There wasn't anyone in my family who piloted a plane, so it must have been pretending to fly that inspired me later in life ... along with wanting to learn something new."

When Charlotte soloed in June 1993, she said, "I was very disappointed when my instructor said I couldn't just fly off any direction, that I had to complete three touch-and-go landings and come to a complete stop before I could take it around. After complying with my instructor's plan, I was given the go ahead so I could take a look at the landscape around the Matanuska Valley." With the look of a mischievous, excited child, Charlotte said, "I couldn't resist the chance to fly over my home before I landed, so my family would know I had soloed."

Charlotte's income from driving school buses and her annual Alaska Permanent Fund dividend check paid for her lessons. She received her instrument rating in June 1994, her float plane rating in August the same year, and in 1995, both her commercial rating and commercial flight instructor license. Today, Charlotte is quick to say, with wide eyes and a big smile, "Having a float plane is my favorite kind of flying because I can land on rivers and lakes, not only airstrips!"

On her first long distance cross-country flight—a trip she calculated would take her from Birchwood to Talkeetna and eventually to Gulkana (396 air miles), where she'd land, refuel, and return—taught her a lesson. Charlotte checked the book and determined how much fuel she needed, but by the time she was past Talkeetna, she knew something was wrong.

"The gauges warned of low fuel. The spring lakes were still frozen and a few roads were open but I couldn't raise anyone on the radio. I believed the gauges as I looked for the nearest airport and followed a roadway till I put down at Tazlina, on fumes, with the engine sputtering! I heard an airplane engine across the road and walked over to ask for some gas. There were two or three men standing around talk-ing, and several large gas cans nearby. The first man told me there was a gas station just down the road. I explained that I needed about five gallons of 'av gas' to get my plane on to Gulkana where I'd refuel. The second man scolded me for running out of gas, but eventually took my 20-dollar bill and gave me five gallons of fuel, mak-ing a profit off my misfortune."

Before venturing off on long-distance flights after this experience, Charlotte said she talked to other pilots with more experience, no longer satisfied to go only by the book. "I always give myself at least a one-hour reserve, and check the terrain and look for airports."

Recently, Charlotte and another Bush pilot ferried six men from out-of-state to the Stony River Lodge, some 220 miles northwest of Anchorage, on the other side of the Alaska Range. Once there, Charlotte ferried the fishermen from one waterway to another, landing on floats. "There was one place we only flew about a mile but it would have been impossible for them to get in there because they would have had to slog their way through the swamp."

Charlotte ferried the men from Stony River Lodge to Holitna River, Nushagak River and Telaguana Lake, waking at 5:00 A.M., and donning a pair of chest waders to pump out the floats and ready the Cessna 180 for another day of flying and fishing. "I even learned to fly-fish on this trip. I caught a two-pound grayling. It was a blast!" In the evening, sitting on the porch back at the lodge, the men said they were impressed with her skill and would be returning next year with their wives.

On this same trip, Charlotte and the fishing guide flew out to scout the best fishing holes and spotted a male bear charging a newborn moose, the unsuspecting mother cow a few feet away. The fishing guide dived and chased the male grizzly, but unfor-

tunately the Cessna 180 was no match for the massive bear as it snared the young moose in his large jaw and made off with his kill.

Charlotte then explained how she became an instructor at Palmer Airport for RIS Unlim-ited, later O'Hare Aviation at Birchwood Airport. In April 1998, she was the lone instructor and did all the office work for Mustang Air Flight School, working for Gary Baker at Palmer Airport. In November 1999, she obtained her multi-

Charlotte Luckett at the controls of Pen Air's Metro-liner, near Adak, Alaska, in the Aleutian Islands.

engine rating. Eventually, she would instruct as many as six, sometimes seven, days a week. Then Mustang Air hired four more instructors before she took a job with Pen Air out of Anchorage, flying a 19-passenger Metroliner. Charlotte was hired by Pen Air in March 2001 and flew the Aleutian chain to the Pribilof Islands, all over the West Coast of Alaska, to Unalakleet, McGrath, Cold Bay, Dutch Harbor, Adak, Dillingham, St. Mary's, St. Paul, and St. George. She even shuttled a Metroliner from Anchorage to San Antonio, Texas, for repairs. After the terrorist events of September 11, 2001, Pen Air cut back on their flight schedule, but Charlotte wasn't furloughed until March 2002.

Even though Charlotte could pursue work with the airlines, her brief career with Pen Air, flying the Metroliner, convinced her she enjoyed teaching others to fly more than anything else. "I get a real kick out of telling someone they can go around alone now, they can solo." This was attested to when the Federal Aviation Authority (FAA) recognized Charlotte as the 2002 Alaska Region Flight Instructor of the Year.

Reflecting on her career, Charlotte told me a story. While she was still at Mustang in Palmer, a man came in because he'd received a letter from his son, that made it sound like the young man would not return—a suicide letter. The man pleaded with Charlotte to fly him up the Knik River towards the glacier to look for his son's red pickup truck. She was more than happy to oblige, hoping, of course, to find the young man alive and safe. Even though her passenger was an airline pilot, Charlotte was quick to point out that they'd be in for a bumpy ride with 35- to 40-knot winds. He didn't mind; he was desperate to reach his son.

"I knew the area well and after searching all the possible roads and passable trails where his son could drive his truck, I suggested we check at Jonesville. Sure enough, we spied the red truck on a ridge and could see the young man in the cab, but he wasn't moving. My heart sank, but I knew how determined the man was to contact his son so I buzzed the truck twice and finally the young man stepped out to see who was overhead. I tipped the wings to signal that we were there to find him. I was so relieved that he was okay. We returned to Palmer Airport and the father drove to the site to be with his son.

"He wrote to me in a letter that it might well have been his saddest moment if we hadn't found his son. He also offered to give me a recommendation to his airline, which was flattering. My reward was finding the young man alive and well."

At the time of this interview, Charlotte was chief pilot for Thunderbird Air, based at Birchwood Airport. During the summer months, her teenage daughter Charity worked in the office. I remembered sitting in the middle of a rolltop desk, hand-stamping mail at two years old, because my mother was a postmaster in a small town in the 1940s. I didn't become a postmaster, but maybe Charity will become a pilot.

Reflecting on the "wild hair" that brought her to Alaska when she was just 16, Charlotte knows she has carved a niche for herself in the Last Frontier, unlike anywhere else she could have chosen to put down roots, raise a family, drive a school bus and become a pilot.... a highly respected pilot and flight instructor.

26

No Strings:
GINNY JACOBER

"I wore a motorcycle helmet and had no radio to talk to my instructor, who was standing on the ground watching me when I took off. It was like putting a ten- or 11-year-old in the driver's seat of a Suburban and telling them to make a run to Palmer," Ginny Jacober said with a laugh. (When Ginny learned to fly an ultralight, it was a single-place aircraft, and the instructor could not ride along as they can today.)

"It was exhilarating, but terrifying to be up there alone!"

Ginny described the feeling when she soloed: "It's like a spiritual elevator. Take-off almost brings me to tears every time. In fact, I like takeoff and landing the best."

We first met in 1996 when I stopped in at Arctic Sparrow Aircraft at Birchwood Airport (about 25 minutes north of Anchorage) to ask Mike Jacober if he would participate in the Wasilla Air Show. He smiled and said, "Sure. I'd like to do that." Ginny was behind the counter, but I didn't have a chance to get acquainted with her then. Our paths crossed again in February 2003 when I attended an Alaskan Pioneer tea at the Captain Cook Hotel in Anchorage. I had no idea who the tall, friendly auburn-haired woman seated across the table from me was until everyone was introduced. At break time, I spoke with Ginny and asked for an interview. I didn't have to beg. She was eager to talk about ultralights and flying.

We met a few days later at Arctic Sparrow. No one was in the office, so I walked around and looked at the large array of awards and certificates presented to Mike Jacober. I spied a poster near the entrance with an eagle in flight. Beneath the majestic bird were the words, "Gear Down … Flaps Down … Cleared to Land." Across the room I spied a mock green frog with fake wings outstretched, dangling from the ceiling by a string. A small sign on the counter said, "Get your butt off the ground!"

Several times since 1996, I've stopped in at Arctic Sparrow. Every time, Mike Jacober tried to get me to take up flying ultralights. "You should try it," he'd say.

Ginny Jacober in an Antares MA 32 Flexwing Trike ultralight at Birchwood Airport, near Eagle River, Alaska.

"You'll love it." Each time I insisted my feet had to stay securely planted on the ground and thanked him for the offer. Mike would always smile and wave as I drove away. Often, I'd see him at the Chugiak Post Office and we'd have a friendly chat.

This day, Ginny arrived and invited me to sit with her at the long table in the office. She talked of going flying with a friend of the family when she was 12. "I always wanted to learn to fly. I went to college and pursued a Fine Arts degree, married and had two sons. Then we came to live in Alaska in 1972 when the oil pipeline was being installed."

Specific and precise, Ginny continued. "My husband was an engineer who worked to develop airports around the state, so he was usually hanging out with the guys. We got an amicable divorce in 1975, each going our separate ways. I worked in graphic design and had a second job at night as a grocery clerk. It was hard raising two children and working a second job," Ginny said with a sigh.

"In 1981 my friend, who was in sales with me in the graphic design business, handed me Mike's card and told me to call on him. I balked, because by then I had so many customers I was swamped." Ginny laughed. "Nothing could have prepared me when I made that first business call. I walked into Mike's warehouse and here was this guy who looked like he was all of 12, sweeping the floor."

Mike Jacober is one of those men whose age will never show.

Ginny continued. "I had an awful time trying to get him to sit down and go over his ideas for the brochure we were developing to help promote his new business. He wouldn't focus on anything except talking to me about flying. I explained that the more time it took to agree on the layout and design, the more it would cost, but he wasn't listening."

I suspected if the truth were known, Mike was infatuated from the minute he met Ginny and that was the real reason he seemed unwilling to focus on plans for a brochure. He probably wanted their first meeting to last forever.

"Before long," Ginny said, "a friend who was an architect tried to convince me that I should follow my dream and buy an airplane. He kept saying, 'You're entitled,' and I just didn't believe him. I thought about my dad, who was a World War II pilot and instructor and how he always encouraged me to learn to fly, even though my mother felt just the opposite. Finally, in the fall of 1981, I went to Mike and asked him to teach me to fly. I was one of three women in ground school, with the number of men triple that. One guy flat out said he didn't think women should fly. That was all the challenge I needed. I wasn't the first woman to solo in Alaska in an ultralight, but I passed my written exams with nearly 100 percent."

"On weekends, all of us would load up the equipment. Mike only had one plane back then, and we'd all drive out to Big Lake to practice. I got very frustrated because Mike kept holding me on the ground," Ginny said, rolling her large brown eyes. "I was so ready and yet he still wouldn't let me lift off! He would crouch beside me on the ski and give me instruction, letting me taxi around on the ice that covers Big Lake, but he wouldn't let me fly!"

At that point Mike came into the office from the shop so I asked him why he was overly protective. He laughed and said, "Because I know her!" He scribbled something on a chart from where he stood behind the counter. "Tell her about the time we were out there flying around together at Big Lake."

Ginny glanced over her shoulder at Mike and smirked. "I was happily flying along but I had no radio. I soloed on November 12, 1981, and had only been flying ultralights for a few months."

Mike interjected, "I was flying behind her in another aircraft and knew that if she rounded the bend in front of her she'd probably encounter some air turbulence and there was no way I could warn her. I was terrified knowing Ginny was in grave danger and there was no way to catch her or warn her because I was fighting a headwind."

"When I came around the bend," Ginny said, "I got blasted, like I was inside a clothes dryer. I was just scared to death as the wind tossed me around. I thought the airplane would disintegrate at any minute. I didn't know how I was going to come out of it alive, but I leaned forward and pushed down on the bar in front of me with both hands."

Mike added, "There were no strings! I couldn't do anything! It was horrible, but after Ginny made a perfect landing, I convinced her to get back in the air right then and fly back to the Klondike Lodge. She was very brave."

Ginny rolled her eyes at Mike. "I was so mad at him, but it wasn't his fault. I didn't want to get back in the airplane ever again, but Mike talked and talked to me and I finally agreed."

At this point, Ginny urged Mike to take me outside and slide me into the seat of an ultralight. I half expected he would climb in too and we'd be airborne, but it was raining and fog surrounded the airport. The ground under my feet was icy slick as Mike held my hand and helped me "plant my butt" in the two-place red ultralight. It was very comfortable, almost cozy, with a seat belt and a shoulder harness. Mike explained, while Ginny observed, that I should put my hands on the long horizontal bar in front of me that's connected to the wing overhead. Leaning forward and pushing the bar towards the windshield would cause the aircraft to lift off when the power was turned on. Pulling back on the bar the nose or prow of the angled wing would cause the plane to go faster, and without doing anything more than just turning the bar left or right, I could easily maneuver in both directions, even make a 360-degree turn … if the power was on and I was in the air!

The sensation was positive. I wasn't the least bit afraid and caught myself about to say, "Okay Mike, I'm ready for a lesson."

He also showed me the on-off switch just inside my left thigh. Beside the switch was the cotter pin to pull to dislodge the parachute. Mike explained that the chute would deploy to my left and rise above the aircraft, where the canopy would allow for a slow, safe descent to earth again. "No one is allowed to fly here without a parachute," Mike said. "Safety is our number one rule."

Ginny interjected, "Women make better pilots because they're more cautious. I always figure if the sky isn't blue I can go the next day."

The single-place aircraft Ginny first flew in 1981 and '82 cost $3,500 and had 22 horsepower. Today, a two-place ultralight runs about $18,000, including a parachute, with 52 to 65 horsepower. In 1981 Ginny had to purchase her chute separately. It wasn't standard equipment like it is today.

On many occasions, I have stared skyward and observed hardy Alaskans dressed in heavyweight winter Carhartts, arctic boots and warm gloves, a helmet protecting their head and ears, lazily flying around our neighborhood. I always envied their outdoor spirit that's typical of many northern people, like Ginny and Mike Jacober. Ginny recalled traveling with Mike to Kodiak, Alaska, an island southwest of Anchorage, where she was planning to demonstrate to fishermen how an ultralight could be used to scout the waters for fish at low altitude.

"I accidentally hit the kill switch mid-air," Ginny said. "All I could think was 'Oh crap!' I didn't want to come in with no power in a new area with wind and trees and unknown turbulence in front of the fisherman. I was scared I'd beak it in, but I didn't. I landed safely."

Ginny is cautious and precise, smart in my book, but her accomplished, daredevil husband Mike sets no limits to his challenges. He was fined $250 and his right to fly was almost revoked by the FAA when he tested a Staggerwing biplane with a 12-horsepower go-cart engine and a 24-inch propeller when he flew across Fire Lake, just north of Eagle River, Alaska, in 1977. The mini-prop from the Staggerwing hangs above a door in his office at Arctic Sparrow, reminding him of the surplus wooden Army skis he used to take off and land at Fire Lake.

Mike said, "By 1974 there were 30 or 40 hang gliders flying in Alaska, long before it took off in the Lower Forty-Eight. Today there are probably 300 ultralight pilots across Alaska and about 10,000 in the Lower Forty-Eight."

Ginny proudly allowed Mike to tell me a bit about his own flying career. Mike participated in air shows at Gulkana, Alaska, on the same program with famed aerobatic pilot Patty Wagstaff, known as Patty Beck in 1984 when she gave her first performance. Seemingly fearless, Mike holds the title of first to summit Mount McKinley with an ultralight after he and a friend camped on Kahiltna Glacier.

"We spent seven days at base camp on Kahiltna at 7,200 feet, and we flew to Mount Foraker, which is 17,400 feet above sea level. On the sixth day, I picked the right day and worked my way around McKinley for two hours and forty-five minutes in minus-35-degree temperature. Once I soared to the south buttress at 18,000 feet, it seemed feasible I could make the summit of McKinley, which is 20,320'. I had to use oxygen, of course, but once I reached the summit, I circled twice then I turned off the engine and glided back to base camp at Kahiltna ... ridge-soaring all the way back, with the approval of the National Park Service in Talkeetna."

Ginny and I listened intently to Mike matter-of-factly describe his solo to the summit of Mount McKinley and safe return to base camp. It was as if he relived the experience, the exhilaration, by telling us about it. I should have asked Ginny if she knew beforehand what her daredevil husband planned. I think she would have said, "Heck no. He probably didn't know himself until he did it."

I thought about Ginny's earlier comment that for her flying is a "spiritual elevator." I remembered how Ginny Wood, World War II ferry pilot in the WASPs, talked about the solitude and having the sky to herself. I remembered that Phyllis Tate and other women pilots described flying as a boost to their confidence, and a chance to be alone with God. I remembered how Ginny Jacober described her feelings about flying: "What a gift. It's such a joy to lift off, not only physically but emotionally." I believe there is nothing that compares with flying — and I'm sure Ginny Wood agrees.

Note: On June 5, 2003, Mike Jacober and a student pilot crashed near Birchwood Airport. On June 7, 2003, the FAA presented Ginny Jacober with a coveted Safety Award in recognition of Mike's dedication to safety throughout his flying career in Alaska. The award had been planned before Mike's untimely death.

Fellow ultralight instructor Rick Huggett said, "Jacober was one of the best ultralight pilots in Alaska and probably the country."

Ginny had the world's best teacher when she learned to fly ultralights.

27

Invincible:
PHYLLIS TATE

To know Phyllis Tate is to know Fairbanks, Alaska, and the people in the community. While I was in the heart of Alaska to do interviews, Phyllis put me in contact with other key women pilots and went with me on a tour of the Aviation Museum in Pioneer Park. Her eyes scanned the exhibits as if it were her first time at the museum, but that wasn't the case. Phyllis was keenly aware of the names and history of northern aviation being preserved for future generations. A Wien Airlines exhibit, an airplane flown by local pioneer aviator Jim Magoffin, and a display commemorating the ill-fated trip of Wiley Post and Will Rogers all captured our interest. Fairbanks is where early-day pilots began tempting fate in the skies of Alaska in 1924.

Next stop, the hangar housing Phyllis's Cessna 206, with its nose pointing north, waiting for Phyllis to hop in the cockpit and take it for a spin. The Cessna was surrounded by boxes of supplies from her trading post at Lake Minchumina, and assorted fishing gear ready for next season in Valdez, Alaska, on Prince William Sound. Weather kept us grounded that day.

Phyllis laughed. "I should clean this place up!" We agreed to leave before we got an urge to start sorting and stacking boxes. During lunch, Phyllis expressed hope that preservation efforts will succeed in downtown Fairbanks too. Phyllis proudly pointed out buildings her father or husband helped construct as we strolled through the downtown area.

I teased her. "I think you must know everything there is to know about Fairbanks."

With her infectious laugh, she said, "Well, I've lived here most of my life."

"I've been told Fairbanks has a population of about 50,000, but you make it sound like a small town."

"Oh, yes, definitely," Phyllis said beaming. "That's what I love about Fairbanks. The people."

So did Ginny Wood and Celia Hunter, and Pearl Laska Chamberlain, when they arrived in the 1940s, and claimed the frontier town as their home.

Phyllis Tate greeting Paul Herbert, former mayor of Fort Yukon, while campaigning for Alaska State Senate in 1998.

It's easy to understand why Phyllis came close to winning election to the state senate in 1998. The handout she gave to voters read: "I'm a lifelong Alaskan. Born in Fairbanks, I've lived just about everywhere in the state, from Biorka Island to Kotze-bue to Valdez to Lake Minchumina, my current home."

"I came close to winning," Phyllis said. "I thought I had an advantage over my opponents because I could fly to the villages to meet everyone, but two weeks in the hospital with appendicitis slowed me down. I still had a month left, and I tried to get back to campaigning too soon, ending up back in the hospital. It was fun to fly to the villages, pitch a tent overnight and talk to people about their concerns, which had a lot to do with subsistence … living off the land. Oh well. Maybe another time."

Even though appendicitis derailed Phyllis, she only lost by 19 votes in the primary election. Her flying campaign to some 93 villages (100,000 square miles) took her to the lower Yukon River, to the Canadian border and Tyonek, Nenana, Delta, Valdez, and Cordova, Alaska.

"I learned to fly in Chico, California, in 1965. I remember when I soloed. I was so ready. I felt like the instructor was holding me back. When I returned to Alaska a few years later, I got an instructor and went up to become current again. I was practicing touch-and-go's at Metro Field in Fairbanks in an Aeronca Champ and it was an overcast day with about a 1,100 foot ceiling. I'd done everything right and was on final approach when a Piper Lance pancaked on top of us, mid-air, slashing the fuselage from the tail to the wing. We were about 200 feet above the ground when the propeller cut all our control cables. The stick was loose. I remember saying, 'I can't control the airplane.' Then we nosed over, the ground started spinning and down we went, nose first, and flopped over on our back."

Phyllis was strapped in upside down and hung there for over half an hour with a broken neck and back while medics worked to remove her and take her to the hospital.

"Was your instructor injured too?"

"Yes. He had a broken back and his arm had been sliced clear to the bone by the propeller from the other plane. He's lucky he didn't lose his arm."

Phyllis paused then she added, "After I had the mid-air crash in 1980 and survived, not much scares me now."

Phyllis showed me photos of the Aeronca, lying upside down, the doors removed to allow the ambulance crew and firefighters to safely remove Phyllis and her instructor from the plane. She also showed me a photo of the Piper that caused the incident, resting on its belly in a swampy area, only tearing off its landing gear in the crash. The Piper pilot was uninjured.

"After that," Phyllis said, "I never felt afraid to die. I was slow to heal and I remember feeling so helpless after the first month because I couldn't even dress myself. But I never felt afraid to fly again because the accident wasn't my fault.

"It was about a year before I was able to take the controls by myself again, but before that, I went up flying, wearing my support collar."

"How many hours have you logged to date ... approximately?"

Without hesitating, she handed me her log book. "Twenty-five hundred."

I glanced through the log book while she answered a phone call. For October 12, 1985, Phyllis had written, "Just Me." After her phone call ended, I asked about the notation.

She laughed. "That was when I had the trading post and I never got to fly anywhere alone. My father had a cabin at Lake Minchumina, and that's when I first fell in love with the place. Then, years later, there was a fire in the area and there were about 300 firefighters working the fire. They'd ask me to bring back soda pop, and

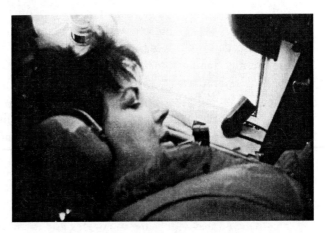

Phyllis Tate in the cockpit of her Cessna 206 returning to Fairbanks from Lake Minchumina.

147

sometimes they'd ask me to bring pizza. Sometimes I made three trips in a day. That's when I began to think about opening a small trading post. I went around and talked to everyone who lived there and they all thought it was a great idea."

"What sort of things did you sell?"

"Anything. Nails, a frozen pig, a keg of beer, lumber, cement, insulation, and baby chicks that rode in a box on the seat beside me. Whatever people needed."

"You loaded and off-loaded all these supplies, by yourself?"

"Oh yeah," Phyllis responded, smiling as usual. "At first I sold everything out of the back of the plane. That winter, my husband, Murray, built a store for me. In the summer I used a four-wheeler [ATV] to haul things from the plane to the store, and in the winter I used a snow machine. I started this in the summer of 1986. We carried over 400 items. Our motto, jokingly, was 'If we don't have it, you don't need it!' Sometimes I did medevac flights too.

"One evening I received a call from a stranger named Red, in Eagle River, near Anchorage, 350 miles south of Fairbanks. He asked me to pick up our mutual friend John about 60 miles south of Lake Minchumina. Red and John communicated regularly via sideband radio. John radioed he was suffering from a bad tooth, too sick to fly himself to the dentist. He had a runway marked out with spruce trees in the frozen lake and that night I put heat on my C-206 to warm up the engine, and took off the following morning to pick up John.

"When I got over John's lake, I could see the wind had swept the lake clean. I lined up for the long makeshift runway and set my wheels down on glare ice. As we rolled out, I tapped the brakes to see how slippery it was. We immediately started sliding sideways. I released the brakes and let the plane roll some more, braked, and slid again. Brake, slide, roll," Phyllis said, her voice quickening as she spoke. "I had visions of the plane piling right into the snowbank and all of us looking for a ride out! It was one of those heart-stopping moments.

"The most amazing part is this was a Sunday morning. When I got within radio range, I called Fairbanks Flight Service and asked them to call my dentist, explain the situation, and ask for an appointment as soon as possible. Flight Service called back in a few minutes to say we should go to the dentist's office as soon as we landed. He would be waiting for us ... on a Sunday, no less!"

"Who is the most memorable passenger you delivered to Fairbanks?" I wondered.

Phyllis chuckled. "A two-month-old baby named Katie that traveled alone with me. It was a snowy November afternoon flight. I strapped the baby into the seat alongside me, armed with baby formula, pacifier and plenty of blankets. I wondered how I would comfort the baby and fly the plane, if necessary, but Katie fell asleep shortly after take off and never let out a peep until we landed."

"Do you use your plane to go back and forth to Valdez for the summer fishing season too?"

"Um-hum," Phyllis said with a nod. "We used to do a lot of shrimping on our boat, the *Nuliaq*, and I'd fly from Fairbanks to Gulkana, then drive the truck two hours on to Valdez, load up and return the same way. We'd sell the shrimp in Fairbanks.

"Probably the most difficult trip I ever made was when we received a call in Fairbanks from a friend in Minchumina asking me to come out and fly him and his youngest son. They were not allowed to fly on the medevac flight that just left with his unconscious wife and fatally injured older son. In a small community we all know each other very well. I was so glad Murray accompanied me that trip."

"I think I understand why you wrote in your log book, 'Just Me.'"

Phyllis smiled. "Flying is an escape. I can be with God, with nature, and appreciate the beauty of the world."

"Did you always feel that way?"

Phyllis made a funny face. "Oh no. I used to get air sick all the time before I learned to fly. I never liked flying between Fairbanks and Kotzebue. It was always too long. I finally discovered that I was much better off getting sick and getting it over with. I still carry my little one-pound coffee can with a plastic baggie in it. In those days, I'd take an apple, put it in the coffee can, close it with the plastic lid and climb aboard the plane. As soon as I felt sick, I'd take the lid off, pull out the apple, get sick, cover the can and eat the apple. Then I'd feel fine the rest of the trip. Once I discovered that, the three-hour trips were much better."

"Did you ever consider becoming a commercial pilot?"

"I passed my written test three times," Phyllis said, raising her eyebrows. "I'd retake the test every two years, each time I got the urge to be a commercial pilot. I'd pass, then I'd have second thoughts. Bush air-taxi operators and their pilots constantly push the weather, and some of them die."

Phyllis paused to drink some water. "You start out working for an air-taxi operator in the Bush to build your hours—probably in Bethel, Nome or Barrow—all places with bad weather conditions a great deal of the time. Then after you get a couple thousand hours you could try for a 'real' pilot job with the airlines. I figured I'd get myself fired right off the bat by refusing a flight. I didn't want to put myself into that position—working for someone who insisted I take a flight when I didn't think it was smart or safe to fly. So, I guess I wanted to be a commercial pilot, but I wasn't willing to put my life on the line.

"I do other things that give me satisfaction. I volunteer with Big Brothers and Sisters and tutor at a nearby school. I really enjoy doing that," Phyllis said.

"Anything else ... in your spare time?"

"I serve on the Board of the Arctic Games and have been as far as Greenland for the competitions. The games are held every two years for athletes in the Circum-Polar Region and include about 20 different winter sports. They are a mini–Winter Olympics. About 2,000 people attend, and the Board is in charge of financing and logistics for the Alaska team, which numbers about 350 athletes."

I probed one more time. "Anything else?"

I learned that Phyllis had been a contestant in the Miss Alaska contest, that she was president of the Valdez Harbor Users, vice president of Minchumina Home-owners Association, and currently chairman of the Midnight Sun Chapter of the Ninety-Nines in Fairbanks. There was more, but it would probably fill a book. I began to wonder when Phyllis found time to sleep!

A smile crossed Phyllis's peaches-and-cream face as she blushed. "Well, I was a weather observer for the National Weather Service from 1987 to 1992 at Lake Minchumina. That's about it.... No ... I just remembered I also taught creative writing in a one-room school at the lake.

"I have to give credit to my husband, Murray. When we met in 1978 his first words were, 'I understand you are a commercial pilot.' He had just bought a Cessna 206 a month before we met and was looking for a pilot. Murray is not a pilot. I told him I had my private pilot's license. Twenty-five years later, I still have all three — Murray, the Cessna and my license!"

A trading post in Bush Alaska, marriage, divorce and remarriage, a daughter to raise, a mid-air crash, and working with her husband in the fishing charter business in the summer is what keeps Phyllis Tate active and happy. The commitment to her community and the concern Phyllis has for family and friends paints a picture of a very busy, but well-rounded, caring person, a gutsy woman who would not be deterred in 1980 when she almost lost her life, and got a second chance.

28

Drop Zone:
CAROL REDDING

Twelve years ago, in Taft, California, Carol Redding was a "stay-at-home-mom," raising and home-schooling her five children. Today Carol's life is nothing like it was in 1993 when she learned to skydive. "My desire to jump out of a perfectly good airplane was put on the back burner because family needs came before my own desires … or ambitions."

Athletic as a child and teenager, Carol was named Most Athletic Student in the seventh grade. She described herself as very active: a swimmer, a lifeguard, and a girl who played football just because "I liked the game." Carol pushed her wavy red hair out of her eyes and laughed. "I've had more injuries roller-blading than skydiving!

"I married young. I was 20 when my first child was born. Four more followed in less than six years. I had a B.A. degree in Education and was also trained as a medical technologist. When my daughter was born, I figured I'd stay home six weeks and then return to work, but I found I couldn't tear myself away from her for a minute. I decided to stay home so I'd be there when she spoke her first word. I didn't want to hear it from someone else when I came home from work.

"I was trapped in an unfulfilling, unhappy marriage and my self-esteem was at an all-time low. It was after completing a marathon that a real awakening occurred. It became clear to me that if I could run a marathon, I could learn to skydive. I'd been struggling to reestablish my self-esteem, and the marathon was my key."

While we sat in the shade of a tree on a breezy afternoon in Wasilla, Alaska, batting pesky mosquitoes away, Carol explained that she took lessons in Taft and paid for them by packing parachutes for five dollars apiece. At the time, her oldest child was 14 and her youngest eight. At the time of the interview her 18-year-old daughter already had 70 jumps in her log book and Carol had 1,500.

After she divorced, Carol met and married Bill Jones, and as he put it, they ran away from home to be "Snowbirds"—a name given to people who spend summers in Alaska and winters in the Lower Forty-Eight in a warmer climate. All of Bill's six children skydive.

In the summers of 1996 and 1997, Carol and Bill taught skydiving in Girdwood, Alaska, near Alyeska Ski Resort. Bill sold his skydiving school in California and they went looking for an airstrip to purchase in Alaska. He phoned all the realtors in the Mat-Su Valley, about an hour's drive north from Anchorage, and no one knew of an airport for sale. Bill drove around and saw a sign alongside the road on Fairview Loop Road, "Airport For Sale." The owner had just placed the sign there that day. It had originally been homesteaded as a potato farm and had an old style stucco house where the Jones family now resides.

The 20 × 65 acre parcel soon became the Alaska Skydiving School and boasts somewhere between 300 and 400 students from May to September every summer. They have extended the grass runway to 2700 feet and have added a hangar and more outbuildings for skydiving classes. Carol explained that 85 percent of their students are men, but when I visited again and watched the jumpers, one young woman, probably no more than 25, said she first jumped with her mother. The young woman was proud and anxious to be airborne to make her 104th jump.

Carol explained, "There's no particular background that leads each person to take this risk. We have firemen, oil slope workers, a computer guru, accountants, a graphic designer ... even a guy who customizes Harley motorcycles."

In May, 2000 Carol also learned to fly an airplane and obtained her private pilot's license at the Palmer, Alaska, Airport. All of this is a far cry from the "stay-at-home-mom" she talked of earlier. She said she flies simply for personal enjoyment, while Bill is a commercial pilot, which is a necessary rating to ferry parachutists making jumps. Carol's a parachute rigger and has taught her daughter, Rachel, to repack the chutes. "The FAA requires this procedure every 120 days," Carol said.

Every spring Carol and Bill host a Safety Day. Typically, about 70 skydivers attend to review ground and air safety and check their equipment. "We always stress safety," Carol said. "There are no timeouts in skydiving, like there are in basketball or football. You can't step over to the sidelines and plot your next move. You have merely seconds to pull the rip cord and complete your dive."

With a sense of pride and confidence, she said, "You land and go up and try again!"

She explained the basics of skydiving. "Each diver keeps a log book slightly different from pilots, but they record the date, place, aircraft, equipment, free-fall time and their total time. Many times they note what went well and how they could improve. Like a license to drive a vehicle, skydivers must receive an A card given out by the United States Parachute Association in order to dive from another drop zone. The USPA is a self-regulating organization, and there is no physical exam required unless the individual instructs and dives 'in tandem' with a beginner. Then they must have a third-class medical certificate."

When you drive onto the grounds at the school, a sign reads, "We sell skydives and smiles." I had the good fortune to observe Carol and three other skydivers

Carol Redding grasping Canadian flag in her right hand and the Alaskan flag in her left. Also pictured is Bill Jones on the left, and Lyal Waddell. Photograph by John Smith.

descend from 12,500 feet to the drop zone. One young man in a bright-yellow dive suit made his first solo dive, which only occurs after 20 successful student dives. Carol and two others descended to the ground ahead of Stephan while he circled for a long time, no doubt enjoying the experience and the view from overhead. When I learned this was his first solo, I wondered if he was reluctant to attempt a landing with the earth rushing up to meet him at a rapid pace. Carol was standing on the ground, guiding Stephan by radio. While Carol had landed ever so smoothly, without a hop or extra steps, the young man had to run a few steps to come to a final stop on the grass, but he didn't stumble. He walked over to his red-headed instructor and said, "I had to turn before I landed in the trees! It was awesome!" Stephan appeared numb, overcome with the sensations and exhilaration of his first successful solo jump, but he had a broad smile on his face.

Privately, Carol said, "I love to see their faces when they land. They are scared to jump out of the plane, holding their breath, afraid to breathe, unsure if they'll remember what to do, and if they can do it. Before they know it, their feet are squarely on earth again and their confidence soars ... like mine did in 1993."

While Carol had been aloft, I talked with a man who was waiting to jump with the next group. He learned to jump a year ago and said he does it because it's an "uncommon thing to do; it fills my sense of curiosity and exploration."

During the winter months, I phoned Carol to ask for a photo. She called back on her cell phone from a mountaintop in Moab, Utah, where she was hiking with Bill and some friends. "I've got a great photo I'll send you tomorrow," Carol said. The photo (shown on previous page) turned out to be a shot of Carol, Bill, and a Canadian friend holding Canadian and Alaskan flags as they jumped together. Carol has also participated in a "relative jump," or group jump, with 40 other skydivers to form a geometric design in the sky before they deploy their chutes.

When they returned from Utah, Carol said, "I can't think of anything I'd rather be doing. Bill and I live and work and play together here. I'm the manager and chief instructor, Bill is the pilot. We're partners in business and in life." When I asked which she enjoys most, jumping out of a perfectly good airplane or seeing the ground rushing up to meet her, she laughed and said, "I have a new canopy and it's very fast. I love it!"

29

A Million-Dollar View:
Jeni Hunter

From her office, Jeni Hunter has a 270-degree view that encompasses Knik Glacier, Mount Gannett, and majestic snow-covered Pioneer Peak to the southeast, and Matanuska Peak and Lazy Mountain to the east. Looking north, Jeni has a view of the Talkeetna Mountains and Arkose Ridge. In other words, Jeni has a million-dollar view.

I met the vivacious woman several years ago when I stepped up to the counter in the Flight Service Station at Palmer Airport. She was very friendly and open, willing to help me, but she was all business when she handled air traffic. I watched Jeni's hands point and motion to the inbound pilots, as if they could see her from their cockpit, giving directions. Her animated gestures amused and fascinated me. I thought of Jeni again when the seeds of this book began to germinate. Surprised, she said, "You want to talk to me? I'm nobody. I'm just here to do a job. That's all."

Just shy of 5'2", Jeni said that when she was a child she told everyone she wanted to grow up and be a giraffe. In the Flight Service Station at Palmer Airport, where Jeni has been an air traffic control specialist since November 1984, she no longer needs to fantasize about being taller.

Born in Alameda, California, Jeni moved to Utah in 1968 and took a job at Dugway Proving Ground, an Army post, in 1980. She worked as a civilian for the FAA, as a word-processing operator. "We turned data into usable reports, and I literally hated my job!" Jeni said. "One day this woman came around to talk to us about a federal program to train women in 'non-traditional' jobs. They were recruiting for air traffic controllers. She told me, 'It pays more, and you'll like it better.' I signed on and they sent me to Oklahoma City to the FAA Academy for four months of training.

"At the time I went to the academy, I thought all high-wing airplanes were Cessnas, low-wings were Pipers and big silver ones were made by Boeing," Jeni said, laughing. "Boy, did I have a lot to learn! They gave us a deck of cards with airplanes on each one. There were 27 in all and we had to identify at least 20 to pass the course.

Jeni Hunter, Palmer, Alaska.

I memorized the tail numbers and remembered 26 of 27." Jeni's face turned crimson when she admitted, "I didn't know a Super Cub from a Bonanza back then!

"I had to pick a region before I was hired. I chose Alaska because I knew folks who had been at Fort Greeley, near Big Delta in Alaska, and it sounded great." Candidly, Jeni said, "It was also as far away from my relatives as I could get and still be in the United States."

Jeni came from Oklahoma to Alaska to continue her training when the academy ended. People she met who had been stationed with the Army at Fort Richardson, near Anchorage, told her she'd fit in well up north. The red-headed controller smiled a satisfied kind of smile. "I later learned they put me through an accelerated course because my supervisor decided early on, the first week I was here, that I was the one they wanted to send out to Palmer Airport. I remember my first interview. This guy sat across the desk from me and said he didn't believe women should be air controllers. Fortunately, the second man who interviewed me thought I was a good candidate for the job.

"I drove up the highway ... the Alcan ... and arrived here the third week of September 1984. It was gorgeous. I rented a two-bedroom flea-infested apartment for $760 a month. There were four of us in training at Anchorage Flight Service. It seemed like they asked two or three times more of me than the others. I was convinced I was going to fail."

Palmer, Alaska, is a small rural community about 40 miles from Anchorage, founded by colonists as a farming area in the 1930s. The airport opened in 1966 and today Flight Service provides about 28,000 services annually, including over-the-counter help and radio communications with pilots in flight, checking weather or landing conditions in the area. Jeni said, "I love to get up and go to work. I meet the nicest people in the world, and they think I'm a goddess!" Jeni blushed and laughed out loud when she thought about what she'd said.

"It doesn't bother me that sometimes they call me 'Honey' or 'Janet' or 'Sweetie' when they can't remember my name. But what's really funny is when I answer the phone and they ask to speak to the controller. They're taken back when I say, 'I am the controller.'" (Jeni is the only woman who has ever been stationed at Palmer Airport Flight Service.)

"Pilots come in and file or close their flight plans, ask questions, check maps and weather," Jeni said. "I particularly enjoy orienting students going out to solo for the first time. They're all wide-eyed and nervous … excited. They keep me sharp with their questions."

Jeni admitted that at first some of the pilots had doubts about a 27-year-old "girl" handling the duties in the tower. "Buddy Woods would call in IFR (instrument flying, rather than VFR, which is visual flying), and since I only handled about five a year, he talked me through what I needed to know. I'm grateful to some of the old-timers around the airport who never patronized me when I started out here. They just wanted to help me any way they could. George Palmer, a hunting guide, who talked of places I've never heard of before; John Lee, who patiently talked with me; and Earl Payne, an early pilot we called 'Mr. Super Cub' because he flew all over the state and had lots of stories. They were all so kind and helpful." As if Jeni could see each man's face as she talked, she added, "They had a lot to do with training me."

It's no surprise that Jeni has the respect and admiration of pilots—mutual admiration is the key. In 1997 ace World War II pilot R. A. "Bob" Hoover flew his Aero Commander into Palmer Airport for an air show in Wasilla. Jeni was on the air, pointing and waving just like she would for any other pilot landing there. "I was in awe of the way Hoover would pull up to get fuel, engines off and stop on a dime," Jeni said. "He's an amazing pilot and a wonderful person."

One day sitting at her station with the million-dollar view, mid-field on the runway, Jeni heard something out of the ordinary. She stood up and looked out in time to see a Cherokee and a Cessna on final approach, ready to land. Only the Cherokee had called in on the radio.

"They were one on top of the other," Jeni recalled. "Instantly, without giving it a second thought, I grabbed the mike and told the Cherokee to climb and turn either direction immediately! Both pilots came up to the tower after they landed safely and thanked me."

Even though Jeni had ignored FAA rules and given a direct instruction, she had prevented a mid-air crash and saved six lives.

In 1983 Jeni was invited to go up on a "familiarization flight" with well-known Civil Air Patrol pilot Mike Pannone. Jeni obligingly climbed in the backseat with the other passenger, unaware Pannone needed to re-up his instrument rating. Soon after takeoff, Pannone went under a hood, unable to see outside, with the check pilot riding beside him. Jeni remembers it all too well: "I was sitting in the backseat thinking, why would anyone do this on purpose?"

The next time Jeni flew was in an FAA Convair and they flew west to Homer, Alaska, checking for moose at an altitude of 2,500 feet. "On the way back," she said, "the pilot saw some new construction and decided to do four 360-degree turns to have a closer look. I asked him if he had a wastebasket! I was turning green."

The next time Jeni went flying over the Knik River with a local pilot, she decided, "All pilots are insane and no planes are safe!"

Eventually, Jeni decided it might be a good idea to become a pilot so she'd know firsthand what it's like being on the other side of the mike. Jeni obtainer her private pilot's license in September 1989 and decided it wasn't so scary after all. She did a minimal amount of flying till the spring of 1990 when she went up again with an instructor to refresh her skills. This was the flight that almost ended in disaster when the carburetor iced up due to poor engine maintenance and no fault of Jeni.

"We were 500 feet off the ground and the engine was getting cold. It was still running, but not good. I could smell gas because the engine was flooded. I yelled, 'Your plane!' and threw my hands up. We landed in a muddy field and the plane nosed over on its back. The yoke was in my hands and had broken off. If I hadn't been wearing a shoulder harness, I would have been impaled!"

The woman who owned the field where Jeni and her instructor landed gave them a ride back to the airport where the old-timers told Jeni not to wait, but to get in a plane and go right back up again — "get on the horse again," Jeni said. "We totaled the airplane, but I lost my fear of flying and could ignore all the Hollywood movies because I walked away…. But I never got the bug." It was three weeks before Jeni got back on the horse.

On September 11, 2001, Jeni Hunter was at work when the World Trade Center in New York City was hit by two kamikaze airliners. "I was on the phone most of the day because everyone was in disbelief. They wanted to talk, to grieve. And, of course, all planes had to stay on the ground, but only for five days in Alaska, although general aviation was grounded in the Lower Forty-Eight for 14 days. The flights were highly screened, of course, but up here we have no alternative way to get around. Airplanes are our only reliable means of transportation."

Jeni remembers a flight service call from a pilot about ten miles out of Palmer who said an Air Force F-15 was tailing him. The confused pilot was returning from a hunting trip and had no idea what had happened in New York, Pennsylvania, or Washington, D.C. The F-15 lowered its landing gear, which was the signal for the pilot to land immediately. Jeni remembered the pilot's nervous voice: "I didn't realize an F-15 could fly that slow! Should I land in a field?"

Jeni told him to land at the airport and contact her when he was on the tarmac. When he landed, she explained what had happened. This was one of about ten airplanes still in the air in Alaska that received a surprise escort from an F-15.

Just for fun, the adventurous, happy-go-lucky redhead has traveled to Africa where she went into the bush on a safari and saw a giraffe firsthand. I picture Jeni talking to the animals, her hands waving and gesturing to them while she was on safari.

Miss Hunter, "Jeni" to all who know her, is an asset to aviation in Alaska. Her knowledge, experience, zest for life and her wicked sense of humor make Jeni one of a kind. She made the transition into a "non-traditional job" seem natural.

30

Two Babes and a Bird:
KELI MAHONEY and LEEANN WETZEL

Talkeetna, Alaska, is a "funky little town at the end of the road," according to locals. K'Dalkitnu is the early name given to Talkeetna by Indians, known as the Mountain People, dating back 1,500 years. Gold mining, fur trapping, and the railroad helped to establish the quaint village at the end of the road where tourists, mountain climbers, and locals mix and mingle today.

Two well-established annual events draw hordes of people into town. One is the Moose Dropping Contest, held in July each year. The contest isn't about dropping a moose from the sky, it's a contest to hit the mark with a "moose nugget"—the roundish waste product that looks like chocolate candy, but isn't.

In December, the popular Bachelor Auction is held, and women from the Lower Forty-Eight make their way to Talkeetna by train, plane and car to bid on scruffy, bearded bachelors who may or may not have taken a bath. Each bachelor is attired in a Talkeetna tuxedo ... which is a pair of grungy coveralls. The women bid for a dance and a drink, and whatever else the bachelor agrees to on the side.

Running concurrent with the auction is the Wilderness Woman Contest. Each woman must wear "bunny boots" that look like over-sized Popeye work boots and keep your feet from freezing. Each contestant must haul two empty five-gallon buckets about three blocks, from the Fairview Hotel to the old Road House, and return with two buckets filled with water. The winner is chosen by how much water is still in her bucket when she crosses the finish line.

Other contests require shooting a gun, casting a fishing pole, and donning snowshoes to pull a sled filled with wood. The final event requires making a sandwich that must touch a bachelor. Typically, the contestants don't bother to walk up to the tuxedoed fellow and politely hand him the sandwich; they take aim. After all, the rules say the sandwich only has to touch the bachelor.

Judy Marie, of the *Talkeetna Good Times* newspaper, is quick to say, "This place attracts strong, beautiful women and hairy, laid-back men."

Keli Mahoney and LeeAnn Wetzel, co-owners of McKinley Air — "Two Babes and a Bird."

Talkeetna is also the jumping-off place for climbers attempting to summit Mount McKinley — or Denali, as Alaskans call it, which stands for "Oh Great One."

A phone call to the ranger station in Talkeetna put me in contact with Chief Mountaineering Ranger Roger Robinson, who has climbed the highest peak in North America 20 times, reaching the 20,320' summit of Mount McKinley six times.

"We have about 1,200 people who register with us to make the climb up the mountain between late April and mid–July, and about 50 percent will succeed," Robinson said. "They must apply two months in advance of their planned climb, provide us with a résumé of their climbing experience, and pay a $150 fee. We expect people to have a minimum of five years' climbing experience under their belt before they attempt Denali. There are 30 different ways to go up Denali, but 85 percent use the West Buttress.

"Most people plan a year ahead before they attempt this climb. It's a challenge — a great adventure for climbers from all over the world. Once they arrive here, we give them a Power Point presentation covering the importance of self-sufficiency, the environment they will experience, and safety. We also explain about rescues and go over their gear to make sure they are prepared."

The experienced ranger chuckled. "Some of the climbers assume we're paper pushers and never get out from behind our desks, that we've never done what they're about to attempt, but every ranger here has and does climb Denali, and is also trained in rescue operations."

Once climbers make their way to Talkeetna, register with the National Park Service and listen to the required briefing, they must fork over more cash to a local air-taxi operator to fly them and their gear to one of two base camps, located at 7,000 or 14,000 feet. This is where "Two Babes and a Bird" come into the picture.

LeeAnn Wetzel and Keli Mahoney started McKinley Air Service in April of 1995. Keli, an athletic woman in her 30s with a dry sense of humor, was a pilot with another base operator in Talkeetna. LeeAnn was the office manager. Both are experienced pilots.

Curly red-haired Keli Mahoney learned to fly on the East Coast, in New Hampshire, Boston and Long Island. She soloed at 16 and became a flight instructor at 18. After receiving her Bachelors degree at Bridgewater State College, she began flying the East Coast corridor for TWA regional commuter shuttle in 1989, at age 21. Keli's father, Roy Mahoney, was a mechanic for Delta Airlines, but none of her five siblings pursued a career in aviation.

"I grew up around boats," Keli said, "so I figured I'd go to the maritime academy, but my dad thought there were more opportunities in aviation. I flew commuters for TWA in the northeast before they went out of business, landing at Kennedy and LaGuardia, then I headed north in 1991 ... for a couple reasons. I wanted to mush dogs and run the Iditarod, which I did twice. And I knew I could get a job and make a living as a pilot. I ended up in Bethel, Alaska, where I flew for Hageland Aviation." Keli paused to reflect. "Bethel is a far cry from Boston!"

Her hazel eyes brightened as she talked about dog mushing. "One minute it's pure tranquility, the next it's pure chaos! Mushing is way more challenging than flying. I have 25 dogs now and I've run the Yukon Quest and the Iditarod twice finishing once in each race. I had to drop out of one race because I had a dislocated knee, pneumonia and a broken sled, plus my dogs had a bout with salmonella during training season."

Dark-haired LeeAnn, the other "Babe," suppressed a smile and listened, occasionally interjecting a funny aside as her partner told her story, sometimes finishing Keli's sentences.

"Winters were too short in Boston," Keli said. "I love the outdoors and enjoy cross-country skiing, so Alaska is perfect for me.

"I gave up a $50,000-a-year job in Boston for a $200 mongrel in Alaska," Keli said while LeeAnn smirked and nodded, and the three of us enjoyed a good laugh at Latitude 62, a popular rustic log restaurant, just a stone's throw from the Talkeetna airport.

The verbal tennis match continued when LeeAnn said, "It's an addiction as bad as heroin!" She was referring to dog mushing.

Keli added, "There's no Betty Ford Clinic for dog mushers. And it kills relationships."

It was LeeAnn's turn to explain how she came from Nebraska to the "funky little town at the end of the road."

"In college I planned to become a physical therapist, but after four years in school, I lost interest. Some of my friends talked me into coming to Anchorage in 1990, where I went to work as a trainer and manager at a fitness club.

"One day I drove past Merrill Field in Anchorage, stopped and signed up to take lessons at Wilbur's Flight Service. It was that simple. I was ready to learn to fly. I'd flown a little in Nebraska and knew it was the absolute best way to get around, but I never could afford it before I moved here. I took lessons in the daytime and worked nights."

Keli prompted LeeAnn to tell about her first time in Talkeetna. The verbal tennis match continued.

LeeAnn's face came alive as she leaned forward. "I did my first cross-country flight to Talkeetna and just before I landed, the cockpit started to fill with smoke. It wasn't serious, but I was a little panicked. Everyone here was so helpful. I fell in love with the place. It was like coming home for me. I'm from a small town, so I decided I'd move to Talkeetna and open an espresso stand — me and my cat and my dog — but I ended up as the office manager at Doug Geeting's Flying Service, and...."

"That's where we met," Keli said as she glanced at her watch.

"Keli was a pilot at Geeting's," LeeAnn explained. "One day we talked about going into business on our own, so I contacted a friend in Anchorage for financing to buy a plane, a Cessna 185, and told her the name of our business was McKinley Air Service.

"My friend said that wasn't a very interesting name, so I admitted we'd been thinking of calling it Two Babes and a Bird."

LeeAnn glanced at Keli and both laughed again as they recalled the first steps they made to start their own charter service.

LeeAnn sat on the edge of her chair, as if she were going to wave multi-colored paper pompoms any second. She bubbled over as she shared the story of their start-up. "We got an 800 phone number. I put together a brochure and went to travel shows to promote the business ... and ordered T-shirts and hats." LeeAnn broke into laughter as she remembered how much work it took to start a fledgling air-taxi service.

"Tell her about the shirts," Keli suggested, with a wry smile.

LeeAnn nodded. "We ordered half the shirts with the tag line 'Two Babes and a Bird' on the back and McKinley Air on the front. People loved them. They wouldn't buy the ones with only McKinley Air Service on them."

Keli pointed to her partner repeatedly during the two-hour interview. "She's the sales person, not me! She's good with people. I'm no good at sales. When we first started, LeeAnn went up to the overlook where people stop before they drive into town, and —"

"I'd hand them a brochure and talk about taking a scenic flight. They wanted their money's worth, so I'd tell them if they didn't like the trip or it wasn't worth it, I'd give them a full refund." Both women smiled as they looked at each other. "No one has asked for a refund yet," LeeAnn said, displaying great pride on her face.

"Sometimes people pay to take a second trip, the same day!" Keli added.

"It's not cheap," LeeAnn chimed in. "For a group of four, it can cost a thousand dollars, but our insurance for five months of the year that we're in operation runs $25,000."

"I get such a big kick out of people who come to our kiosk and talk price, then they say they might be back," LeeAnn said.

Red-haired Keli rolled her eyes and waited for LeeAnn to deliver the punch line.

"In a couple hours, they come back and they're ready to fork over the money because they've found we all charge basically the same rate. We don't undercut each other, but when they come back, sometimes we're already booked and they've lost a chance to fly today."

"Seven of us have a concession with the Park Service to land on Ruth or Kahiltna Glaciers," Keli explained. "In 1998 we were grandfathered in, and we have to deal with three entities: the Park Service, the State of Alaska, and the FAA.

"At least seven days a month," Keli added, "you can't fly here anyway because of weather, so people are really disappointed then."

Marketing person that she is, LeeAnn had more to share. "Eighty percent of our customers are walk-ins. We come to work with nothing scheduled, then we end up running eight flights that day. We never know what to expect, and the first two years, I was really scared. If it was sunny and we didn't have customers, I was a nervous wreck. Or if weather kept us grounded and we couldn't fly, I panicked. But I've learned to roll with the punches. It works out okay and we don't need winter jobs."

The natural banter between the two Babes was refreshing. It was hard to interrupt the easy flow of conversation, but there was one question I needed to ask.

"Is it a treacherous flying around Mount McKinley and landing with wheel skis on glaciers?"

Keli shrugged, responding as if she believed it's about the same as driving down a six-lane freeway. "The first time I landed on a glacier was mind boggling, but what makes it enjoyable now is the first-timers who remind me how unique it is. People are overwhelmed. You see it through their eyes again every time you fly. For some people, this is the first time they've been in a small plane and they tend to get a little claustrophobic, then they forget and start to enjoy the view, the experience."

"Do you have lots of turbulence to contend with?"

"Not really. Talkeetna isn't windy and the glaciers keep the air cool so it's like

LeeAnn Wetzel and Keli Mahoney at Kahiltna Glacier, Mount McKinley, Alaska. Photograph by Melanie Stephens.

flying a highway in and out of peaks and valleys. The passengers get to see the mountain climbers and see their camps too."

With a serious look on her face, Keli said, "I've only had to stay overnight on the mountain once, the same day that Don Bower from Hudson's Air crashed. We didn't dare take off in a thunderstorm, which is what brought Don's plane down. With

Keli Mahoney flying a Cessna 185 in the McKinley range, Alaska.

the exception of one passenger, everyone on my plane understood it was smart to stay put and they helped calm the woman down who wanted to get back to Talkeetna."

Keli was the last person to talk with Bower on the radio from the mountain before he crashed and died.

"Eighty percent of our business is scenics," LeeAnn interjected. "The rest are climbers." She turned to Keli on her left. "Tell her what it's like when you pick up the climbers after three weeks on the mountain." Both women scrunched up their faces.

"Sometimes they won't come back with the person they started climbing with," Keli said. "Three weeks out there makes or breaks relationships. If you're married when you start, you may be getting a divorce when you come off the mountain. It's a good idea to know your fellow climbers very well. And all of them need a bath and they're still wearing the clothes they had on three weeks ago when I fly them back to town."

Keli and LeeAnn broke up in uncontrollable laughter while I tried to imagine a small cockpit filled with over-ripe people and their smelly gear.

"They're usually excited when they see rocks and trees again after three weeks of ice and snow, and no other stimulus," Keli said. "Most of them just want a pizza and a beer, then a shower ... well, the women want to shower first."

"They don't haggle over the price either," LeeAnn said, still laughing. "They'll blow a $100 bill on pizza and a couple of beers."

Keli checked her watch again, and I had a sense we'd been talking for two hours, the allotted time. I had no idea then that Keli was a member of the volunteer ambulance service as well as volunteer firefighter. In the off-season, when she wasn't flying, Keli also built cabins in Talkeetna.

"How would you sum up living and working in such an isolated area, with competition, a very short season, and weather to contend with, where the biggest thing that happens in Talkeetna is the Moose Dropping Contest or the Bachelor Auction?"

My question brought more laughter, then sighs and side glances between Keli and LeeAnn. Keli was ready to explain.

"I could never live in the city again. I enjoy flying in Alaska and running with my dogs."

"Besides," LeeAnn said, "Talkeetna is a town full of women in business. We're very supportive of each other. It's a good life."

I had to agree with both women, that living and flying "in the funky little town at the end of the road" is unique and rewarding.

Keli and LeeAnn are two strong, smart, beautiful, adventurous and fun-loving women capable of making a life anywhere, like the pioneer women pilots of the 1920s and 1930s who arrived in Alaska with hope, and not much more.

Keli Mahoney
February 20, 1968–May 28, 2003

It was a warm, sunny afternoon that day in May. I was outside planting flowers and came inside for a glass of water. That's when I heard the evening news. Keli Mahoney and three passengers perished at South Hunter Pass in the Alaska Range, near Mount McKinley. Stunned, disbelieving my eyes and ears, I went outside and planted white petunias in Keli's memory.

A memorial service in her honor was held in the elementary school cafeteria in Talkeetna the following Monday evening. There was standing-room only for the crowd that numbered around 500 people — people who flew with Keli; people who volunteered with her at the fire department; park rangers, Alaska state troopers, mountain climbers, fellow dog mushers, friends, pilots, and her family.

A close friend said, "You didn't tag along; you ran to keep up with Keli."

Another said, "She believed in setting the bar high and higher. The message was always the same: try!"

Tigger, a male friend who worked with Keli building houses, said, "She sang bad and when we played poker she won. She was the sister I never had."

Fighting back tears, Keli's father, Roy, said, "Keli found a community in Alaska."

A woman friend said, "Keli was a woman who inspires you to live your dreams."

Then her partner at McKinley Air, LeeAnn Wetzel, summed it up: "Keli never backed down. Anything you want to do you can. Don't wait. Don't put it aside."

Following the hour-long memorial, everyone was asked to step outside into the school yard where four local air-taxi operators flew in formation. As they passed over the school, the plane on the left cut away towards Mount McKinley in memory of Keli Mahoney.

Note: Mount McKinley claimed the lives of 13 pilots between 1967 and 2003. Keli Mahoney is the first female pilot to lose her life on the mountain, raising the total to 14.

31

Choices:
ROBERTA DEGENHARDT

Roberta Degenhardt sat down beside me at an Alaska Ninety-Nines meeting. There was no speaker, but a lively two-hour discussion was held to make plans for the 2003 Centennial of Flight, commemorating the Wright Brothers flight at Kitty Hawk in 1903. "Berta," as she prefers to be called, offered some great ideas.

I'd heard her name and knew she was a pilot with FedEx. I asked for an interview and with a friendly shrug, she said, "Sure, why not." I inquired if she would be in town for the next day or two, depending on her flight schedule. Berta replied, "I'm not going anywhere for a while." Rolling her eyes, she explained. "I broke my back last year and I'm still recovering."

I assumed she'd been in an accident involving an airplane, and was surprised to learn otherwise. "I broke my back skiing at Alyeska," Berta said.

Two days later, I pulled up at her apartment in Bootlegger Cove on the edge of Cook Inlet in Anchorage. I was 15 minutes early and Berta wasn't home from her doctor's appointment. It was about 10 degrees so I waited in my car until a red SUV backed in beside my car. I thought to myself, "Must be a pilot. No one backs into their parking spot." It was Berta. I followed the 5'8" brunette into the building, her long, straight hair trailing down her back as we ascended the stairs. I would have opted for the elevator.

Berta said, "I do this because I can, and to help rebuild my strength."

It was mid–January, but Berta's Christmas tree still twinkled in one corner of her living room. With only six hours of daylight in January in Anchorage, it lifts the spirits to keep lights on, especially holiday lights.

Next, I was drawn to the bay windows in the living room with a view of the Sleeping Lady (Mount Susitna), the Alaska Range and Mount McKinley. "Here comes the boys," Berta said, pointing to the Air Force jets on final approach at nearby Elmendorf Air Force Base. "I can see everything from here. Even the FedEx building over there to my left … and the runway."

Berta made hot tea and we settled down to talk. The awesome view and the ornaments on Berta's Christmas tree kept distracting me. "Where did you find all these unique ornaments?"

"It's one of my obsessions when I fly around the world. I pick them up everywhere I go. Let's see.... I've landed in every state in the U.S.A. and I bought some of them in Europe ... Scotland, Ireland, England, France, Italy, Germany, Switzerland, and even in Russia."

I asked Berta how long she'd been living in Bootlegger Cove.

I think it's about two years," she said. "I'm still based out of Memphis, Tennessee, but I choose to live here because I love Alaska. The first time I saw Anchorage when we were coming through here and we were on final approach, I said, 'Oh my God. Someday I will live here.'" Berta laughed. "My brother George teased me when I decided to move here. He asked me if I'd have to kill animals for food and use their antlers for utensils!"

Roberta "Berta" Degenhardt, in cockpit of FedEx MD11.

Our interview was disrupted again when Berta spied another pair of Air Force jets. "I tried to get into the Navy in the fall of 1980 before I graduated from college. I took the physical and the written test, then the recruiter phoned me from Jacksonville or somewhere to give me the news after I graduated in the spring of 1981. He had a deep southern accent. 'Roh-berta,' he said, in a husky voice, 'we don't need any more girls in the Navy. If you were a guy we'd take you. We just don't need any more girl pilots. But we do need mechanics.'" She laughed. "I turned him down because I wanted to fly.

"I remember one time when I was flying as a charter pilot this guy said he didn't believe I was a pilot because I'm a woman. I just smiled at him and said, 'Yes, they let us fly and you know what else? They let us smoke and they let us vote! Can you believe it?'"

170

As Berta's story unfolded I learned that her father was a private pilot and often took her with him, along with her three brothers, when he went on scenic trips.

"My dad worked for ABC as a TV cameraman and director and he absolutely loved his work. Even though I had a scholarship and thought I'd pursue a liberal arts degree, or maybe become a forest ranger, or a TV cameraman — something non-traditional — I just didn't know what I wanted to do my senior year of high school.

"My high school counselor suggested that I get a degree in psychology, and so I applied at a local college and was accepted, but when I thought it over … sort of meditated about it, I knew I had to do something I loved, like my dad. When I told my counselor I had decided to fly she said, 'Great! You can be a stewardess, then.' But I said no, I wanted to fly the planes.

"I couldn't go to college for a year after high school because it was too late to apply anywhere else so I stayed on working at a fabric store. My father had a friend whose son had gone to Embry-Riddle so we planned a trip to visit the campus at Christmas."

At this point I expected Berta to say she took flying lessons during that year after high school, but I was mistaken. She worked and saved the money for school, enrolling at Embry-Riddle Aeronautical University in Daytona Beach, Florida, the following year.

"The university where I could have gone right out of high school had 25,000 students. At ERAU there were only 2,500. It was great. I loved it. I received a Bachelor of Science degree in Aeronautical Science with a minor in Management.

"I needed a biennial flight review and went to the local FBO [Fixed Base Operator] at Westchester County Airport. While I was waiting to go fly, I was approached by the director of flight training, who ended up offering me a job as the receptionist on weekends. Instead of being insulted, I took the job because it afforded me the chance to fly at a discount and complete my CFI [instructor] rating and CFII [instrument instructor] rating."

Her sparkling blue eyes lit up when Berta said, "I gave flight lessons during the week and padded my own schedule on the weekends. I liked teaching, but the students weren't as dedicated as we had been at Embry-Riddle. Flying was only a hobby to them, so they would be late, or not study for the lesson. That bothered me because I didn't want someone to hurt themselves if they weren't competent in the cockpit of an airplane."

I asked Berta if she'd ever had a close call in the air.

"I don't think being scared goes hand in hand with danger. I think that the more experience we get the less likely we are to be frightened by dangerous situations because we know how to deal with emergencies. Actually," Berta said, "the one time I've really been scared was when I was still a student pilot. The weather in Daytona had gone IFR [instrument flying] while I was out on a cross-country flight. I knew I could not go home, but wasn't quire sure what to do. The controller suggested I go land at the Deland, Florida, airport and wait it out. I was so shook up by the time I got to Deland that I entered the traffic pattern in the wrong direction. It was very embarrassing and, fortunately, no one else was in the pattern at the time."

I told Berta about a friend I flew with in the late 1970s who told me the first time he did a cross-country flight, he landed in Hayward, California, went up to the tower and had the air controller sign his log book. Then he climbed back into his 180 Commanche and went through his preflight checklist. When he started to taxi, the plane wouldn't budge from the spot where he'd parked. He'd forgotten to untie the plane. He said he never returned to Hayward airport again.

Berta chuckled. "How embarrassing! I know how he felt."

"Between your job at Panorama Flight Service [the FBO] and FedEx, what did you do?" I simply assumed Berta had climbed the ladder of aviation with small commercial operators, finally landing her dream job.

"After three years at Panorama I had moved from receptionist to flight instructor to first officer in the charter department, and finally made captain. Westchester Airport is home to some of the best corporate flight departments and pilots. I set my sights on Wayfarer Ketch, which was the best corporate job on the field. I'd show up and try to convince them to hire me. I hung around, gave them my resume — which I updated every 100 hours of flight time — and drank a lot of coffee. They said they finally hired me so they could get me out of the office!

"Wayfarer was owned by the Rockefeller family. I worked for them for 10 years. I flew as captain on the Canadair Challenger 601, the Falcon DA20, the Hawker Siddley HS125, and the Cessna E550. I also flew helicopters for Wayfarer, including the Agusta A109, an Italian helicopter with retractable gear — the fastest civilian helicopter. And I flew their Bell BO105 helicopter."

This is when I realized Berta is dual-rated. She flies airplanes and helicopters and is one of approximately 530 women in the entire country with these credentials.

She explained that the Agusta (pronounced "Ah-goo-stah") A109 helicopter flies faster because it has retractable gear instead of skids for landing. This reduces the drag and you can take off and land like an aircraft. Berta said, "There is not that challenge at the end of the day to land on an 8' × 10' dolly!"

Laughing, Berta recalled the first time she landed on a dolly. "Everyone in the company, from the director of ops on down, came out to watch. All of the mechanics had made up rating cards like they have for the diving competition: 8.5 … 7.8 … 9.9. It was quite funny! The also made me a little model of a helicopter on a dolly and presented it to me. It was made out of a Falcon 20 nav lite, some bolts and ice cream sticks. I still have it!"

Berta had a unique description of flying helicopters: "Flying helis is the freest sense of flying, but you have to be able to rub your stomach, pat your head and tap dance all at the same time! Helicopter flying is a different kind of flying. It's a sensory thing you have to feel. You have a control in each hand and pedals for both feet.

The cyclic control allows you to move left, right, forward or backwards. The collective control allows you to move vertically, to lift off. By comparison, it's like wind surfing.

"You can see a lot more of the world in an airplane because you can go farther and faster. The airplane is the means to the end, which is seeing the world, but there's something really nice about flying along at 1,500 feet in a helicopter. Helicopters can't fly in icy conditions because there's no way to de-ice them. Most helicopter pilots learn in the military, then they learn to fly fixed-wing, and most fixed-wing pilots don't care to fly helicopters."

Berta learned at Bell Helicopters in Fort Worth, Texas, in a BA105 — a German-made multi-engine helicopter. She advanced to the BO 105 for a commercial check-ride in a twin-turbine in 1987, obtaining both her ATP (airline transport) and instrument ratings. "The Bell 47 that I learned to fly was like the helicopters on *M*A*S*H** on TV. I soloed after ten hours."

I listened in awe, but I still hadn't abandoned my bad habit of making assumptions. I just figured Berta was the Rockefeller's family pilot.

"Over the years Wayfarer had become more like a management company. We also operated the aircraft for Chase Bank, Time-Life, ABC Television, Warner, HBO and others. We carried passengers like Henry Kissinger and Bruce Willis."

Berta stood up and walked across the room. She pushed her hands deep into her sweatshirt pockets and lowered her head. "This is how Bruce Willis came walking toward the helicopter, his baseball cap pulled down over his eyes, his head down. As he approached, he raised his head and winked at me. He was definitely one of my favorite passengers, and he wasn't the least bit surprised to see a woman flying a helicopter."

"Can you remember other passengers that flew with you at Wayfarer?"

"Sure," Berta said. "John F. Kennedy Jr., Natalie Cole, several ambassadors from the United Nations, and I flew Dan Quayle to Scotland to play golf as a guest of Time-Life, but it was after he was out of public office. I also flew the cover models for the 25th Anniversary of Sports Illustrated Swimsuit Issue to their L.A. press party."

Berta leaned back in her chair. "There are so many I can't list them all. It was a great job. We flew state-of-the-art equipment, stayed in the best hotels and ate in the best restaurants.

"Nelson Rockefeller died in 1985, before I was hired, but his death had made them realize that the ownership of the company had to change, and so the business was sold to a Rockefeller venture capitalist group and was operated as a management company. We were on call 28 days a month. It just wasn't the way it used to be, and I was ready for a change."

Did I dare ask Berta if she simply applied at FedEx and was hired? No, I waited for her to explain. I was learning.

"Wayfarer sent me to Texas to get my ATP. At that time I only had my commercial rating in helicopters. On weekends I stayed with friends from college. They had a friend who was a captain at FedEx. Two years later, in September 1995, I was fed up with my schedule and they put me in contact with their friend. I interviewed in November 1995 and was hired in February 1996 as a flight engineer on a 727. Before long I moved to first officer on the 727, and now I'm the first officer in their hundred-million-dollar MD11, with a type rating. We fly all over the world. Most of the Anchorage flights go to Asia, but I prefer the around-the-world trips that go eastbound, first stop Paris!"

Berta is a member of the International Society of Women Airline Pilots and recently flew from New York to Paris with two other women pilots. "We had an all-woman crew and on the return leg the French men gave us long-stemmed roses. The male pilots back in Memphis, Tennessee, were jealous when we stepped off the plane carrying roses. They said, 'Oh those French, they know how to charm the women.'"

Berta has never felt any limitations because she's a woman in the cockpit of an airplane or helicopter. She made the choice to pursue a career in aviation that has taken her around the world. A choice to live anywhere, fly anywhere, and follow her dreams.

32

All Trails Lead to Here:
TERRI LaCLAIR

There are no roads leading to Naknek, Bristol Bay or King Salmon in southwest Alaska on the hostile waters of the Bering Sea. There are only 1,082 miles of actual highway in the expansive state, compared to 1,100 in the greater Los Angeles County California area alone. In December of 1984, Terri "TQ" LaClair hopped on a plane from Portland, Oregon, to Anchorage, Alaska — some 1,539 miles by air. Then she changed planes and flew another 300 miles to the salmon fishing capitol of the world, King Salmon, where she was given the opportunity to help an old friend open a new hotel named the Quinnatt Landing in Naknek.

The gregarious caramel blond gave up a job as a bartender in a trendy hotspot in Portland, gave up a boyfriend, and left a college scholarship behind to move to Alaska to follow a dream. All her life Terri's grandparents talked of going to Alaska — the fishing, the hunting, the beauty of the land — but they never made the trip. But through their eyes, Terri fell in love with the Last Frontier. She said, "The lure of Alaska was too much. I bailed!"

On the last leg of her trip, from Anchorage to King Salmon, TQ — to her friends in Bristol Bay — was one of two people on an eight-passenger Cessna Conquest twin-engine airplane. The pilot invited her to sit in the right-hand seat where the co-pilot would normally ride. From her vantage point in the cockpit, Terri could look around outside and see that Alaska was the place for her. She said, "The sheer vastness of the land hooked me. It was rugged and foreboding yet held a peacefulness that takes hold of your heart."

Once there, TQ had offers to go fly every day. "Since there are only 14 miles of road, between King Salmon and Naknek, if you don't go by boat to get somewhere you have to fly," she said. "The guys tried to impress me because I was new in town and it was the dead of winter. They offered to take me flying all the time."

Originally an Air Force installation built during World War II, King Salmon and Naknek residents survive by fishing for herring and salmon when in season. Students from King Salmon are bussed to school in Naknek, but students from South

175

Naknek in grades six through 12 are flown across the Naknek River to their school. This appears to be the only school in the United States to do this. Children in outlying villages in Alaska learn about flying at an early age.

Medical care is offered at Camai Community Health Center, also in Naknek, but patients with major injuries and surgeries are flown to Anchorage for treatment. Terri mentioned two stores—one owned by the Red Salmon Cannery, the other owned by Alaska Commercial Company, where residents buy supplies including food, appliances, hunting and fishing gear, furniture and clothing, among other things. But Terri pointed out that milk typically costs $7.00 a gallon and there is no fresh meat and very little produce. This is an accepted way of life for Alaskans in outlying villages like Naknek, where Terri chose to plant her feet in 1984.

"Most everyone goes to Anchorage a couple times a year," Terri explained, "and stocks up on everything. There is a 24-hour post office at the Anchorage Airport and we'd be in there in the middle of the night with our grocery boxes shipping things home. You inevitably ran into someone you know at the post office. You also get pretty good at ordering things by phone or over the Internet. This has really improved the quality of life in the Bush. People in the city are pretty good about accommodating us too. When you knew you'd be in town you'd try to get everything done: doctor appointments, dental work, clothing, shopping, gifts for future events. You'd have to go to at least one or two movies and you would also want to eat as much Chinese and Mexican food or fast food as you could consume … and still you would take home some Kentucky Fried Chicken for later!"

Terri talked about the flat landscape, devoid of mountains, with water outside her front door, and bears. "You can see in all directions and I like that. One night I had gone to bed when I heard a bear on my deck. I was scared. I got up and started into the living room. Just then this bear stood up with his paws against the door leading to my deck and *slam*, the glass door came crashing open in front of me right there in my living room! My little dog, Tonka, a Pomeranian, scared the bear off, much to my amazement and relief."

After numerous flights with her new neighbors and friends, TQ said, "I did a lot of recreational flying but I didn't see myself learning to fly or owning an airplane. There wasn't much purpose in it for me at that point. During my second summer I was hired as a laborer to help build a bunkhouse at Nelbro Cannery. I got a phone call from a man named Dave Lax. He said he did not know me but had heard that I was a hard worker. He wanted to start a ground-taxi service to help haul incoming fisherman from King Salmon to Naknek.

"In the late 1980s there was generally an influx of between 6,000 and 10,000 people showing up from May to June and then leaving after the fishing season ended. This diverse group included fishermen, crew members, cannery workers, mechanics, waitresses and many other adventuresome and money-seeking characters. The only catch was I had to be self-motivated and would have to compete with two other taxi companies that had been running for years. Always up for a challenge, I said yes! So Lax bought a big, shinny red Ford van and away I went. When he sold the business five years later there were six vans and Redline Taxi was a success story in itself.

"At that point the construction end of Dave's business was really taking off. He had always been interested in helicopters and decided to invest in one for personal use and maybe do some construction-related flying. He asked me if I would also like to learn to fly."

Terri's soft gray-blue eyes warmed to the memory of going to Fairbanks to learn to fly helicopters as she retold the story. "For three weeks, I trained with Larry Larivee, a Vietnam pilot who also flew charters for federal and state wildlife programs in Alaska. He's a one-man flying wonder and a great instructor. He has done everything from herding cattle at Unimak Island to bear and wolf collaring for Fish and Game, and some caribou herding on Nunivak Island. He sling-loads barrels of fuel, fishing nets and everything from skiffs to pizza.

"I learned a lot in March of 1994 there in Fairbanks with Larry's expert guidance," TQ said with a laugh. "He wears a helicopter like a pair of pants! March in Fairbanks means temperatures well below zero and snow on the ground. Everything was white." Speaking of learning to handle the various controls of a helicopter, Terri smiled and

Terri "TQ" LaClair, in front of Robinson 44 (R44) helicopter "somewhere between Fairbanks and Anchorage." Photograph by Larry Larivee.

said, "One day it seemed easy, but the next day it didn't make any sense. It's like learning to drive a car. One day you think you won't know what to do and they next day you do." She leaned back in her chair and sighed. "Like anything, it's a learning curve."

The technical description involves the pilot using rudder pedals with their feet, which turn the helicopter to the right or left; a cyclic pitch stick in one hand that tilts the helicopter forward, backward, or sideways; and a collective pitch stick in the other hand that allows the helicopter to climb and descend vertically.

FedEx pilot Roberta Degenhardt, a dual-rated ATP in fixed-wing aircraft and helicopters, described learning to fly rotor wings like tap dancing, patting your head and rubbing your tummy all at the same time. Anchorage pilot Ann Wilbur added, "You may as well be making a quilt too!" But Terri LaClair from Naknek took it in stride, like everything else in her life. She was determined to learn. She soloed in a Robinson R-22 in Fairbanks in July of 1994 and later flew an R-44.

Terri pointed out that her instructor, Larrivee, also "reads the fish." "He knows exactly where to find pools of fish and their spawning grounds." TQ flew with her mentor to places like Nunivak Island, Togiak and Unalakleet to scout for fish. She remembered one landing on a herring fish tender with between 30 and 40 knots of wind pushing the tail of the helicopter. She had to gently land on the heli-pad, facing the wheel house. There was no room for error. "When it was time to take off, with the 'copter fully loaded, the wind was so strong I was reluctant to move off the pad, but Larry assured me it was easy, then he took control of the duals and backwards we flew, tuning around once we were airborne." The next time, Terri didn't hesitate, she just did it the same way … backwards.

Terri has no desire to learn to fly fixed-wing aircraft. "The reason I prefer helicopters is because I can land anywhere, without wheels, a runway, flat ground, or on water if I have floats. I don't have to look for someplace to put down. I can just set down anywhere with a helicopter."

At the time of the interview Terri had moved from Naknek to Anchorage with her new husband, Ronnie LaClair. "I feel like I'm in a box here," she said. "I like wide-open spaces of the Southwest coast and the tundra flats." (Anchorage is the largest city in Alaska and the snow-capped Chugach Mountains buttress the eastern edge while the waters of Cook Inlet border the western edge of the community.) In other words, TQ would like to return to Bristol Bay on the Bering Sea where she keeps her two-bedroom house at the edge of a cliff overlooking the bay where the bears frolic in the sand and water and Beluga whales scour the sea for smelt. "In the summer, hundreds of fishing boats and tenders and barges would pass by my windows and in the winter the huge ice chunks would flow in and out with the 17- to 22- foot tides, and bald eagles would swoop into the water and scoop up fish."

For a girl from the bustling city of Portland, Oregon, were everything you could ever want or need is at your fingertips 24/7, this sounded crazy, but then Terri was born on the Oregon coast so no doubt the aura of the sea keeps her anchored to Southwest

Alaska. With a wry smile, she said the wind blows almost constantly from the north and west to Naknek. She added, "But the sunrises and sunsets are always beautiful."

When TQ first took up flying, her friends in Bristol Bay were convinced she'd be killed. Everyone in the Bush flew airplanes and it was thought that anyone who would fly without wings was courting disaster. But now they're all very proud, especially Terri's husband, Ronnie, and her 27-year-old-son, Damion Robinson.

The active, outdoor woman is a member — member number 1048, she pointed out with pride — of the 1258-member-strong international organization of Whirly-Girls, women helicopter pilots representing 41 countries. Each year Terri attends their annual meeting, called a "Hovering," in Las Vegas, Dallas or Anaheim, California to rub elbows and share flying stories with her peers, some who pioneered in rotor-wing aircraft 60 years ago. Terri said, "Everyone meshes together at these conferences and no one takes it for granted."

TQ knows the trail for women pilots was blazed by others decades before she first took the controls of a helicopter, and today it's not so unusual to be a woman pilot, yet her eyes filled with tears as she acknowledged those who came before her. "It's more acceptable, I think, in Alaska because there are so many places where you can't get to if you don't fly."

As the purchasing agent for Southwest Alaska Contractors, with an office in Anchorage, TQ makes arrangements for people, supplies, equipment and goods to be sent out to the Bush for construction of airports, underground utilities, and underground infrastructure such as water and sewer lines. Some of these areas include Kwethluk, north of Bethel, Clarks Point, South Naknek and Egegik.

There's no doubt sometime in the future TQ will take up residence again in her small house on the bluff in Naknek, maybe only during the fishing season so she can return to flying, doing what she loves in a place she loves. "I have always thought I'd be there when the bank finally erodes and my house slides into the Naknek River!" This is always a threat to coastal villages on the treacherous Bering Sea and if it happens in Naknek, Terri will take it in stride. She said, "I live for today. Yesterday is gone."

If Terri "TQ" LaClair hadn't come to Alaska, she would have become a teacher with a desire to work on an Indian reservation because she has Blackfoot Indian heritage. She is an avid collector of Native American art and always buys art in the remote places she is lucky enough to travel to in Alaska.

Summing it up, Terri said, "All trails lead to here. If I die tomorrow, I had a blast ... a wonderful life. I'm blessed."

33

Flying Across the Tundra:
Diana Moroney

The forecast was for rain as I pulled on a pair of old jeans and a stained sweat-shirt, and laced up a pair of worn out tennis shoes. Before I grabbed my car keys, my husband suggested I should take along my rain coat, not just a jacket. "You're liable to get muddy," he said. I tucked the yellow slicker under my arm and left. It was about 9:30 in the morning when I pulled into Diana Moroney's steep downhill driveway just off Birchwood Loop in Eagle River, Alaska.

A pair of dogs yelped to greet me as I knocked on the etched-glass door. Inside the large log home, Diana, in a T-shirt and heavy fleece pants, sat at the end of her dining table, a 9' × 12' cookie sheet upside down in front of her. She politely intro-duced the other two people and continued moving small magnets around the cookie sheet. It took a minute before I realized each small magnet had a name on it.

Diana said, "We'll run three teams of ten today."

Her long, auburn-blond hair draped over her shoulders, her soft brown eyes concentrating on the cookie sheet, Diana called out names: "Tracks … Squid … Vic-tor and Vector — no, we can't run them together. We'll run Vector here," she said, placing the small magnet in the second line-up. "We've got Rosebud, Dolly, Coho, Indy, Shish." She paused to move a couple of magnets. "Teller, Laser, Angel, Jedi," her eyes transfixed on the cookie tin. "Dakota needs to run today. He's ready." After juggling more magnets, Diana was finally satisfied with her three-team line-up of husky dogs.

"Okay, let's go," Diana said. "I'll put on jeans and meet you downstairs."

She suggested I follow her downstairs, where she handed me rubber boots that belong to her husband and one of his jackets, which was layered with dog hair. "Look in that basket on the floor and find a pair of matching gloves," Diana suggested, don-ning a red jumpsuit and rubber boots.

Outside, we proceeded down a slippery, wet hillside into her dog lot, where 45 four-legged animals began a boisterous chorus at the prospect of hooking up to an ATV (four-wheeler) for a four-mile run through the woods. "Here's a brush.

Dawson's real friendly," Diana said matter-of-factly. "He needs to be brushed. He's right over there." She pointed toward six dogs that all looked alike to me. "Make him stay on top of his dog box while you brush him."

The chorus of yelps and loud barking engulfed me as I wove my way through a maze of excited dogs, all wanting attention, but not necessarily eager to be brushed. It occurred to me that ear plugs would have been a good idea. I called out to Diana when I thought I'd found Dawson and she nodded yes, because I couldn't hear what she said.

The enthusiastic dog leaped onto his four-foot-square wooden box and licked my face and pawed my chest. The attention he gave me was great, except that his face had the smell of muddy animal urine on it, so I tried to discourage him from giving me a bath. His thick hair came off easily as I brushed one side of his long muscular body. Then he lost interest and leaped to the ground. Diana

Diana Moroney with her lead dog, Rhythm, a ten-year-old husky, during the Iditarod Dog Race from Anchorage to Nome, Alaska.

yelled at him from across the yard to get back on his box, and he did. A self-professed coach and animal psychologist wrapped into one, Diana knew what to do. I didn't have a clue.

Carla Kelley, who ran in the 31st Iditarod in 2003 as a rookie, driving a team of dogs that Diana had raised and trained, was busy scooping poop into a large pail while Diana hooked up the long gang line needed to connect ten dogs to her four-wheeler for strength training. I continued to groom several other mischievous, 50-pound huskies, until Diana enlisted my help to put on their harnesses.

A rack holding all the dog harnesses hung between two trees, each identified with a name, in a variety of sizes and lengths, depending on the weight and size of the dog. The cookie tin hung from a nail, close at hand, to prevent mix-ups in the line-up.

Diana held up a red harness and explained. "You place it over the dog's neck, turn it, reconnect their collar, pull their front legs through like this and drape the straps back across their body where I'll hook it to the gang line."

Diana had to show me how to do it twice before I was somewhat comfortable with the process. I was amazed how well the dogs responded to my inept handling, but they knew they were going to do what they love to do—run and pull a dog sled. Only on that September day, without winter snow, it would be an ATV the dogs would pull, not a sled.

Diana, who had recently been diagnosed with pneumonia and had instruction from her doctor to rest and take it easy, had hold of Solo, the lead dog, by her collar. Holding Solo's front feet off the ground, Diana gingerly walked her over to the gang line and connected her harness. "If I tried to let her walk on all four paws, she'd be dragging me," she explained without breaking a smile as she trudged back across the muddy dog lot for another eager animal. At this point I noticed that the ATV was secured to a tree with a large rope because the dogs could easily have taken off down the hill without Diana in the driver's seat. In less than ten minutes, ten dogs were harnessed and ready for action.

I was sweating inside my clothes, short of breath and dirty, when Diana and Carla took off with the eager dog team. Diana whistled and Solo raced down the muddy hill, nine dogs in hot pursuit, running happily behind the leader. They were gone for a half hour. I peeled off my jacket and groomed another dog and drank some water. The dog chorus ceased and so did the drizzle from overhead.

Diana had promised to take me with her on the second run, but I was feeling uneasy. When she returned, I took a few pictures and suggested that Carla probably should go with her again, but Diana gently persuaded me it was my turn on the back of the ATV as soon as the second team was hooked up.

No roller-coaster ride could compare with racing through the brush over clumps of tree limbs and debris, a cow moose with calf standing off to our left, a large water hole to negotiate in front of us as we raced along. For the first quarter mile, I kept asking myself what in the world possessed me to do such a foolish thing. I wanted to ask Diana to stop and let me off. I gripped the handles tighter to keep from bouncing off the ATV into prickly flowering Devil's Club bushes alongside the trail. For a fleeting moment, I pictured myself in a full-body cast!

A mile farther down the trail, where the ride was smoother, I asked Diana, from my seat behind her, if this was what she called taking it easy—resting, like her doctor said. She simply replied, "Yes," followed by "Gee" to make her dog team stay to the path.

Diana was in her element. She was at ease, relaxed, at home behind a team of ten huskies winding their way through the damp woods. I settled back and began to relax, picking up on Diana's calmness. After a safe four-mile ride, with Diana fully in control, calling out "Gee" to make the team turn right or "Haw" if she wanted them to go left, I realized I'd just had the thrill of my life—an exhilarating ride that helped me understand why Diana mushes dogs and runs the Iditarod, even if she has pneumonia.

Diana has competed in nine Iditarods— the grueling 1,049-mile dog sled race from Anchorage to Nome, Alaska, that commemorates the lifesaving Serum Run of 1925. She has crossed under the famous Iditarod Arch in Nome in the top 20 twice — no small feat, given that about 60 racers participate annually. Only a handful of mushers are women.

Self-portrait of Diana Moroney at the Braeburn check-point on the Yukon Quest in minus-45-degree temperatures, 2001.

"I had to scratch in one race," Diana said, "after I dislocated my shoulder, but I still would have continued to Nome if the doctor hadn't made me quit." She paused to reflect. "I'm not a quitter. I was very disappointed."

Born in Sacramento, California, Diana went to college with plans to become a lawyer. But her life took a different turn when a friend recruited her to work in Barrow, Alaska, for the Naval Arctic Research Laboratory on contract with the University of Alaska Fairbanks, where she also first began dog mushing.

"My first team of five dogs came from Willow, Alaska, with a slip of paper, about 5" × 7", with a hand-drawn diagram showing me how to set up the harnesses and gang line and connect to the dog sled, with a list of commands to give the dogs. Five months pregnant, I harnessed them and mushed out onto the frozen tundra to train. A couple of times, the dogs got away from me and beat me back home. Fortunately, I never met up with a polar bear while I walked back into Barrow.

"In 1986, we relocated from Barrow to Willow, which is home to many Iditarod mushers. I became a single parent in 1987 when my husband and I divorced. I was commuting to Anchorage to work, a two-hour drive each way, working on the Exxon Valdez oil spill cleanup at the Joint Transportation Operations Center. The center coordinated the boats, airplanes and trucks that worked to clean up the spill.

"I had begun working on my private pilot's license in 1990 with the help of Bert Hanson, a friend who was a captain for Reeve Airways and also an Iditarod pilot. He wanted to learn to run the Iditarod, and I wanted to learn to fly. Bert competed in the Iditarod in 1990 with my help, and I soloed in October 1990 with his help. With a son to raise, long hours working on the Exxon case and managing a kennel of racing dogs, I had to quit flying." In her usually accepting manner, Diana said, "Something had to give."

After coordinating clean-up efforts on the oil spill, it was a natural transition for Diana when she began helping the support flight group that volunteers to deliver people, supplies and dogs, popularly called the Iditarod Air Force (IAF).

"In 1992, I met Bruce Moroney, a captain with Mark Air, who volunteered every year with the IAF. I was in Nome awaiting the start of the Hope '92 race from Nome to Anadyr on the Chukota Peninsula in the Russian Far East. Bruce met me at the finish line." Diana smiled. "It was then I thought I should keep him around. After all … how many guys would chase you to the Russian Far East!

"Bruce helped me finish up the requirements for my private ticket. He gave me encouragement and training and helped me advance through my ratings. I obtained my private license in 1993, followed by my instrument rating, multi-engine rating, private and commercial instructor licenses in 1995, and a marriage license in June of 1994. Bruce proposed during the running of the Iditarod that year." Diana chuckled softly. "Our engagement made national news. CNN picked up on the story.

"I applied for a job at Woods Air in Palmer, Alaska, in 1995 because I wanted to fly their DC3, a plane that some describe like 'flying on a pillow.' Shy of 500 hours in the air, Warren Woods turned me down, saying his insurance required a minimum of 500 hours of flight time."

Fiercely competitive, Diana would not be put off. "I spent hour after hour in the air, traveling to Talkeetna, Skwentna, Kenai — wherever I could log more time. Then I went back to Woods and handed him my log book. He agreed to hire me, and I flew co-pilot in the DC3 for two years and flight engineer in the DC6. In November of 1997, I was hired on as co-pilot on a DC3 with Majestic Air, flying out of Anchorage International Airport.

"Arctic Transportation Services wooed me away in April 1999," Diana said. "ATS, formerly known as Ryan Air, is a cargo company based in Nome, Alaska. I flew cargo in a Cessna 207 all over western Alaska and left to do a five-month stint for Frontier Airways in Fairbanks, flying passengers in a Navajo airplane. I returned to ATS in January 2001 and primarily fly their Cessna 402, working one week on and one week off."

As a commercial pilot, Diana can boast that she "knows every crook and bend in the trail" because she's flown over it so many times. "I love to see the land and to travel anywhere my plane will take me. It's the freedom and the challenge in Alaska because there are so many non-standard airports where you have to land. In the Lower Forty-Eight, air traffic is probably the biggest concern, where here it's the terrain and the weather conditions." With the shrug of one shoulder, she said, "I've landed the DC3 on a beach. It's no big deal."

In 1998, one of the years Diana did not compete in the Iditarod, she volunteered to fly with the IAF with a hand-picked group of 20 volunteer pilots. As of this writing, she is the only IAF woman pilot. All of the pilots must follow strict guidelines, and complete survival training that includes dealing with hypothermia. A checklist of items needed by each pilot includes food to sustain life for two weeks, an ax or

Diana Moroney with her son, John Dronenburg, also a commercial pilot, at Unalakleet beside a Cessna 402.

hatchet, a first-aid kit, a gun and ammunition, a knife, two boxes of matches, two small signaling devices, snowshoes, a sleeping bag and a wool blanket. The list continues for two full pages, including other items like flares, signal mirror, whistle, compass and a hypothermia thermometer. Survival gear and training are necessities year-round when you fly in Alaska, not just when the IAF is in the air. In the winter, snowshoes are important; in the summer, a head net to distract swarms of mosquitoes is a darn good idea.

The IAF handbook given to each volunteer pilot provides tips for dangerous landing areas. At Rohn, one of the checkpoints along the 1,000-mile trail, 83 miles from McGrath, pilots are instructed to land to the east whenever possible because the landing will then be uphill. The handbook says, "Getting stopped can be a problem. Whenever possible, take off to the west (downhill). If the wind is blowing hard it is advisable for the pilot to walk the entire length of the runway before attempting to take off because the wind sometimes blows from one direction on the east end and from the opposite direction on the runway's west end. If the wind and/or turbulence is too severe to land on the airstrip, it may be possible to find a clear stretch on the Tatina River, a short distance upstream from its confluence with the South

Fork of the Kuskokwim River. Check this area carefully; conditions change from year to year. There may be too much open water, or ice may be too rough for a safe landing."

Additional instructions explain that the runway is narrow with trees on either side. There are snow machines, airplanes and people everywhere. And, "If you don't feel comfortable, don't land."

"Two thousand pounds of food and supplies have to be delivered to the checkpoints along the race course for each dog musher before the race ever begins," Diana explained. "This means that 120,000 pounds of food, hay bales, and supplies have to be transported by 20 airplanes and pilots to all the checkpoints. This poundage does not include the 30 volunteer veterinarians, race officials, ham operators, and all their supplies, that must also be dropped off at the various checkpoints, and later retrieved. All of this is dependent on weather conditions," she pointed out.

"Once the race is underway, the IAF picks up injured or sick dogs for care and treatment. Mushers drop dogs along the race route at predesignated checkpoints for return to Anchorage." With her firsthand knowledge as an Iditarod musher, Diana explained, "A dog may be dropped for a number of reasons: illness, sprained wrist, pulled muscles, or just plain tired. All the same type of reasons humans have in marathon-type races." She paused, then added, "Television crews and newscasters charter their own planes to get to the checkpoints and on to Nome for the finish."

I couldn't resist asking Diana if she'd rather be mushing dogs on the Iditarod Trail of flying with the IAF. With a toss of her head and a big laugh, she replied, "When I'm mushing, I wish I was flying, and vice versa. And I fly the trail as if I'm mushing."

It's obvious that Diana doesn't lack the physical stamina or self-confidence to do either one; she just considers what she does her "lifestyle."

Diana is a sought-after speaker at area schools. "Sometimes the kids ask real basic questions, and I don't consider anything they ask me a dumb question. I'm glad to explain. I give the children a chance to pet one of my dogs and show them a dog sled." She paused, remembering something special.

"One of my greatest pleasures is bringing Make-A-Wish children to my home to handle the dog team and ride on the sled before the running of the Iditarod. My reward is their smiles when they interact with a dog team and the letters they write to me after they return home."

Asked why she likes to dog mush 1,049 miles from Anchorage to Nome, Alaska, in below-zero temperatures, across ice and snow, deprived of sleep, risking life and limb, Diana had the perfect answer: "I must be crazy."

But after riding with her on the trail, I know she's not crazy. She's happy. Diana's at home in an airplane or racing a boisterous team of dogs to the finish line at the Arch in Nome, Alaska. It's apparent that Diana has learned to juggle her family life — raising, training, and caring for huskies so she can mush dogs — and make a living with her flying. Yet, with all of this on her plate every day, Diana never lets on if she's having a bad day, even when she has pneumonia. It's just not her nature to complain. She takes care of the business at hand with the same ease she uses to fly an airplane or direct a team of 16 dogs down the Iditarod Trail on their way to the finish in Nome, Alaska.

34

It's Never Boring:
CARRIE LICHT

Imagine having 315 people living in your house, and it's your job to keep track of them. You have to respond to endless questions and concerns. You have to make sure they get to the doctor on a regular basis. And you have to plan their itinerary, make sure they have lodging when they travel.

"My job is herding cats," Carrie Licht said, shaking her curly blond hair and shrugging, "But I love it!"

Carrie is the Northwest Airlines pilot base manager in Anchorage, one of five bases that includes Honolulu, Minneapolis, Detroit, and Memphis, Tennessee. Carrie is second in charge behind the chief pilot assigned to the Anchorage base, and in many cases, she is it. She has a degree in Aerospace Studies and Aviation Safety, with minors in both Aviation Psychology and Aviation Business, from Embry-Riddle Aeronautical University in Prescott, Arizona.

Around 5:00 A.M. on September 11, 2001, a friend phoned Carrie from Arizona and yelled, "Turn on your TV! Turn on your TV!"

Carrie said, "Nothing could have prepared me for the terrorist attacks on the East Coast. No one ever imagined this could happen. For the next three hours, while I tried to shower and dress, my cell phone, my house phone, and my pager were in constant use. Our chief pilot was stranded in Seattle, so it was up to me to handle things in Alaska. We had several wide-bodied planes diverted into Vancouver when all flights were grounded. We had no outbound flights from Anchorage for several days."

The tall, athletic blond's voice raced as she relived the nightmare of September 11. "I barely slept for three weeks … maybe getting two to four hours a night of sleep. We couldn't get our pilots up here from Seattle because they fly on Alaska Airlines. We were up and ready to fly again when the FAA lifted the ban, but all passenger planes were still grounded." Carrie's green eyes, which change to hazel, flashed as she remembered. "I had pilots calling me from everywhere, day and night, asking me what they should do. Some of the pilots were ready to charter small planes and fly to Anchorage if necessary because we have flights leaving here that go to Tokyo

Carrie Licht, Northwest Cargo Airlines pilot base manager, Ted Stevens International Airport, Anchorage, Alaska.

and Asia, not just domestic flights. After 9/11, we threw the old rule book out ... literally. Nothing's the same anymore.

"I had to give updates from the FAA every day because it kept changing. I briefed every crew for two weeks following the attacks," Carrie said, expelling air through her cheeks, as if talking about it made her tired. "On a slow day we have six outbound flights. On a busy day it can be as many as 27 flights. I had to give them verbal and written updates and answer their questions. I'd go over to the Westmark Hotel, where we house our pilots, and brief the captains, and the flight attendants— something I don't typically do."

Carrie responded to an incoming phone call in her office, as soft music played in the background. My eyes were transfixed on an undulating mint-green lava lamp on a side table. Stacks of paperwork covered the table. Carrie ended her phone call and continued to explain.

"Within one month, one in five employees at Northwest lost their jobs. I'm talking about managers with ten and 15 years on the job, too." She paused. Her demeanor changed from cheerful to somber. "I don't mean to say that losing your job can compare to losing your life. It's doesn't, but so many people were affected, and no one realized the overall impact. It was devastating for so many families."

Carrie needed to change the subject as she relived the tragic domino effect of September 11, 2001. She paused to wave to a pilot checking in, which was her way of letting pilots know she's aware of their arrival. Then she continued. "In some cases, both the husband and wife were employed here, and both lost their jobs. This happened to all the airlines, not just Northwest, of course. No one could have predicted the long-term impact, but I felt it because I'm a pilot advocate…. I care about these people and their families."

Carrie checked her watch, standing up to her full height of 5'10". "We have a plane on the ramp. Let's go outside." She donned a florescent-green vest and handed me a similar one with an official Visitor pass clipped to the front of the garment.

In the open area outside her office, Carrie acknowledged several pilots checking in for their flights. Eyeballing one, about her same height, she looked him straight in the eye and said, "Need your medical certificate today." He reached into his shirt pocket and waved his certificate at her. Carrie made small talk with another pilot ascending the stairs. Then we made our way outside to the ramp. The sound of nearby airplane engines required ear plugs to buffer the noise.

Facing us was an enormous wide-body Northwest cargo plane, with a large lift delivering palleted loads to the second story of the aircraft to be placed inside on a conveyor system. "The nose opens too," Carrie said as we approached the awesome metal giant.

On the stairs leading inside the airplane, a food-service provider greeted Carrie, and they talked above the noise. She was friendly, but direct in her instructions, making it clear the food service company must provide what's in their contract, to the letter.

Inside the gutted giant there were no seats or amenities. Carrie said Northwest handles all kinds of cargo, even giraffes, buffalo, rhinos, and miniature horses. She pointed to the floor where the conveyor system tracks were placed. "Be careful. Don't step on those. Here, I'll hold your camera while you climb up these steps. I'm used to doing this."

The flight engineer ascended the crude metal steps first, to prepare for the flight. Carrie joked with him while I watched my step.

"I'm the steward on this flight too," he said with a grin. "Would you like coffee?" His offer was genuine, but I declined.

Inside the cockpit, which is no more than six feet wide and deep enough for the captain and co-pilot, the engineer sits behind them. There is a mind-boggling electrical panel facing him and overhead are more gauges, switches, buttons and lights. The subtle noise of a fan cooled the interior of the cockpit. On the console in front of the pilots and overhead were a maze of maybe 200 more gauges, switches, buttons and lights. They seemed more complex than any video game ever designed, or ever imagined by Nolan Bushnell, the Silicon Valley guru of video-game fame.

The co-pilot arrived and busied himself preparing for the flight. We made our way down the ladder, stepping carefully back across the conveyor system again, then outside, where it looked as if we were standing on the fourth-floor balcony of a moving hotel.

We walked across the tarmac, or "ramp," as Carrie called it. Another pilot approached, black case in hand, a smile on his face belying the fact he was the captain of the wide-body about ready to lift off. He stopped to talk with us.

"I think I'll just distract you while they take off," Carrie teased. The captain was friendly and polite, but eventually tore himself away as Carrie chided him a little more.

"I may not always be on time," he yelled to us, walking towards the waiting aircraft, "but our flights are!"

Carrie's natural, easy style of engaging everyone she encountered made it clear to me why she has the respect of the pilots based in Anchorage, including the maintenance crew, the office staff, and the security team.

We headed into the maintenance hangar where a security guard scrutinized my name tag. Carrie assured him I was authorized to troop around with her for the sake of an interview, but I didn't mind his questions. He was just doing his job.

Back inside the flight center, Carrie stopped to make more conversation with other pilots. They talked about renting a car and staying over a couple days to drive to Homer, Alaska, just for fun — maybe a last-minute fishing jaunt before the season ended. Carrie was invited to join them.

Inside her office, with the door closed, Carrie exuded self-confidence in taupe-colored slacks and lime-green sweater. "It's like being a diabetic and working in a candy store. I don't allow myself to have a relationship with any of the pilots because it would be too awkward professionally. Eighty percent of what I do is communication, and 5 percent cause about 90 percent of my work load." She turned to her computer and checked for new e-mails. Clearly, Carrie was always on duty.

"As a kid, I managed to bury or break my dolls. I preferred climbing trees and getting dirty. I had trucks and airplanes for toys," she said with a broad grin. "I was a tomboy. And since my mother's an artist and my father's an engineer, I'm a contradiction. Who knows why I turned out like this," she said, laughing. "It doesn't make much sense to me."

Ted Stevens International Airport, formerly Anchorage International, is going through major construction upgrades, and it's not uncommon for Carrie to sit in on construction meetings. "I remember one meeting in particular," Carrie said. "The architects came in, dressed in suits and ties, and other key people like engineers and planners, and then this guy with a hardhat. Anyway, he made some kind of crude comment to me, and the guys in suits turned white. I said to him, "I heard the odds in Alaska are good, and that some of the goods are odd." Carrie folded her arms and leaned on the edge of her desk. "We get along fine now.

"I've been here two years, and it took six months before the pilots would walk into my office. Now, even if the door is closed, they don't hesitate. Sometimes they've come off an international flight and need sleep, but they've got some problem they want to tell me about. I listen and listen some more, and it's obvious they are still in the last time zone, so I usually suggest they get some sleep and come back tomorrow and we'll iron it out, and they do.

"Eighty percent of what I do is interpret the contract between the pilots' union and the company," she said, holding a three-inch-thick binder, with an index that's nine pages of fine print. "I'm always juggling. I could work 24 hours a day, seven days a week and never get it all done. That's probably the only reason people burn out doing this job. You never get any closure. It's like being a rat on a wheel that never stops turning round and round."

Carrie placed a hand-held e-mail unit on the desk, along with a cell phone. "I'm attached to these everywhere I go. It's like having two leashes. Even if I have a day off, and I'm hiking or camping, I'm connected. I've been yanked out of a movie when my pager goes off. It's just part of the job."

Carrie ended our interview by saying, "I originally went to ERAU to be an airline pilot. I never imagined I'd be a pilot base manager, and it's the best job I could ever have. There's never a dull moment!"

35

A Love Affair:
Dee Hanson

The 6th Alaska State Aviation Trade Show came off without a hitch in May 2003, because Dee Hanson was the chief pilot of this formidable project. Fifteen thousand aviation enthusiasts attended the two-day trade show and conference, held in the FedEx hangar at Ted Stevens International Airport in Anchorage, where 230 vendors and exhibitors lined up to participate. Outside the hangar was a unique collection of static aircraft on display, including a vintage 1939 Stinson from the Aviation Heritage Museum in Anchorage.

"The Alaska Airmen's Association needed to have a source of income, so I approached FedEx about having an aviation trade show in their hangar, the largest at the airport," Dee said. "It took a while to get approval from corporate headquarters in Tennessee, and in spite of a short four-month lead, we succeeded in putting on a great trade show in 1998."

I had chased Dee for five or six months before she agreed to be interviewed. Dee is a "doer" who probably has to schedule time to sleep, but when our paths crossed at a Ninety-Nines meeting, I pressed her one more time. She said, "Are you sure you want to interview me?" We set up a convenient time, but two days beforehand, Dee phoned to cancel. She had taken a sledge hammer to a wall in her new home, with plans to remodel, when a piece of metal landed in her eye.

I figured Dee probably weighs about 100 pounds if she's encased in ice — a fact she disputes, admitting to 120 pounds. Anyway, 5'5", blond Dee Hanson had no intention of hiring a demolition crew just to tear down a wall in her home when she could do it herself!

We set up another appointment and with a laugh, she explained how to find the Airmen's office on Aircraft Drive. "It's behind a large blue building, upstairs.... There's a small decal in the window." Two days later, I literally stumbled into the hard-to-find office, because the stairs leading to the second floor were slippery with ice. The Airmen's office overlooks the Lake Hood Seaplane base with a view of the snowcapped Chugach Mountains in the east. Dee wasn't there. She had gone over to the Alaska Aviation Heritage Museum, two blocks from the Airmen's office. The museum is Dee's second home, another key facet in her love affair with aviation.

When we finally sat down for the interview, Dee's voice wasn't monotone or matter-of-fact. Her face was animated when she said, "I live and breathe aviation!"

After seven years as executive director of the Airmen's Association, Dee still has the momentum and zest she first brought to the job when she was hired part time to drum up new members, publish a quarterly newsletter, and organize a Christmas party.

Dee explained that she is a third-generation Alaskan. "My grandparents came here and homesteaded in Anchorage in the 1930s. My grandfather had a Supercub and my dad would throw the three of us kids in the back and we'd go fishing and camping." Dee smiled. "You know, the typical Alaskan thing—fishing trips."

You'd expect that Dee learned to fly in her teens since both her father and grandfather were pilots, but after high school, she headed off to Baylor University in Texas to get a degree in Business, with emphasis on marketing and real estate. Dee said, "I loved going house hunting and figured I'd be a realtor after college."

Dee Hanson with her Piper Super Cub at Lake Hood, Anchorage, Alaska, wearing hip waders.

But when she returned to Alaska for the summer, her dad asked if she'd like to take flying lessons. "He sent me to Wilbur's Flight Service over at Merrill Field for a quick flight around the Anchorage bowl with an instructor, and that was it. I was hooked! I couldn't wait to take lessons! Dad paid for ten hours of dual, ten hours of solo, and video tapes, which I took back to college with me. During the school year, in Texas, I got my license and could hardly wait to come back and tell my dad." Dee smirked. "I think he expected it and wasn't that surprised."

When I first met Dee in 1996, she owned and ran a bed-and-breakfast in Anchorage with one hand, and with the other hand, she

194

guided the Airmen's Association on a full-time basis. The other facets of Dee's busy life amazed me as I listened to her talk about her journey.

"After college I took a part-time job for a company called Air Logistics, doing fixed-wing marketing. I loved being around helicopters and airplanes, the people, and everything to do with aviation. When they closed their doors, I went to work for *Alaska Flying* magazine and I was the only pilot on staff for a while." Dee paused. "When they closed, I took a job at Standard Aero, selling parts and turbine engine overhauls. I didn't know squat, but I could talk flying, and what I didn't know I learned about and got right back to the customer ... immediately. I also didn't wear a business suit when I made sales calls. I wore jeans and 'extra-tuff' boots, like the fishermen wear. If I had to make a sales call in Barrow, Alaska, I wore long johns, and if I went out to King Salmon or Dillingham, I took along rain gear."

Dee rolled her blue eyes as I anticipated the next chapter in her journey.

"Standard Aero closed their doors too. I began to think I was a jinx, but I got a job at Pen Air in the parts department for five months, setting up an inventory control system, working alone, and I missed being around people. That's about the time I went out on my own to market sport fishing trips for the next 10 to 12 years."

Two years ago, Dee agreed to help guide the Aviation Heritage Museum, while continuing in her full-time role with the Airmen's Association It seemed to me that either organization could consume the normal person's time and energy, but not Dee's.

"Actually, the museum and the Airmen's Association compliment each other," Dee said. "We're in it together. One promotes and one preserves. We all fly the same skies here. I love airplanes and antiques. We have 25 rare historical Bush planes housed at the museum, dozens of rare photographs and memorabilia exhibits gathered from famous pioneers and veterans, plus exclusive pioneer film collections we show in this theater where we're sitting right now."

A large new hangar, alongside the new exhibit hall and gift shop, vouches for Dee's ability to secure funding for aviation preservation. There is also a hangar for restoration of aircraft, which is accomplished by dedicated volunteers.

"Inside the museum, the 1920 Stearman, flown by early aviation pioneers in Alaska, including Noel Wien, Ben Eielson and Joe Crosson, is on exhibit," Dee said. "And once a year at the Fourth Avenue Theater in downtown Anchorage, we recognize early Bush pilots. In 1903 we will recognize Ben Eielson, the father of aviation in Alaska.

"The Airmen, along with other groups and individuals like Alaska Airlines and Richard Wien, have commissioned a bronze statue of an early airman that will be placed on the downtown Park Strip in 2003, during the Centennial of Flight. The Park Strip was an airport in the early days before it was relocated to Merrill Field on the east side of Anchorage, and before Ted Stevens International Airport was built."

As she spoke, it was clear Dee had a vision for the future, with a deep appreciation of the past. "Reliving history keeps all of us enthused about the significance of aviation in Alaska." Dee leaned back in her metal folding chair to reflect. "I'll never be bored. The variety keeps me going."

When Dee is at home — the home where she knocked out a wall with a sledge hammer — she is mother to Rosie and Mr. Jigs, her two family dogs. "When I got Rosie, a weimaraner, I had no idea she was pregnant! I woke up one morning and she had given birth to nine pups! It was so much fun to go home every evening and lay on the floor and let the pups crawl all over me. I interviewed people to make sure each pup got the best home, then I think I went through 'puppy postpartum' after they were all gone. Luckily, Mr. Jigs came back after three weeks." Dee paused to catch her breath. "I can't leave them home alone, or they'd destroy the place! So it's a good thing I don't have kids. They'd be spoiled rotten too."

When we returned to the Airmen's office, Mr. Jigs, a mix of American bulldog and weimaraner, was resting beside Dee's desk, waiting for his favorite human. Her desk was stacked with papers, phone messages, photographs, reports and miscellaneous. A chart hung on a nearby wall with the outline of the trade show booth spaces. Dee was quick to invite me to the Airmen's Open House being held at the office the following evening. Just one more project she handles without breaking a sweat.

Dee believes her job is akin to owning her own business. "I treat the association, the trade show, and the museum like they are my own," she said, with conviction. "Like I said when we sat down to talk, I live and breathe aviation."

But Dee admits that when she needs a break, she takes to the skies in her Supercub to regain her focus and just relax.

36

Juggling:
DR. PETRA ILLIG

"I was always somewhere between the thrill of flying and the fear of piloting," Dr. Petra Illig admitted while we had lunch on the patio of the Millennium Hotel in Anchorage. The float planes took off and landed at Lake Hood as Petra's cell phone rang. She asked the caller when he would solo and set up an appointment following our lunch to give him the required flight physical. We ordered lunch and continued the interview.

A float plane from Rust Flying Service carrying fishermen to a remote area or tourist on a flight sightseeing trip lifted off. The waiter delivered our food as Petra's cell phone rang again. "Hi," she said with a smile on her face. "I'm having lunch with a friend. Come on over and join us." We managed to talk a little more about her life, in between bites of food, as her cell phone rang for a third time. Once again, Petra invited the caller to join us. The midday sun beat down on us as a float plane landed nearby.

The second caller arrived, a FedEx pilot based in Tennessee on layover in Anchorage. We moved to a larger table. The last caller arrived, Carrie Licht, Pilot Base Manager for Northwest Airlines in Anchorage. Carrie bought along a friend who was visiting Alaska for the first time. They ordered while Petra concentrated on our interview again, determined not to let airplanes, waiters, or the other three people at out table distract her.

Petra was the third child, with two older brothers, when she was born in Germany in 1953, daughter of an eye surgeon who was also a private pilot. "My parents never thought they'd have another child.... Mom was 42 when she had me. She thought she was sick with the flu when she found out she was pregnant. When I was two we moved to Ethiopia, where my father worked as an eye surgeon in Haile Selassie Hospital in Addis Ababa. My memories from that time are from pictures and childhood stories.

"Two years later our family received their immigration papers to come to the United States, and we arrived in New York City in 1957, where my mother worked as a cleaning lady in a synagogue because my father did not have a license to practice medicine in the United States. We moved to northern New York state where my father worked as an orderly in a psychiatric facility while studying to pass his medical licensure exams. Then we moved to South Dakota, where I entered kindergarten and learned to speak English. In 1967, when I was 14, we moved again, to Washington state, where we stayed and my father built a successful ophthalmology practice."

Petra spoke of her family background with a somber face. "I grew up in a strict environment with lots of criticism, never meeting my parents' expectations. Although my father was a doctor, I don't feel like I followed in his footsteps because I never wanted to be a doctor while growing up. I wanted to be an astronaut, or some other similar exciting career ... but really had no mentors or understanding that such a thing was possible. I also wanted to fly and liked to go flying with my father, but because of an emergency landing when I was 12 — my mother and I were passengers— she made him quit flying. I suspect that had this not happened, I would have gone on to get my pilot's license at a very early age, and I would have gone on to some sort of flying career. Perhaps even as an astronaut."

Petra watched a float plane overhead come in for a water landing, then shared, "It's funny when I remember it — when my father made an emergency landing. I don't remember feeling scared, or scared to die. I took it in stride and accepted that my time on earth might be over, and that was okay. I was full of lofty ideals at that age." Petra raised her eyebrows. "My mother was screaming the whole time, but somehow my father managed to land that plane and we all walked away."

Dr. Petra Illig, senior FAA aviation medical examiner.

It could have been that Petra was used to suppressing her feelings, I thought. But this incident also taught her that nothing is forever, that she needed to grab hold of the brass ring and make her life good.

"I applied to medical school to receive validation of my abilities and intelligence," Petra said. "In our family, medical school was a badge of honor. If I made it to med school, well then, I was good enough. I convinced myself it was a worthy and distinguished thing to do.

"Through an interstate program called WAMI between Washington and Alaska, I was able to get out of the rat race and off the freeways by transferring to the University of Alaska in Fairbanks for my first year of medical school. After completing two years of academic courses and two years of clinical studies in the Lower

Forty-Eight, I returned to Alaska and flew to Athabaskan villages to do a research project, which I published in the *Alaska Medical Journal*. I'd been hired to do the examination and data collection. This is when the flying bug caught me — all those neat little bush planes.

"My second year of medical school in Seattle, I began taking flying lessons, along with learning to tune pianos and repair bicycles, and I sang with the Seattle Chamber Singers to take my mind off the pain of medical school." With a laugh, Petra added, "I guess you could say I was a hyper maniac!

"After medical school, I thought I would like to be a Bush doctor in Alaska, so I signed on for a basic rotating internship at Cook County Hospital in Chicago. That's where I discovered emergency medicine and liked the excitement as well as the advantage of shift work. For the next 17 years I worked as an emergency-room or urgent-care physician in a variety of hospitals in Washington state. I was tired a lot, and also had no flying community to tap into. I barely stayed current in flying during those years. I always admired others who went on for higher ratings, but because of my work schedule — I always seemed to work at understaffed hospitals — I didn't have time to further my flying.

"I married and had two children, but my husband was unsupportive of everything I did — except work and earn money — so even then, flying went on a back burner. It was up to me to earn the living and rear my son and daughter."

Eventually, Petra divorced and resumed flying, developing a large circle of flying friends.

"After 17 stressful years in the ER, I knew I had to do something else so I developed myself as an aviation doctor. I did flight physicals, working from my home office, and made sure the FAA knew who I was. After many years, it paid off and I was hired by Delta Airlines to be their first full-time flight surgeon. I started the Department of Air Crew Health Services and was regional

Dr. Petra Illig in the cockpit of a home-built Christavia, with her daughter Lena Illig and her son Peter Illig, Anchorage, Alaska.

medical director for that department based in Salt Lake City. Three years later, the department was downsized, and I left Delta."

This was a turning point for Petra. She didn't want to return to emergency medicine, and as a single parent, she dreamed of Alaska again, so she sold her home in Salt Lake City, moved to Anchorage and started her own private practice. "I considered other options first: working for the FAA in Oklahoma City for NASA, traveling between Houston, Texas and Russia, but fortunately recognized that none of these options really suited my personality nor my career goals."

Petra is the first to admit that it was scary at first, being without a regular paycheck, but she knew her experience and ability would carry her through. Her practice has grown rapidly. She said, "I thoroughly enjoy my work and most of all, I am able to take care of my kids without child care. And of course, I am flying more than I ever have before!"

As an aviation doc, Petra provides physicals for pilots taking their first solo flight, private pilots who need to renew their license every two to three years, commercial pilots who need to renew every two years, and airline pilots who are required to renew every six months.

One of her greatest challenges is working with pilots who have special medical issues. "It's not like it was ten years ago," she said. "Today you can usually continue to fly after a heart attack because of advances in technology and pacemakers. The same is true for diabetes. Insulin levels can be maintained and appropriate dosages administered with a pill rather than an injection." She continued to explain. "This is also true if a pilot has high blood pressure. What I'm looking for when I give a flight physical is any condition that would bring on an incapacitating incident unlike when a person goes to their doctor for an annual physical, to prevent illness."

Petra said, "Medical standards for pilots first came about during World War I because it was discovered that the mortality rate wasn't caused by enemy fire. Pilots were fatigued, they had medical problems before they took to the air, or they had been drinking before they climbed into the cockpit. Through observation and scientific evidence over the years, new civilian and military standards were developed for the safety of the pilots. Military standards are the most rigorous, requiring ongoing physical strengthening. In foreign countries, this is the norm for all pilots."

When Petra finished medical school, her mother told her she would rather she had married a doctor than be one. What Petra does now reflects her desire to make a difference in other people's lives, especially young people.

"I admire those young people I have met who sought me out and quizzed me to death about flying and medicine. I never did much of that. I just knew that what I wanted to do was different than the routine, but didn't know how to find others who had been there!

"I suggest to young women: get as much science education as you can stand—

no matter what career you end up in, that will help you make it further in a 'man's world.' And don't ever demand recognition on the basis of being female! Think outside the box. Most of us are hesitant to do anything out of the ordinary. Look for mentors that have done things out of the ordinary. Ask questions and don't take no for an answer. But listen to sage advice."

At 2:30, I reminded Petra of the flight physical she agreed to do at 2:45 P.M. She ran her fingers through her short blond hair and within a few minutes said her good-byes and left the rest of us to get acquainted. We all laughed and agreed that Petra is masterful at juggling work, family and friends.

Fortunately, before Petra made her exit, I had my story. The story of a woman who is driven to succeed, driven to perfection, to high achievement. But with time in her life for her son and daughter, her friends, and flying.

Recently, a pilot friend of ours was suffering with an aggravating migraine headache. I knew that Petra was her doctor and asked my friend if she'd told her how miserable she felt for the past two weeks. Sheepishly, she replied, "No." I encouraged her to phone Petra. Within the hour, my friend phoned to say that Petra had come by her house and given her something that made her feel much better. Doctors don't make house calls anymore. Petra did because she cares.

37

The Future:
AUDREY COLE

Audrey Cole was boxed into a workaholic job in Texas in 2000, engaged to be married, when she fantasized about coming to Alaska. She dreamed of flying in the Last Frontier and wanted to learn more about the opportunities for women pilots.

A friend handed her the phone number of 747 pilot Louise Gettman, who lived in Anchorage. Louise told Audrey the best thing she could do was hop on a plane that weekend and come meet other pilots at the annual Alaska Airmen's Trade Show being held at the FedEx hangar. This was May 2000.

In her mind, when Audrey hung up after talking with Louise, she was already airborne. She announced to her fiancé that she was going to take a weekend flight to Alaska. He was stunned by her decision, but Audrey bought a $298 round-trip plane ticket and for the next 72 hours, she barely slept.

"I'm an adventurer," Audrey said of herself. "I went to the University of Houston and got a Bachelor of Science degree in Biology with a minor in Chemistry, but found the work too inactive. In school I was a long-distance runner. Sitting at a computer just didn't do it for me.

"In college I went flying with a friend, a flight instructor. He allowed me to hold the yoke, and I logged it in my book because I was hooked. It was a fantastic adventure. When I got my private pilot's license in February 2000, it gave me a sense of freedom."

Audrey laughed, remembering her first instructor. "He was very conservative and patient. I often wished he'd do a wing over or fly low to the ground, but he was a good role model."

While we sat around a large table with a bright blue-and-yellow sunflower table cloth, enjoying some herbal tea, I ask about Audrey's family. "I am the youngest of seven children and when my mother remarried I had a blended family of 12 siblings. It was really funny when I started flying," she said. "Two of my step-brothers said they should have thought of it. I'm the only pilot."

Audrey returned to her story, while on her 72-hour visit to Alaska, she even vol-

Audrey Cole flying a C-46 at Lake Clark Pass, Alaska.

unteered in the Aviation Heritage Museum booth at the trade show, selling belt buckles. "I didn't know anything about the museum, but I read their brochure and actually sold a few buckles," Audrey said with a chuckle. "It was a perfect place to meet and talk with pilots about opportunities in Alaska."

Everyone Audrey met that weekend, especially women pilots, assured her the best place to advance her career and become a commercial pilot was in Alaska. "They talked about age not being a factor. I was 32 and beginning to feel like it was too late for me, but I met a woman who didn't learn to fly till she was 40. I heard about Bush flying around the state. I talked with a woman who was a captain with an airline. And I discovered the Civil Air Patrol. I was intrigued by their low-level flying to help locate lost aircraft, stranded hikers, or snow machiners."

The 72 hours ended in a flash, and Audrey, running on two hours' sleep each night, had to fly back to Texas and her fiancé. He probably knew from the moment she stepped off the plane that her heart no longer belonged to him. It belonged to Alaska.

"I think the glue that kept us together was working side by side, frantically, in his theatrical lighting and sound company. There was never time for us unless we stopped working long enough to grab something to eat in a restaurant. Every idea I put forth to develop long-range plans for the business he passed off as worthless, a waste of time and money. I didn't realize it then, but we really weren't good partners in business and making a marriage work would have been even more difficult."

With a heavy heart, but a desire to fulfill her dream, Audrey announced she wanted to spend three months on sabbatical in Alaska that summer. She planned to take more flying lessons and obtain more ratings. Her fiancé helped her get a $12,000 low-interest loan, but he didn't bother to make time to see her off at the airport. Audrey phoned from Alaska every couple of days, but he was unavailable.

"In August I asked his secretary to book him a flight. I felt sure if he came here and saw the wonder of Alaska, we could cement our relationship. We went on a flight-seeing trip the next day and he sat in the small plane, shuddering, unable to look at the landscape that simply enthralled me. His visit was supposed to include five days of sight seeing, but the following day Malcolm flew home, leaving a note for me while I was taking flight training at Merrill Field.

"I was devastated at first," Audrey said. "I had convinced myself it was time to settle down, like my siblings. Marry, have a house and 2.5 children. All the cultural mores women are raised to believe tugged at my heart."

Audrey Cole proudly holding a 25-pound King Salmon she caught at Clear Creek, near Talkeetna, Alaska, photograph by Mio Johnson.

On her first trip north, Audrey had met Mio Johnson, an engineer at the Municipal Power and Light Company, a pilot she has since nicknamed the Queen of Networking. Mio invited Audrey to stay with her for the summer months in 2000. Audrey still resides at Mio's rustic home on the outskirts of Eagle River. Mio is a wonderful mentor and friend to young people.

Audrey was fortunate to be mentored and inspired by another woman in Texas, a very successful business woman and counselor who was not a pilot. "My counselor in Texas called me a Warrior Spirit," Audrey said, tucking her long honey-blond hair over her right ear. "She's probably right. When I came to Alaska I felt like I'd come home. I found a new family in aviation."

Audrey found work at the Elmendorf Aero Club in dispatch operations for general aircraft. She did sales and customer service for an avionics and pilot shop where she made valuable contacts in the aviation community. To

Audrey Cole, relaxing on top of a Grumman Widgeon, Anchorage, Alaksa.

earn extra money for other licenses and training, she worked part time during the Christmas holidays for the postal service. She became an active member of the Alaska Ninety-Nines and the Civil Air Patrol. She is also a member of Women in Aviation International, the Aircraft Owners and Pilots Association, and the Anchorage Running Club.

One of the people Audrey met in Alaska was Greg Ashwell, a local news media traffic reporter who takes her with him in his Cessna 172 twice a week. "I fly for Greg while he reports the news on Tuesdays and Thursdays," Audrey said. "One day we were flying over downtown Anchorage and the winds were so strong they reduced our airspeed, keeping the plane stationary. It felt strange, like we might fall out of the sky, even though I knew we wouldn't. Basically, we were hovering like a helicopter. Flying for Greg while he gives the traffic report helps me build up my hours."

Audrey talked about another unique Alaskan experience. "I flew in a Maule to Lake George, near Knik Glacier, and we did touch-and-go landings on glacier silt. Basically, we were doing short field landings, without the benefit of lights and lines, or numbers, or the kind of visual clues you would have at an airport. There were no wind socks to tell us which way the wind was blowing. We had to check which way the leaves were blowing and fly close to the ground to eyeball where we could land. It was an incredible experience when we got out and walked around — definitely a part of flying I could never have done in the Lower Forty-Eight."

Anything's possible in the Last Frontier. Audrey is part of the new breed of pilots with a bright future. She's full of adventure and she's committed to succeed. As she put it, "There's no way I'm going back!"

As I listened to the young woman, who doesn't appear to be more than 24, it was clear to me that she had moved on with her life and her future. With over 1,000 hours logged since we met in January 2003, her instrument, commercial and commercial flight instrument instructor exams completed, Audrey Cole, the young woman from Texas with a big dream, is fast on her way to achieving her goals.

Index

Index

Index

Index

Index